Best Broadcasts of 1939-40

Best Broadcasts

of 1939-40

Selected and Edited by

MAX WYLIE

Director of Scripts and Continuity,
Columbia Broadcasting System;
Lecturer, New York University
Radio Workshop

New York WHITTLESEY HOUSE *London*

McGRAW-HILL BOOK COMPANY, INC.

PUBLISHED BY WHITTLESEY HOUSE

A Division of the McGraw-Hill Book Company, Inc.

Printed in the United States of America by the Maple Press Co., York, Pa.

Preface

THIS book is Volume II in a series of annual collections of outstanding radio material. Some of the pieces reprinted in the following pages are very good from every standard, and some of them are very bad from every standard except radio's.

American radio shares the standards of the public it serves. It does not, in contrast to British radio (before the war), decide what the public should have, put it on, leave it there for months, and ignore the fact that it brings small delight to few people.

English friends have told me, for example, that you can learn how to flash the chimney of your smokehouse, how to tell the Douglas plaid from the Cameron plaid, and how to keep bees—all this over the wireless. American radio tries to teach, too; but we somehow act on the assumption that a man will be coming around to flash the chimney, that a good Cameron will know his own plaid. As to the bees, we, too, approve of them as the English do, and we believe in them; but we seem to feel that a bee knows his business. As a race we feel that bees have been around a long time and have done well. As a race we do not believe we can bring much to the bee. We do not see a commercial in it. Over here we don't bother with bees; so radio doesn't bother with them either. But Englishmen hear a great deal about one thing and another that has no possible affinity with their life. It is the difference between arbitrament and volition.

Nor does American radio, in contrast to German radio, decide what the public should have, put it on, leave it there, and see to it that all Germans behave as if they were having a whale of a time listening to Goebbels' romancing and Mr. Schicklgruber's helminthic fiddle-faddle.

English radio is a schoolmaster. German radio is a drill-master. American radio is the reciting pupil of its own 130 million tutors. In Germany you take your radio and like it. In England you take it or leave it. In America you get what you ask for; and if you don't like what you get, it is taken off for you. In general, American radio gives out what it has taken in. This is healthy, this is sensible, and this is fair.

It would seem logical to go on from here and point out that our great national genius for "squawking" is America's best check and balance to keep radio doing the things Americans want it to do. But it is at this precise point that we encounter a severe, and in some ways inexplicable, breach in our logic. Radio hears much squawking, to be sure, and it considers each squawk according to its merit; but thus far its millions of listeners have not yielded a true critic of the industry.

To me this is very strange. Nothing in this world has impinged upon the active consciousness of a whole people as radio has impinged upon Americans. I have heard many explanations as to why radio or the great body of its listeners has not supplied broadcasters with good critics.

It is claimed that art produces critics and that radio is not an art and so does not deserve and does not need critics. It is said that critics are concerned with form and that radio is innocent of form. Another and far too popular answer to the whole thing is this: criticizing radio is as futile as criticizing the Atlantic Ocean. Here the reasoning seems to be that you can say all you want about the ocean without changing its temperature or moving it out of its bed.

All these arguments make a lot of sense, and they have all been enunciated at one time or another by sensible people. But they do not make enough sense. They bring no direction of development to the world's most overgrown baby, no dietary control, no educational toys, nothing but diapers. All of this is to be deprecated because it is all negative.

The simple fact of the matter—with a few scattered exceptions that I wish presently to mention—is this: radio is its own critic and has been so ever since the business began. With much patience, many mistakes, and great trouble it has written millions of letters, called people on the telephone, rung doorbells, and Q.S.T.'d entire networks to see what listeners were listening to and why, and to see what they were not listening to and why. It has spent millions of dollars and millions of man-hours in finding out as much about its own business as its public would let it know. Terrific energy has been put into this search by radio people. Little energy has been put into it by radio listeners. Broadcasters want to know where they are, and the public is not helping them as much as it should.

Few discerning men within the industry itself would claim that broadcasting as a whole is an art or even that broadcasting as a whole has artistic form. Most of them know pretty exactly what radio is. Most of them know that it is the most fluid medium that we have for bringing some of the arts (and only some) to their largest audiences. That much is a good deal, but it can never reach its peak of self-realization without the assistance of intelligent and sympathetic public review.

To lump radio with the Atlantic Ocean and say that one might as well criticize the one as the other is a very dangerous thing to do. The risk and the fallacy in this rugged analogy are at once apparent; several people have criticized the Atlantic Ocean with very good results. They have navigated her, fished her, flown her, scraped her bottom for oil, sucked her middle for gold, skimmed off her top for perfume and pipe bowls, backed up her tides for power, and browbeaten her generally into a docile and producing accessory for sixty-three separate nations. Critics did all this—Schoutens, Drakes, Magellans, Fitzroys, Darwins, Melvilles, Sarmientos, Columbuses, Dampiers, Shackletons, Ladrilleros, and Lindberghs—with fleets and astrolabes and microscopes, with whatever they had and whatever they knew. All these men were critics of the Atlantic Ocean. They all thought that they could improve it, and they all were right. It is a much better ocean than it was.

Sooner or later adventuresome spirits will begin to perceive the challenge that the very immensity and heterogeneity of radio offer to the restive and exploring mind. People will begin to dissect its social implications; to discover why, when Stokowsky plays for it all the time,

Kreisler won't play for it at all; to bring the right people together in order to bring the right program to the grave and grasping minds of small children; to find out how to move more merchandise without so many commercial plugs; to teach languages; to persuade adults to drop an old idea as soon as they have evidence enough to accept a better one.

Some of this is being done. Within the business itself NBC has the most just, the most catholic and impartial appraiser of written show material in radio today. He is Lewis Titterton. NBC also has radio's most experienced theatre man in John Royal, vice-president. His knowledge, his irresistible personality, and his chatoyant brilliance make it possible for him to meet and reach all types of people on their own ground, a capacity neatly demonstrated two years ago in London when, in the course of a single afternoon, he had tea with a cabinet member, a conference with Toscanini, and highballs with Mike Jacobs and got everything he wanted from all three. Mutual has its shrewdest analyst of popular values in Julius Seebach. Among executives in the creative divisions, CBS has radio's boldest innovator, its most exciting experimenter, and its most inventive showman in W. B. Lewis, youngest and nimblest vice-president in American broadcasting.

Two newspapermen stand out as the most astute and knowledgeable critics that have brought their offices to bear on radio from the field of journalism. They are Robert Landry of *Variety* and Leonard Carleton of the *New York Post.* They are widely read, and they should be. Their perceptions are accurate; their evaluations incisively gauged and arrived at; their observations readable, searching, and fair. All these men are useful and productive, and radio today is better than it would have been without them.

Another type of critic should be mentioned. They are the members of the "We Are Not Listening" societies. These groups have sprung up in the past two or three years, principally in the East, and are increasing slowly in numbers. Almost all their members are women. They are bad for radio. Anybody who doesn't listen to radio is bad for radio. The forming of these groups of total abstainers had its rise in an increasingly articulate protest against the fecundity of the daytime serial.

It is much easier for me to understand their attitude than to find intelligent justification for their militance. The reason so many daytime serials are on the air is that so many millions of women want to hear them. There are millions of women in America who work much harder than the "We Are Not Listening" women, who live on less money, and who find in these tales of family life and typical or atypical romance their only exercise of reverie, their solace, and the sustaining, if imaginary, extension of their own lives, their own personalities, and their own best conception of themselves. The daytime serial makes life endurable to many millions of women who never before have experienced the thrill of being told how wonderful, how resourceful, how valorous they were. Daytime serials don't have heroes; they have heroines. A whole matriarchy has built itself up around these resilient, albeit fictional, females. The listeners identify themselves with the best types in all these endless stories. They do it in the same way that readers do with all fiction. The serial makes it possible for those to live a little in their own spirit who are domestically surrounded by dishes, money worries, empty lives, tired or unromantic husbands, ugly back yards, or flat feet.

The serials are for these women. There are about twenty-five million of them. The serials are not for the "We Are Not Listening" women, were never intended for them, do not claim to interest them or to bring them anything experiential, social, or cultural that they can possibly enjoy.

But for these very women (and it is interesting that there is rarely an underprivileged one among them) to rebel at the whole output of radio in order to press down on its (to them) most reprehensible feature is not only completely selfish but completely indefensible. Shall we put on the Budapest Quartet for two hours every morning and three every afternoon for the two million who would like it, and shall we do so at the expense of the twenty or thirty million who listen all day long to what they are already getting? Certainly not.

American radio is for all the people, and there is much for all the people. For any group to refuse to listen to anything and everything merely because there is much that they object to, merely because there is much that they consider blatantly stupid, is in itself blatantly stupid. It is like going through the whole of life and saying, "We found some ugly sights, and we are not looking." It is like going through the whole of literature and saying, "We found some vulgar doggerel and we are not reading."

I do not know as much about radio as I should like to, but I know as much as my slender talents for absorption have made it possible for me to learn. I've taught radio in universities, written it, produced it, lectured about it, listened to it, defended it, attacked it, heard charges and acquittals from many sources. I have brought several people into it and urged a few out. Radio is not unlike any other great business in so far as its two basic needs are concerned; it needs people who know things, and it needs people who can do things. It goes to considerable expense to supply the relatively proper amounts of them both. For myself, if I may be permitted the slang, I think that radio is "the stuff," but I would not think so if it were made up of people who were as myopic and unrealistic about radio as are the good ladies who will not listen. Creative criticism never has anything to do with groups or movements. Creative criticism is a peculiarly individual thing. It will be time to take the daytime serials off the air when the women who don't like them now can persuade the women who do like them not to like them any more. I doubt if they can do this. Most of the women who do not listen have a boiled dinner on top of their head instead of a hat; and in the case of some, I fear, a boiled dinner inside their head instead of the machinery of thought.

There are differences in this year's book from the one that appeared last fall. I have not put individual properties into so many separate classifications. Six or seven pieces appear under the general heading "Best Scripts," five or six under "Best Comedy," some under "Best News Reporting." A few still get their necessary independent billing, but on the whole I have tried to simplify the reader's problem by setting before him the broad field of radio activity in its entirety and not confusing him with discrete snatches of this and that.

Last year's book was more instructive than entertaining, and I deliberately put it together that way. This year I hope the reverse is true. It is a hard year for everyone, and it is going to be worse. Empires have subsided overnight; friends have betrayed one another and themselves; everybody is telling lies. There is not much to cling to in the world.

In these moments and in these months our own country, of all those still remaining afloat, is blessed and sustained by the truth that we may read every day in our press and hear every hour on our radios. Moreover, these two great forces of public information in America are reflecting another side of our vast and incorporated life together—the American sense of humor. It is robust and joyous, occasionally vulgar, but always full-throated—qualities that in themselves describe us as well as any others I can think of. No race is lost that can still laugh together at itself.

MAX WYLIE.

Contents

BEST SCRIPTS

My Client, Curley

by Lucille Fletcher Herrmann

and Norman Corwin

Lucille Fletcher is responsible for the basic idea and the original story on which "My Client, Curley" is based. Miss Fletcher for many years was one of the most valuable members of the CBS publicity staff. She is a free-lance writer today and the wife of Bernard Herrmann, CBS composer-conductor. Miss Fletcher has an immense gift of fantastic invention, and it is all lively and amiable. She has done little professional writing as yet, aside from her staff work in radio, but two or three of her pieces have appeared in *The New Yorker*, and the Columbia Workshop has produced another of her half hour radio shows—a story about a man who wanted to be a locomotive. It was called "The Man with the One-track Mind."

Norman Corwin, radio's most unspoiled prodigy, in a brilliant and intensive collaboration with Miss Fletcher, expanded the basic idea of the caterpillar story to the proportions it has achieved in the script which follows. In two weeks of work Miss Fletcher conceived and outlined the career of her very implausible bug, and in two more weeks Mr. Corwin, by dialoguing the whole and replotting many of the amiable excursions of the principal, converted a fine piece of architectural blueprinting into last year's most irresistible fantasy. The program was first produced by the Columbia Workshop on the evening of March 7, 1940. An immediate public response required a repeat performance four weeks later.

Here is Miss Fletcher and Mr. Corwin's caterpillar.

My Client, Curley

ANNOUNCER.—Ladies and gentlemen, in the following play, any similarity to caterpillars, living or dead, is purely coincidental.

MUSIC.—*Symphonic treatment of "Yes, Sir, That's My Baby."*

ANNOUNCER.—The Columbia Workshop presents "My Client, Curley," a new radio play by Norman Corwin, based upon a short story by Lucille Fletcher Herrmann.

MUSIC.—*Up and out under.*

AGENT.—There are some things a man doesn't like to talk about because they're . . . (*breaks off*). Well, I'll just tell this story about my client, Curley, and then I'll go back to the agent business and try to forget it. But if I should get a lump in my throat while I'm telling it, I hope you'll understand, because this whole thing was so recent, I still feel pretty upset about it.

To make a long story short, I'm out walking one day in the suburbs where I live, when my attention is attracted by two kids sitting on the side of the road (*harmonica in, well off-mike*), and one of them is playing a harmonica. They're bent over watching something on the ground, and I, being curious, go over to see what it is.

SOUND.—*Fade in harmonica playing "Yes, Sir, That's My Baby."*

AGENT.—Hiya, boys, what you got there?

SOUND.—*Harmonica stops abruptly.*

FATSO.—We got a trained caterpillar.

AGENT.—What's trained about it?

STINKY.—He dances.

AGENT.—(*Laughing*) I don't believe it.

STINKY.—He sure *does.*

FATSO.—(*The business brains*) Give us a nickel, and we'll show you.

AGENT.—(*Good-naturedly*) Oh, a racket, eh? All right, I'm a sucker. Here's two nickels.

FATSO.—Thanks, mister. Okay, play, Stinky.

SOUND.—*Harmonica begins tune.*

AGENT.—(*Fascinated . . . after a moment*) Well, what do you know! (*To Stinky*) Now stop. (*Harmonica out*) I'll be darned. Stops right when you do.

FATSO.—(*Proudly*) Sure. That's the way Stinky trained him, didn't ya, Stinky?

STINKY.—Aw, it was nothin'.

AGENT.—(*Still incredulous*) Play some more, Stinky.

SOUND.—*Harmonica starts and plays through briefly to finish.*

AGENT.—(*Laughing with delight*) Lies right down when you're finished!

STINKY.—Sure, he's talented, ain't he? (*To Curley, affectionately*) Come on up on my finger, Curley. That's a boy!

AGENT.—Does Curley dance to any kind of music?

FATSO.—Nope. Only "Yes, Sir, That's My Baby."

AGENT.—You mean to tell me he dances to only *one* tune?

STINKY.—That's right. I tried lots more, but I guess he only likes that one.

AGENT.—Well, why is that, do you suppose?

STINKY.—Feller I know says he got a real musical ear.

FATSO.—I guess that's what those two branches are on his head, huh? Musical ears.

AGENT.—No, that's his antenna.

STINKY.—*Antenna?* (*Laughs*) He ain't no radio set! (*Vastly amused by his own joke, he laughs again, Fatso joining him.*)

AGENT.—Say!

FATSO.—What!

AGENT.—I wonder if he's got any snake blood in him? You know there are some snakes who dance.

FATSO.—No kiddin'?

AGENT.—Here, let me take your harmonica a minute. Curley may be related to one of them Asiatic snakes or something. Lemme play it a minute.

SOUND.—*Plays "Hootchie Kootchie" (Danse de Ventre).*

AGENT.—(*Stopping*) Nope. Won't budge. I guess it's an American caterpillar, all right.

STINKY.—Oh, sure.

AGENT.—(*All business*) Look, fellers, I'll make you a proposition. How would you like to *sell* Curley?

FATSO.—(*Commercial minded*) How much?

STINKY.—(*Sustaining minded*) Wait a minute. I own Curley, and I don't wanna sell him.

AGENT.—Why not, Stinky?

STINKY.—(*Ashamed to confess that he loves the bug*) Well, because I—well—just *because.*

FATSO.—(*Interpreting*) Know why he don't wanna sell?

AGENT.—Why?

FATSO.—On account of he's *stuck* on him.

STINKY.—Aw, shut up, Fatso.

AGENT.—You mean you like Curley so much you don't want to part with him?

STINKY.—I just don't want to sell him, that's all. Not even for a *dollar.* (*Afterthought*) Not even for *two dollars!*

AGENT.—Well, of course I don't think anybody'd ever offer you *that* much money.

STINKY.—I don't care. He's my pet, and I want to keep him. I trained him from a pup.

AGENT.—Now look, kiddo. I think you're a very bright and sensitive boy, and because of that, I'm going to make you an immediate cash payment of *five dollars* for Curley!

FATSO.—Hey! *Five bucks!* Holy smackerels! Whadda ya say, Stinky? Huh?

STINKY.—(*Almost in tears*) Well, gosh, I dunno.

FATSO.—Take it, I'm tellin' ya! Now you can buy a bike!

STINKY.—(*Deserted by Fatso and now a martyr to his affection for Curley*) Well, that sure is a lot of money, but y'see, I *like* Curley, and I guess Curley likes me, too; and when we're alone I talk to him, and he understands me. (*Warming up, finding reasons to support his refusal to sell*) Curley likes me around. He's very intelligent, even though he don't look so smart.

AGENT.—Oh, he looks smart, all right.

STINKY.—Fatso or my old man or nobody else can't never get him to move. He won't do *nothin'* when *they* ask him. He lays down, just like on spite, almost. (*Deadly serious*) You know, if somebody took him away from me, Curley would die.

AGENT.—Think so?

STINKY.—Sure. He's only human, ain't he? He would absolutely die.

AGENT.—Listen to me, Stinky. I'm going to talk to you man to man. This caterpillar you've got is very valuable. He's worth a lot of money, way more than five dollars, maybe.

FATSO.—No kiddin'?

AGENT.—Now this is what we're gonna do, Stinky. You're gonna *stay* with Curley, and I'm gonna manage both of you. Curley will be my *client!*

FATSO.—What's that mean?

STINKY.—What's a client?

AGENT.—Well, you wouldn't understand very well. That's something I'll have to explain to your parents, because I've got to get their signatures on a long-term contract. You're a minor under the law, you see.

STINKY.—(*Apprehensive of the terminology*) I didn't do anything wrong, did I?

MUSIC.—*Harmonica with orchestra in transitional treatment of "Yes, Sir."*

AGENT.—That was how it began. I get Curley under my management and take him and Stinky with me. The first thing I do is start out after some publicity. And boy, do those reporters eat it up. Front page, with pictures. Pictures of Curley and pictures of Stinky and pictures of me. Pictures of my client dancing on a leaf, curling around the mayor's finger, climbing up a pretty model's leg, sitting in a tiny box at the opera. And *headlines!* Headlines, like in the *Times:*

TIMES.—Swing Caterpillar Sways to Strains of "Yes, Sir, That's My Baby"; Fred Astaire of Insect World Demonstrates Almost Human Sense of Rhythm.

MUSIC.—*Motif . . . Phrase from "Yes, Sir" builds progressively each time it is repeated after.*

AGENT.—The *Post.*

POST.—Curley in Custody of Stinky, Young Svengali of Caterpillars.

MUSIC.—*Motif.*

AGENT.—The *Herald Tribune:*

HERALD TRIBUNE.—Insect Phenomenon Learned to Truck in Truck Garden, Manager Avers.

MUSIC.—*Motif.*

AGENT.—The *World-Telegram.*

WORLD-TELEGRAM.—The Curley Crawl Becomes New National Dance Sensation.

MUSIC.—*Motif.*

AGENT.—The *Daily News:*

NEWS.—Bug Cuts Rug! Story on Page 2.

MUSIC.—*Finale treatment of motif.*

AGENT.—And sure enough, with all that publicity, things really begin happening. First, Bill Robinson introduces the Curley Capers at the Cotton Club!

MUSIC.—*Effect of solo tap-dancing.*

ROBINSON.—Copasetic!

AGENT.—Then Raymond Scott writes a song called the "Caterpillar Creep."

MUSIC.—*Fragment from "Caterpillar Creep."*

AGENT.—Then, half a dozen agencies bid for the rights to syndicate a comic strip.

BIDDER.—Four hundred and twenty-nine papers, 5 days a week, making a grand total of . . .

AGENT.—Other companies pay me royalties for Curley balloons and spaghetti and dolls and toys and picture books and decorations on the outside of drinking glasses.

CHILD.—Maw, buy me the glass with Curley's picture on it!

AGENT.—And, to make a long story short, I get a vaudeville offer. The money begins to roll in. I hire an expensive suite and a secretary.

GIRL.—Curley Enterprises, good afternoon!

AGENT.—I buy Stinky a bike and a new suit of clothes.

STINKY.—Gee, thanks!

AGENT.—The publicity begins to pile up, and at the height of the excitement, I get a wire from Hollywood!

DISNEY.—*(On filter) Offer ten thousand for Curley appearance in feature-length cartoon Stop Propose using live character for first time among cartoon characters Stop Appreciate immediate answer would like to rush story and production cordially Walt Disney.*

AGENT.—Mmm. Oh, er, Miss Neilson!

GIRL.—Yes?

AGENT.—Take a wire to Walt Disney, Hollywood, California.

GIRL.—Yes, sir.

AGENT.—*Curley price one hundred thousand.*

GIRL.—Is that all?

AGENT.—Do you think I should ask for more?

GIRL.—No. I mean, is there any more to the wire?

SOUND.—*Telephone rings . . . receiver off.*

GIRL.—Curley Enterprises. Just a moment, please. (*To agent*) *Time* magazine on the line. Will you take it on the table phone?

AGENT.—(*Going off*) All right. (*Sound of telephone receiver off . . . following conversation is background all the way through to end of scene*) Hello? Yes, this is him. Yes. Well, you see. Yuh. Uhuh. No, I discovered him in the boy's possession. That's right.

SOUND

Second telephone rings . . . perspective with the girl.

GIRL

Curley Enterprises. Well, he's busy on another line. Who? Oh, yes . . . he wanted me to tell you to order a special air-mail daily shipment of willow leaves from Florida. (*Third telephone rings*) Wait a minute, will you? (*Fourth telephone rings . . . alternates with third . . . finally the flustered girl can stand it no longer, and she shouts to agent*) You better hire some more secretaries!

. . . No . . . No . . . Yes, sure . . . No, he hasn't yet . . . Right . . . I keep him right here . . . Stinky looks after him most of the time . . . Yes . . . What? . . . No . . . Oh, no . . . I beg your pardon . . . Oh, by all means . . . From the very first, yes . . . that's right . . . that's right . . . Hm? . . . Not yet . . . Probably not for another week or two . . . Absolutely . . . Well, we tried all kinds of tunes . . . no, sir . . . which . . . which are you referring to . . . No . . . I don't . . . Hm . . . Yes.

MUSIC.—"*Yes, Sir*" . . . *transitional cue* "*B*" *rides over ringing telephones and conversation.*

AGENT.—Well, things are going in great shape, and Curley is making us a bundle of dough, when all of a sudden I get three visitors I didn't figure on.

DOCTOR 1.—We have been reading about your wonderful specimen in the papers, and we have come to ask permission to examine it.

AGENT.—Examine it? What for?

DOCTOR 2.—We are lepidopterists.

AGENT.—Lepidopterists? But Curley's a caterpillar, not a leopard.

DOCTOR 3.—Ah, no, my dear man, lepidoptery is a branch of entomology dealing with the insect order of which your, er, shall we say, client is a member.

AGENT.—Well, I'm sure Curley doesn't want to be examined by nobody.

DOCTOR 1.—Oh, come, come. If this caterpillar is as remarkable as the newspapers say, then you certainly owe science the courtesy of permitting an examination.

DOCTOR 2.—Exactly.

DOCTOR 3.—It would be nothing short of criminal to withhold such knowledge from science.

AGENT.—(*Grudgingly*) Well, if you want to put it that way.

DOCTOR 1.—It will take no more than 2 minutes.

AGENT.—Oh, I suppose it's all right. Come with me, please.

SOUND.—*Steps . . . as of group passing from one room to another . . . door opens . . . closes.*

AGENT.—Hello, Stinky.

STINKY.—Hello.

AGENT.—This is Master Stinky, gentlemen, discoverer and trainer of my client. He guards Curley all the time.

ALL.—*Ad lib greetings.*

AGENT.—Well, there he is, in that box. Please be careful how you handle him.

DOCTOR 2.—Aaahhh, *here* you are!

DOCTOR 3.—My! Muscular little fellow, isn't he?

DOCTOR 1.—Mmm hmm. (*Examining*) Normal mandible . . . unusually conspicuous first maxillae.

DOCTOR 2.—I say, watch out there, Doctor, he's trying to *bite* you!

DOCTOR 3.—Ha! Never been attacked by a caterpillar before! Astounding.

DOCTOR 1.—See here, Doctor, just notice this remarkable elongation of the abdominal feet.

DOCTOR 2.—Yes, quite. And doesn't this feature make you think of the *aglais antiopa?*

DOCTOR 3.—Incredible!

DOCTOR 1.—Look here! Isn't *this* remarkable! I've never seen such ocelli except in the *melanargia galathea*. And the chitinization!

AGENT.—No kidding?

DOCTOR 2.—(*To agent*) Well, sir! Congratulations! This *is* a remarkable specimen, even *before* we test its reactions to musical stimuli.

AGENT.—Gosh, thanks.

DOCTOR 3.—It is of the ordinary genus *papilio rutulus*, mind you, but it has the most extraordinary features.

AGENT.—Thanks very much.

DOCTOR 1.—But we feel that the specimen would be much more valuable to society, if you, instead of exhibiting it for commercial purposes, were to, uh, loan or donate it to the Museum of Natural History, where it could be further studied by the leading entomologists of the world.

AGENT.—But I . . .

DOCTOR 2.—Yes, and when it dies, we can dissect it, and . . .

STINKY.—No! No! They're not gonna take him away! (*Crying*) Don't let them take Curley! (*Keeps protesting and crying under*)

DOCTOR 3.—Don't cry, my boy, we're not going to hurt him.

DOCTOR 1.—(*Ignoring the commotion*) An insect like this occurs probably once in a million years; and surely, for the sake of a few dollars, you're not going to risk injuring him by overwork!

AGENT.—(*Rising above mercenary motives*) Are you accusing me of sacrificing Curley's health for *profits?* (*Scornfully*) Why, that's ridiculous! Curley is . . .

SOUND.—*Knocking on door . . . all noise stops, including Stinky's protestation.*

AGENT.—Yes, come in.

SOUND.—*Door opens.*

GIRL.—Just got another wire from the coast. Disney's raised his offer to twenty thousand.

AGENT.—(*Heatedly*) *Twenty!* Tell him one hundred thousand or nothing!

MUSIC.—*Sock cue . . . down behind.*

AGENT.—Well, the papers get hold of the lepidopterists' story, and there's another pile of publicity. It gets to be a moral issue, with preachers delivering sermons, and all like that. I'm attacked editorially for exploiting caterpillar labor. But, on the other hand, I am defended as an individualist who refuses to submit to regimentation.

DEFENDER.—A man owns a clever bug. He has the right to manage that bug. There is no question about his status as manager of that bug. Yet he is asked to release his client for scientific purposes. He refuses. He has a right to refuse. Nobody denies that right. Yet, in certain quarters, he is attacked merely because he insists upon his constitutional guarantees. We say it is consoling to find a man, in this day of reckless encroachment upon the individual, who will stand up and fight for his rights. We wish him well. We stand behind him, foursquare, our feet firmly implanted in the soil from which his bug has sprung, to support his defiance of those who would turn back the progress of man.

AGENT.—The American Legion and the Daughters of the American Revolution send Curley an engraved silver-plated twig and a miniature flag to put on top of his box. The foreign correspondents get busy and cable long stories to their papers. In Madrid, the Spanish *Graficano* comes out with a dirty dig.

GRAFICANO.—Mas los norte-americanos no deben olvidar que la danza española es la mejor de todas y que si la oruga del

Señor Stinky tuviese un poquitin de buen oido para la musica, reconoceria los irresistibles ritmos de la jota, y no se limitaria a tocar "Yes, Sir, That's My Baby." Es un insulto a los paises latinos que esse insecto . . .

AGENT.—How do you like that for nerve? But get this. The Curley motif is reflected, as they say, in the latest Paris fashions. Caterpillar doodads on hats and scarfs and all like that. *Le Temps*—that's a newspaper in Paris—comes out with a swell plug.

LE TEMPS.—Tous se réjouiront avec notre république soeur, les États-Unis, de la découverte faite récemment par un petit garçon qui s'appelle Stinky, la découverte d'une chenille dansante que le monde connait affectueusement sous le nom de Curley. Et c'est remarquable de constater que cet insecte ne consent á danser que si l'on joue l'air justement célèbre, "Oui, monsieur, c'est mon bébé!"

AGENT.—Not only that, but my clipping service sends me another pat on the back from Shanghai, China, which I get my laundryman to translate.

CHINESE.—

六月上海電

聲音之道與性情通其感人亦微矣哉故一曲雍門鬼神歆泣成連海上禽鳥移人從未有不定中聲而可言正樂不嫺妙技而可謂知音者也音樂名家士丁記君無所不能復無所不精允文允武担任各劇無不盡量拍演亦現身術界不可多得之人才

STINKY!

AGENT.—The Maharajah of Lahore sends Curley some willow leaves from the sacred willow trees of the Temple.

STINKY.—Gee, look, a package from a place named Lakeshore with a lot of funny-lookin' stamps.

AGENT.—*Lahore*, not Lakeshore.

STINKY.—C'n I have the stamps?

AGENT.—Yeah, here y'are. I sign Curley up for a superspecial movie short, and it sweeps the box office of the country in spite of terrible weather, including blizzards and rainstorms. *Variety* reports:

VARIETY.—Bliz and Driz Fail to Fizzle Biz as Bug Wows B.O. from N.Y. to L.A.

AGENT.—*Life* magazine runs a Margaret Bourke-White picture of Curley on the cover, with the caption . . .

LIFE.—Curley.

AGENT.—CBS does a pickup direct from Curley's box, bringing the sound of Curley eating dinner.

KNELL.—This is Jack Knell speaking to you from the headquarters of Curley Enterprises, where we have a microphone buried among willow leaves to pick up the sound of the world's leading insect danseuse, busy eating dinner after a hard day's work of exhibiting his talents to the press.

AGENT.—*The New Yorker* comes out with a cartoon showing Martha Graham nibbling willow leaves . . .

MAN.—(*Laughter*) Did you see this cartoon in *The New Yorker?*

WOMAN.—Lemme see. (*Silence*) Well, what's funny about that?

MAN.—For heaven's sake, don't you get the point?

WOMAN.—No.

MAN.—Well, don't you know who Martha Graham is?

WOMAN.—Yes.

MAN.—And you know who Curley is, of course?

WOMAN.—The caterpillar.

MAN.—Yes. Well, now, you see, *Curley* lives on willow leaves, and . . .

AGENT.—Walt Disney raises his bid to fifty thousand but I still hold out for one hundred thousand. Grover Whalen invites Curley to do an English country dance on the cover of the Magna Charta at the World's Fair.

Well, to make a long story short, everything's going along hunky-dory until one day some more public-spirited guys get ahold of Curley. Only this time they're not scientists but musicians.

SPOKESMAN.—(*Fading on*) And therefore, in the interests of music, we of the committee feel that you would be rendering an invaluable service to musical knowledge if you would permit us to test the effect of classical music on your client.

AGENT.—But what good will that do anybody?

SPOKESMAN.—Why, it may open up an entirely new field of psychology in relation to music. The world knows very little about the musical instincts of animals and nothing at all about insects. Now . . .

AGENT.—But you're wasting your time. Curley dances to only one tune.

SPOKESMAN.—Have you *tried* other tunes?

AGENT.—Why, sure. Tell him what you've played, Stinky.

STINKY.—I played "It Ain't Gonna Rain No More," "My Country, 'Tis of Thee," "The Beer Barrel Polka," "Shine on, Harvest Moon," "The Music Goes Round and . . . "

SPOKESMAN.—Ah, but no *classical* music!

AGENT.—Sure we did. I myself played "Ah, Sweet Mystery of Life," by Victor Herbert.

SPOKESMAN.—But you haven't tried any symphonies, have you?

AGENT.—(*Straight*) Disney's trying to get us for a "Silly Symphony" right now. His latest offer . . .

SPOKESMAN.—No, I'm afraid you don't understand. Let me explain what we propose to do. (*Fading*) We get Curley in a studio with an orchestra and go through a careful series of tests, using selected symphonic music of dancelike tempi. Now, by the choice of representative works, we can quickly establish . . .

SOUND.—*Rap of baton.*

CONDUCTOR.—All right, I know you're tired, gentlemen, we've now been through 67 pieces already—but let's try a few more and then we'll quit until tomorrow.

VOICE.—(*Off*) Has the caterpillar moved at all?

CONDUCTOR.—So far he hasn't budged once, but maybe we'll get him with the "Habañera" from "Carmen."

SOUND.—*Baton rapping for attention.*

MUSIC.—"*Habañera*" *for about* 12 *measures . . . then . . .*

CONDUCTOR.—(*Perfunctorily . . . this is the sixty-eighth time he's had to stop at the beginning*) Stop! Stop! (*Music out*) All right, try No. 69, "Rosamunde" ballet.

MUSIC.—*Same as above.*

CONDUCTOR.—Stop. (*Music out*) Next, No. 70, Strauss's "Perpetuum Mobile."

MUSIC.—*Same as above . . . fade under.*

AGENT.—For two and a half days this went on, and, finally, after the two hundred and second try, something happened that really made the papers sit up and take notice all over again. The Amalgamated Press next day carried this story . . .

SOUND.—*Fade in printer . . . Establish and down for*

AMALGAMATED.—Curley, the terpsichorean caterpillar, today staggered scientists and musicians when he suddenly went into a stately dance upon hearing the second movement of Beethoven's "Eighth Symphony." The movement, marked *allegretto scherzando*, was the two hundred and third musical sampling performed in an effort to determine whether the supercaterpillar could, or would, dance to anything besides the song "Yes, Sir, That's My Baby." The insect further astonished observers by dancing in a contrapuntal manner to an arrangement of melodies from *both* the song and the movement. Scientists are unable (*fade in music*) to explain the phenomenon. The management of the caterpillar announced meanwhile that Curley will appear as the lead in a ballet entitled "Extravaganza for Insects Only," by William Saroyan and that Curley will also be seen soon in a dance recital at Carnegie Hall.

MUSIC.—*Up full and down under.*

AGENT.—Well, then things *really* begin to break for us. Mrs. Roosevelt writes about it in her column "My Day."

ELEANOR.—It is not often that a creature smaller than one's little finger can completely captivate the imagination of millions. Yet such is the remarkable truth about the caterpillar named Curley, and only today I was telling the President that it has been many years since the country has become so interested in . . .

AGENT.—There's talk among stamp collectors of issuing a special Curley stamp.

PHILATELIST.—And, since the Curley stamp would be the only insect subject in existence, its value to philately would naturally assume prodigious proportions, and . . .

AGENT.—Scientific societies offer to investigate Curley's genius. And would you believe that the annual convention of the American Lepidoptological and Entomological Academy even invites *Stinky* to lecture before it.

STINKY.—(*Echo . . . hesitantly . . . scared . . . obviously no speechmaker*) Er, so I says to my mother, "Ma, can I have a penny, I want to buy a piece of candy." So my mother says yes, so she gives me the penny, er, so on my way to the store, I see a caterpillar, uh, crossing the road, er, um, so I stopped to watch it, see? So then I picked it up, and then I started to . . .

AGENT.—And all this time the money keeps coming in. We're getting along fine, although it costs a lot to keep up my expensive offices and staff of secretaries. But I'm figuring on getting the big dough, the hundred thousand from Disney, and then retiring. Well, to make a long story short, there are a couple of exchanges of telegrams and phone calls, with me holding out for my price, and then one night Disney wires.

DISNEY.—(*Filter*) Will meet your price of hundred thousand please fly out with Curley next plane.

AGENT.—Wow! Am I excited! I rush into the next room, where Stinky and Curley are sleeping.

SOUND.—*Door.*

AGENT.—Stinky! Wake up! We're rich! We're practically millionaires!

STINKY.—(*Sleepily*) What's the matter?

AGENT.—Come on, kid, get your clothes on! Hurry! You're gonna take a long airplane ride with me and Curley! And boy, I'm gonna buy Curley the juiciest willow leaf he ever ate in his life. Now lemme tell the news to Curley. (*As if opening Curley's box*) Here you are, little fella, here you . . . (*Freezes . . . then panicky*) Where is he? Why isn't he in his box? Where's Curley? *Curley!*

STINKY.—(*Refusing to believe*) I put him to bed all right. Ain't he in his box?

AGENT.—Quick! Look all around the room. Under the carpet, under the bed, on the walls, everywhere. *And be careful where you walk!*

STINKY.—(*Half-calling, half-crying*) Curley! Come back! Curley! Where are you, Curley!

AGENT.—Curley! Curley, *listen.* (*Sings "Yes, Sir" in a croaking, terror-stricken voice*)

STINKY.—*Joins in the general desultory singing, interspersed with cries for Curley.*

AGENT.—Curley! I love you! Where are you?

STINKY.—Curley, don't leave us!

AGENT.—A hundred thousand bucks, Curley! (*Sings vehemently . . . breaks off when he gets the idea*) Here, Stinky! Take this flashlight and look for him along the corridor and ask the manager to let you look at the bottom of the elevator shaft. Meanwhile I'll phone the police.

STINKY.—*Goes off half singing, half crying.*

SOUND.—*Telephone receiver jiggles.*

AGENT.—Operator! Operator! Get me police headquarters! Operator!

SOUND.—*Siren.*

POLICE RADIO.—(*Filter*) Calling all cars. Calling all cars. Be on the lookout for a dancing caterpillar. Be on the lookout for a dancing caterpillar. C-A-T-E-R-P-I-L-L-A-R. Caterpillar. That is all!

SOUND.—*Code.*

WINCHELL.—*Flash!* The Federal Bureau of Investigation will neither deny nor confirm rumors that Curley, the hundred-thousand-dollar caterpillar, was *kidnaped.* G-men are investigating closely.

SOUND.—*Single chime.*

ANNOUNCER.—Ladies and gentlemen, we have been requested by the civic authorities to make the following announcement. Whenever you hear the song "Yes, Sir, That's My Baby" will you please watch very carefully wherever you may be, for a dancing caterpillar in your vicinity. This announcement is in (*fading*) reference to Curley, the famous caterpillar whose recent career has . . .

AGENT.—The whole country searches in vain. Nobody's seen Curley. The police throw out a dragnet. Posses are formed. Radio stations play "Yes, Sir, That's My Baby" at intervals throughout the day and ask all listeners to be on the lookout for a dancing caterpillar. Curley fans from all over send in money for a "Find Curley Fund."

SPINDLERIFT.—(*Grating . . . slight echo*) And I am privileged, as president of the "Find Curley Club," to announce to the members that the "Find Curley Fund" has reached the impressive and staggering total of $12,385.14, with the entire South yet to be heard from!

SOUND.—*Great applause.*

SPINDLERIFT.—And I am positive that every mother's son of you, yes, and every father's daughter will pledge his or her heart and hand to the one main and permanent objective—that *Curley* may be *found!*

SOUND.—*Even greater applause.*

AGENT.—But nobody finds Curley. And now that he's gone, I begin to realize how much I love that bug. I begin to understand why it was Stinky couldn't bear to sell him to me, way back in those happy days. I can't bear thinking of willow leaves. I find myself hating all birds and looking suspiciously at cats. And I take to drinking.

SOUND.—*Light background.*

WAITER.—What will it be for you, sir?

AGENT.—A triple Zombie.

WAITER.—Are you sure you . . .

AGENT.—*A triple Zombie!*

WAITER.—Yes, sir.

SOUND.—*Background out.*

AGENT.—And even Stinky tries to drink his way out of his grief.

SOUND.—*Background in.*

WAITER.—And what will it be for you, young man?

STINKY.—A cup of *coffee*—and make it *black!*

WAITER.—Are you sure you want . . .

STINKY.—*Black coffee!*

WAITER.—Yes, sir.

SOUND.—*Background out.*

AGENT.—Meanwhile, sympathizers from all over the world, including Scandinavian countries, send me caterpillars, hoping maybe they have found Curley and are eligible for a reward offered by the "Find Curley Fund"!

SHIPPER.—Mister, here's another barrel of caterpillars from Australia. Where shall I put it?

AGENT.—Give it to the zoo.

SHIPPER.—Which zoo, mister?

AGENT.—Any zoo, any zoo, so long as you get it out of here!

SHIPPER.—Okay, mister.

SOUND.—*Door closes.*

AGENT.—Days go by. Weeks go by. I send Stinky home.

STINKY.—(*Tearfully*) Good-by.

AGENT.—Good-by, Stinky. Well, at least you got a nice suit of clothes on you and a fine automobile and a chauffeur to drive you home in.

STINKY.—I would rather have Curley back again.

AGENT.—Yes, I know. Well, good-by.

STINKY.—G'by.

AGENT.—G'by.

STINKY.—G'by. (*Pause*)

AGENT.—And then one day I'm sitting in my place, playing sadly on the piano with one finger, as is my wont.

MUSIC.—*One-finger plunking of "Yes, Sir."*

AGENT.—All of a sudden, out from under the music rack creeps Curley! (*Piano stops*) Only, he's changed. He's different. He's not dancing any more. He—he's a—a *butterfly!*

MUSIC.—*Orchestra sneaks in with Beethoven movement, softly and very slowly.*

AGENT.—(*To Curley, tenderly*) Curley! Hello, Curley. You're a big boy now, ain't you? (*Low . . . narrating*) He flutters his wings a little when I say that, and I stroke his antennae, which are now very long and beautiful. I see he's getting restless for the outdoors, where he no doubt hears the call of his mate, so I sing a farewell to him. (*Orchestra stops, and agent sings softly, "Yes, Sir"*) He flutters around my head and then flies over to a picture of Stinky on the bureau and then flutters back to me, and after one long look at me he flies out of the window, never more to come back again.

MUSIC.—*Sneaks in lamentation arrangement of "Yes, Sir."*

AGENT.—To make a long story short, I sit down, and I feel like crying. In fact, I do cry. (*Pause*) Yes, who would ever think that a grown man would ever cry about a caterpillar? But *I* did, and I'm not ashamed to admit it.

MUSIC.—*Up briefly, then down again.*

AGENT.—Well, that's the story of my client, Curley.

MUSIC.—*Up to finish.*

ANNOUNCER.—You have been listening to Norman Corwin's adaptation and production of "My Client, Curley," based on the original short story by Lucille Fletcher Herrmann.

In the Fog

by MILTON GEIGER

I HAVE written before of Milton Geiger, radio's most versatile workman. He is still delivering many of the best short sketches in commercial broadcasting. Here is a piece he did for the Kellogg Circle Show. Ronald Colman was heard as the doctor and gave one of the most effective readings in the entire series.

In the Fog

MUSIC.—*Down behind narration.*

NARRATOR.—It is a dense, foggy night somewhere in Pennsylvania. An automobile feels its way slowly over the misty hills. Suddenly, a blur of swaying light swims before the driver's straining eyes. Dimly, the figures of two men materialize out of the darkness. Each carries a rifle under his arm. One wears a canteen slung over his shoulder. The other wears a tattered jacket that looks as if it once belonged to some kind of uniform. The men set themselves squarely in the path of the oncoming automobile; one lifts his lantern, while the other levels his rifle menacingly at the man behind the wheel.

MUSIC.—*Out.*

SOUND.—*Drone of automobile at low speed.*

EBEN.—(*Off . . . strangely*) Stop! In the name of mercy, stop

ZEKE.—Stop, or we'll shoot!

SOUND.—*Grind of brakes . . . engine idles.*

DOCTOR.—(*More angry than afraid*) What—what do you men want?

ZEKE.—(*Coming on*) You don't have to be afraid, mister.

EBEN.—We don't aim to hurt you.

DOCTOR.—(*Indignantly*) That's very reassuring! I'd like to know what you mean by stopping me this way!

ZEKE.—What's yer trade, mister?

DOCTOR.—I—I'm a doctor. Why?

ZEKE.—A doctor, hey?

EBEN.—Then you're the man we want.

ZEKE.—He'll do proper, I'm thinkin'.

EBEN.—So you'd better come out o' that thing, mister.

DOCTOR.—You understand, don't you, that I'm not afraid of your guns. You may take anything of mine you like, but don't imagine for one moment that I'll be quiet about this to the authorities.

ZEKE.—All right. But we're needin' a doctor right now.

DOCTOR.—Oh, has anyone been hurt?

EBEN.—It's for you to say if he's been hurt nigh to the finish.

ZEKE.—So we're askin' ye to come along, doctor.

DOCTOR.—Very well. If you'll let me get out of here.

SOUND.—*Door opens . . . slams metallically.*

DOCTOR.—(*Interrogatively*) Well. Take me to your man. Where is he?

EBEN.—Yonder.

ZEKE.—Under the tree, where he fell. He's bad wounded, we're a-fearin'.

DOCTOR.—I don't know you men, you know. Do you suppose I could have a better look at you?

ZEKE.—Why not? (*Pause*) Raise yer lantern, Eben.

EBEN.—Aye. (*Pause*)

DOCTOR.—(*Appalled . . . gasps*) Good Lord!

ZEKE.—(*Impassively*) That's Eben. I'm Zeke.

DOCTOR.—But great heavens, man, what's happened!? Has—has there been an accident or—or—or what? Your faces, streaked with dried blood. It's in your hair, in your beards! *What's happened?*

ZEKE.—Mischief's happened, stranger.

EBEN.—Mischief enough.

DOCTOR.—But . . .

ZEKE.—So if ye'll be comin' along, we'd be ever so much obliged, that we would.

DOCTOR.—(*Still shocked . . . low*) Yes, yes, of course.

EBEN.—(*Off a little*) This way, doctor. Follow the lantern.

ZEKE.—(*Ruminatingly*) Mischief's happened, that's what. Enough to last these parts a good long while and a day.

DOCTOR.—I don't like this. I don't like it at all!

ZEKE.—Can't say we like it better'n you do. What must be, must. There's no changin' or goin' back, and all's left is the wishin' things were different.

DOCTOR.—There's been gunplay!

ZEKE.—(*Mildly bitter*) Ye'r tellin' *us* they's been gunplay.

DOCTOR.—And I'm telling you that I'm not at all frightened. It's my duty to report this. And report it I will!

ZEKE.—(*Casually sardonic*) Aye, mister. You *do* that.

DOCTOR.—You're arrogant about it now, yes! You don't think you'll be caught and dealt with. But people are losing patience with you men, you—you—moonshiners! Running wild, shooting up the countryside!

ZEKE.—(*Up*) Hear what he says, Eben, moonshiners!

EBEN.—(*Off*) Here we are. (*Pause . . . on*) And there's yer man, doctor.

ZEKE.—(*Anxiously*) He ain't stirred since we left 'im.

DOCTOR.—All right, let's have that light, will you? (*Pause*) Closer. So.

EBEN.—Like this?

DOCTOR.—Yes. That's good. Now help me with his shirt. No, no, don't take it off; just tear it. Yes . . .

SOUND.—*Ripping of cloth, close on-mike.*

DOCTOR.—That's good. Now bring that lantern still closer and . . . (*Deep breath . . . low*) Dreadful, dreadful!

ZEKE.—Reckon it's bad in the chest like that, heh?

DOCTOR.—His pulse is positively racing! How long has he been like this?

ZEKE.—A long time, mister. A *long* time.

DOCTOR.—Well (*With decision*) You! Hand me that bag! Hurry!

ZEKE.—(*Tensely*) Aye, captain.

SOUND.—*Rattle of bag.*

DOCTOR.—Open it!

SOUND.—*Rattle of instruments as bag is opened and rummaged through.*

DOCTOR.—All right, now lend me a hand with these retractors. Draw back on them when I tell you to. Hold it!

SOUND.—*Deep breathing, tensely . . . on-mike.*

EBEN.—How is he, mister?

DOCTOR.—More retraction; pull back a bit more. Hold it!

EBEN.—Bad, ain't he?

DOCTOR.—Bad enough. But the bullet didn't touch any lung tissue so far as I can see right now. All I can do is plug the wound. I've never seen anything like it!

EBEN.—Y'er young. Lot's o' things you never seen.

DOCTOR.—Pass me that cotton, please.

EBEN.—(*Humbly*) Aye, doctor.

DOCTOR.—(*Pause . . . deep breath*) There. So much for that. Now, then, give me a hand here.

ZEKE.—(*Suspiciously*) What fer?

DOCTOR.—We've got to move this man! We've got to get him to a hospital for treatment, a thorough cleansing of that wound, irrigation. I've done all I can for him here.

ZEKE.—I reckon he'll be all right, 'thout no hospital.

DOCTOR.—Do you realize how badly this man is hurt?

EBEN.—He won't bleed to death, will he?

DOCTOR.—I don't think so. Not with that plug in there. But . . .

ZEKE.—All right then. (*A dismissal*) We're much obliged to ye.

DOCTOR.—But I tell you that man is dangerously wounded!

ZEKE.—Reckon he'll pull through, now, thanks be to you.

DOCTOR.—(*Angrily*) Well, I'm glad *you* feel that way about it! But I'm going to report this to the Pennsylvania state police at the first telephone station I come to!

ZEKE.—We ain't stoppin' you, mister.

EBEN.—The fog is liftin', Zeke. Better be done with this, say I.

ZEKE.—(*Slowly . . . sadly*) You can go now, mister, and thanks. We never meant a mite o' harm, I can tell ye. If we killed, it was no wish of ours. What's done is done, though.

EBEN.—(*As sadly*) Aye. What's done is done.

ZEKE.—Ye can go now, stranger. On your way. We don't want no more trouble. There's been trouble enough and grievin' enough, an' we've had our share. Aye. Our share and more. We've killed, and we've been hurt fer it. We're not alone, either. We ain't the only ones. (*Pause . . . sighs*) Ye can go, now, doctor.

EBEN.—Aye. An' our thanks to ye. You can go now, an' thanks. Thanks, mister, in the name o' mercy. (*Fading . . . hollow*) In the name o' mercy we thank you, we thank you, we thank you . . .

MUSIC.—*Bridge briefly.*

SOUND.—*Fade-in drone of automobile engine . . . fast . . . car grinds to stop . . . door opens and shuts metallically.*

ATTENDANT.—(*Coming on*) Good evening, sir. Fill 'er up?

DOCTOR.—(*Impatiently*) No, please. Where's your telephone? I've just been held up!

ATTENDANT.—No!

DOCTOR.—Do you *have* a telephone?

ATTENDANT.—Find one inside, pay station.

DOCTOR.—Thank you!

ATTENDANT.—(*Stopping him*) Er . . .

DOCTOR.—Well? You were going to say something?

ATTENDANT.—Sort of looking fellers were they?

DOCTOR.—Oh. Two big ruffians, with rifles. They won't be hard to identify. Bearded, both of them, faces and heads bandaged and covered with dirt and blood. Friend of theirs with a gaping chest wound. I'm a doctor, so they forced me to attend him.

ATTENDANT.—Oh. (*Oddly knowing*) *Those* fellers.

DOCTOR.—Did you know about them?

ATTENDANT.—Yeah, I guess so.

DOCTOR.—They're desperate, I tell you, and they're armed!

ATTENDANT.—That was about 2 miles back, would you say?

DOCTOR.—Yes, just about that. Now if you'll show me where your phone is and tell me the name of that town I just went through (*Pauses on questioning note . . . no answer*) I say . . . (*Annoyed*) What town was that back there?

ATTENDANT.—(*Oddly . . . quietly*) That was Gettysburg, mister . . .

DOCTOR.—(*Struck*) Gettysburg!

MUSIC.—*In very softly, poignantly, background, "John Brown's Body."*

ATTENDANT.—(*Quiet and solemn*) Gettysburg, and Gettysburg battlefield. (*Pause . . . for effect*) When it's light and the fog is gone, you can see the gravestones. Meade's men and Pickett's men and Robert E. Lee's.

DOCTOR.—Then, those—those men . . .

ATTENDANT.—On nights like this, well, you're not the first they've stopped in the fog, nor the last.

DOCTOR.—(*Softly . . . distantly*) Gettysburg, and the dead that never die!

ATTENDANT.—That's right, I guess. (*Pause . . . deep breath*) Fill 'er up, mister?

DOCTOR.—(*Distantly*) Yes, fill 'er up . . . fill 'er up.

MUSIC.—*"John Brown's Body" up strong . . . cascade of distant trumpets fading away into "Taps" and orchestra in then . . . full and out.*

The Dark Valley

by W. H. AUDEN

IN THE spring of 1940, the Columbia Workshop invited the young English poet W. H. Auden to write an original piece for American radio. He wrote a half hour monologue. I believe it is the first ever broadcast in this country. It was an astonishing piece of work, sinister, mordant, upsetting, gravid with symbolism, luminous in its fears and revelations. It "squeaked and gibbered." Its falsetto exultations shimmered like heat lightning, and its passages of psychopathic uncertainty and frustration pounded like a wreck in the surf. To give any actress the responsibility of carrying the power and the meaning of this monologue to an audience for thirty uninterrupted minutes was to hand out the hardest assignment ever seen in broadcasting. Brewster Morgan, who directed the show, gave the job to Dame May Whitty. The English actress was appearing at the time in Laurence Olivier's production of "Romeo and Juliet." In rehearsal, Mr. Morgan, who is one of radio's most sensitive and resourceful directors, had an interesting time with the problem that Mr. Auden had given him and that he must now give to Dame May Whitty. His comments about this are worth reading. Here is what he said:

In writing "The Dark Valley" for radio, Mr. Auden presented the actress and the director with a terrifying challenge. Here, in a Gothic landscape of crags and crevices and waterfalls and abandoned mining shafts, lives a lonely woman and her goose. The twisted old soul is about to take the final step across the threshold of solitude. She is going to kill the goose. As she goes about the task, all the circumstances that have thrust her toward solitude buzz about in her mind. Here lies the poetic and dramatic action with which the actress must sway and bend and, at the same time, move forward to an inevitable conclusion. But this is only half the problem. The old woman looks down upon the world with the unclouded vision of bitter solitude. She tells the goose what she sees, and it is not pleasant. Here the actress becomes a kind of oracle, discoursing philosophically on the fate of this world—a fate which fuses in the alchemy of poetry with the fate of the goose.

The actress is thus soul and mind—and neither must lose direction or force.

In the playing of "The Dark Valley" we were not always successful in ringing all the changes demanded by Mr. Auden's magnificent music. There were times when even an artist like Dame May Whitty could not ride with the furies of deep feeling and at the same time pause to make footnotes on the state of the world. The author, whose talent is equaled only by his consideration for the practical difficulties of a young dramatic medium, corrected and modified as many of these playing difficulties as seemed compatible with the integrity of the piece. To Dame May Whitty goes the palm for reaching the heights of poetic expression and remaining always believable, as the old woman who lived in a "Dark Valley."

The original title of the Auden piece, when it first arrived, read something like this, as nearly as I can remember: "The Psychological Experiences and Sensations of the Woman Who Killed the Goose That Laid the Golden Egg." You can't get a thing like this into the newspaper listings of radio schedules. Editors look at it, blink, and just write "Drama." The Columbia Workshop changed the title to "The Dark Valley." It was heard on the evening of June 2, 1940.

Here is a brief record of W. H. Auden's life. He was born in York, England, on February 21, 1907, the son of a physician. He was educated at private schools and graduated from Christ Church, Oxford, in 1928. From 1930 to 1935 he taught English in a boys' boarding school and then worked for a time with the General Post Office Documentary Film Unit, under John Grierson. At the beginning of 1939 he came to the United States with the intention of becoming an American citizen and now lives in Brooklyn, N. Y.

He is the author of three volumes of poetry: "Poems," "On The Island," and "Another Time"; part author (in collaboration with the novelist Christopher Isherwood) of three plays: "The Dog Beneath the Skin," "The Ascent of F6," "On the Frontier," and of two travel books, "Letters from Iceland" (with Mr. Louis MacNeice) and "Journey to a War" (with Mr. Isherwood). He has also edited two anthologies: "The Poet's Tongue" and "The Oxford Book of Light Verse." He has written and arranged several programs for the British Broadcasting Company, but "The Dark Valley," commissioned by CBS for their Workshop hour, is his first radio play.

The Dark Valley

ANNOUNCER.—The Columbia Workshop presents "The Dark Valley," an original radio play by W. H. Auden, starring the celebrated English actress Dame May Whitty.

May Whitty, who carries the entire burden of the dramatic action, Dame Commander of the Order of the British Empire, was so honored for her services in the first World War. After nearly 60 years in the English theatre, Dame May began a screen career and gained a niche in the American public's favor by an unforgettable performance in "Night Must Fall." At present, she is playing the nurse in the Laurence Olivier-Vivien Leigh production of "Romeo and Juliet."

And now we take you to the "Dark Valley."

MUSIC.—*Halting and eerie.*

SOUND.—*A goose honks in the distance.*

MUSIC.—*Up and down.*

SOUND.—*Goose honks again.*

MUSIC.—*Up and down.*

WOMAN.—(*Calling*) Na-na. Na-na!

SOUND.—*Goose honks.*

MUSIC.—*Out.*

SOUND.—*Feet breaking twigs as the old woman walks.*

WOMAN.—Na-na. Na-na. The ungrateful creature. If I turn my back for a moment she takes off somewhere. She does it on purpose. Just because I'm old and can't catch her by running. She revels in it. Oh, I know very well why she waddles away. She's ashamed to be looked after by an old hag, a poor old woman alone in the mountains, with not a neighbor near to help her, someone whom the women whisper about in the village and the dogs growl at if she goes near them, and the men spit as she passes by, and the children are dragged indoors by their mothers, in case she should frighten them into a fever.

SOUND.—*Wind.*

WOMAN.—Once this valley was full of voices, effort and action, engines and men. For where a vein pointed promising the golden metal went miners like moles after, hewing into the hill their hopeful way. They sank a shaft from the surface of the earth, they drove through darkness, drifts with a purpose; in somber stopes they scooped out ore, gold-speckled quartz, with their quick hammers. They managed much, those many miners. But father was foremost, first of them all with drill and dynamite and daring hands at deeds deep down where no daylight was, and equally noble was no man living; father moved like a river, riding the world. (*Pause*)

When father spoke the monsters grew mild in the sea, and the roses opened and the eagle hung spellbound over the spellbound lamb. When he smiled it was the shining spaces of summer, but when he frowned it was ages of ice, his anger ended the earth. Oh, but *he* is ended, ended his life, lost, away, a no one, a nothing, as if he never were, his body broken by a blast in the earth. He was drunk, they lied, the low and evil; he was killed by his lack of care, the mine-owners wrote; and their mean hearts were glad he was a ghost, for his greatness galled them. He was a stag among sheep, a star among tapers, alone with fools in a foul field.

SOUND.—*Goose off.*

WOMAN.—Na-na. There you are, you slut. Come here at once. All right. Stay there if you want. Go on, stare at yourself in the water and starve. I don't mind. Nor will the foxes, I'm sure. You'll find them *most* flattering. Na-na. Come here at once. Wait till I find a stone. (*She throws*) You little fool, I'll bash your head in.

SOUND.—*Stone striking in water . . . off.*

WOMAN.—That frightened you, didn't it? A bit too close to be quite comfortable, eh? A narrow escape, from—well—from it, the nasty thing that's always just round the corner but a lady doesn't mention in public. You're quite right. One shouldn't speak of such things. Let's think of something nice like food. Come along, Nana, it's suppertime, time for greedy little geese to stuff their guts and then bedtime. (*She is stalking the goose*)

Hushaby, sleep, sleep and such lovely dreams, flying away away away over the treetops, not even bothering to look back down at the poor old woman waving good-by but just going on and on above the forest, over the tops of the mountains, and then there it is, the fairy castle. (*Goose*)

The gate stands open. There's not a soul to be seen. (*Goose*) Into the courtyard, through the door, up the winding stair to the little room at the very top of the tower. (*Goose*) Ah, how your heart beats. At last I shall meet him, my wonderful gander-husband, my fairy prince. (*Goose*) Knock. Knock. Who's there? Queen Nana? Come in, my dear, I've been expecting you for a thousand years. In you rush with a flutter of feathers. (*She grabs the goose*).

SOUND.—*Goose squawks angrily.*

WOMAN.—Got you, now we'll go my way for a change. (*Pause*) Something funny has happened, eh? There's no handsome rich young gander standing there but only the poor old woman you left behind.

SOUND.—*Goose hisses angrily.*

WOMAN.—Hissing won't mend matters. Yes, there's a nice little coop of wire netting waiting for you while I get things ready.

SOUND.—*Goose being put in coop.*

WOMAN.—In you go, now, and stay quiet till I need you. You're a good respectable goose at last. (*Door fastened*) Not bad is it? Plenty of air? Plenty of room between the wire to look at the view. Food and water and no worries. What more do you want. What's freedom anyway? Ask the boys and girls in the city, ask any of them. Go on, ask them, and what will they tell you? "Dear Goose (*Goose noise*), aren't you a *lucky* girl to have a kind old woman to look after you and feed you and give you a nice coop to live in. Think of all the poor underprivileged wild geese with no roof over their heads, having to lay their eggs just anywhere and liable to be gobbled up any moment by some horrid fox.

"We're lucky too. We can read and write and do sums. Our coops have four walls and a roof and light and heat and hot and cold running water. And all we have to do in return is address envelopes or take dictation or pull levers; which is ever so easy and we only have to do it for eight hours a day. The rest of our times we've absolutely free. We can relax and romp as much as we like. No one interferes. Mustn't it have been awful in the old days before there was any progress, before there was any science to make people safe?" Yes, Nana, you're safe . . . For the time being, anyway . . . Safe until . . .

SOUND.—*Goose honks.*

WOMAN.—Until *what*, you'd like to know, eh? Ah, who knows the answer to that? Do you? Shall we say, until the unexpected happens, whatever and whenever that may be? And until then, we might as well go on happily with our daily routine. You shall stay here in your coop and enjoy your supper, and I'll go and get fresh water. We must have water, Nana, you know. Water's needed for everything. We die without it. (*Chuckle*) We *die* in it. But there are worse ways.

Think of all the babies suffocated in their sleep by large black cats, of all the skaters drowned in millponds when the ice breaks, of all the hilarious parties returning from dances whose cars skid and plunge them shrieking over cliffs. Think of all the geese, Nana.

SOUND.—*Goose noise.*

WOMAN.—You'd be surprised at all the possibilities of hungry hawks and famished foxes and stealthy stoats and lurking lynxes and bold bad bears, at all the varieties of clutch and claw and teeth and talon and snap and snatch.

SOUND.—*Ravens croaking overhead.*

WOMAN.—Cry your curse from the crags; cry it again, black ravens over this ruined place. (*Sighs*) I must get water.

SOUND.—*Footsteps on twigs.*

WOMAN.—(*Sings*) Eyes look into the well.
Tears run down from the eye.
The tower cracked and fell
From the quiet winter sky.

SOUND.—*Fade in stream and waterfall.*

WOMAN.—The shaft is full of water, and the wind whistles through the broken buildings of an abandoned mine. For after father died the lode vanished—in vain they searched.

SOUND.—*Feet on steps continuing . . . Waterfall up.*

WOMAN.—The gold was gone; they got nothing; they lost heart, gave up their drilling; it paid no longer; they departed poor. And none remained but mother and I on this stony farm in a stony silence. She never loved me. I knew it from the first. She was prim and pious and praying always for father's soul and shuddered at his songs and thought him wicked and wept much. (*Pebbles and sand*) For she wanted a dummy who would drive her to church in a blue suit, bowing to the neighbors, holy and hollow and half alive. And she could not *bear me* because I was like him and he knew it and loved me and would lift me up in his great hands as he imitated a lion *roaring* or a rutting stag.

SOUND.—*Bucket in stream . . . waterfall fades, and stream fades.*

WOMAN.—Water, at least we have water.
(*Sings*) Under the midnight stone
Love was buried by thieves.
The robbed hearts weep alone.
The damned rustle like leaves.

SOUND.—*Distant avalanche.*

WOMAN.—The avalanches have been falling all afternoon; for the sun is still shining in the white snow peaks, and the useless wastes of that world are full of useless light and heat that can do nothing. But this deep dale is dark always. (*Wind*) Here summer has no success, and short the distance of noon from night, and near ever are the cold crags to this crevice where roars the glacier torrent in a gloomy twilight, wild waters in a winter dusk. Let the day break its heart on the hard heights, for what it can do. The dark returns, and even up there it is autumn already.

SOUND.—*Goose fades in.*

WOMAN.—Did you think I'd forgotten about you, Nana? (*Bucket of water*) Why do you look at me like that? I know what you're thinking. The old woman is going mad. Only mad people talk to themselves. You wouldn't do such a thing, would you, not a fat sensible tame goose like yourself. Aren't you glad you're not old and mad like me? Old women die; but a sensible goose lives on forever, getting fatter and fatter, while old women have to work, getting everything ready, putting the water on the stove, shelling the peas, sharpening the . . . There now, I nearly said it. You must try to excuse an old woman whose tongue is always running away with her. Stuff yourself till you burst. I'll (*picks up bucket*) be back in a moment.

(*Sings*) Eyes look into the well.
Tears run down from the eye.
The tower cracked and fell
From the quiet winter sky.

SOUND.—*Door opens and shuts off.*

WOMAN.—(*Fades in*) The palace servants sing.
The ships put out to sea.
The form that pleased a king
Swings on the elder tree.

SOUND.—*Goose scolds.*

WOMAN.—Well, what are you fussing about now? You can't still be hungry. (*Chair . . . pan*) What do you want this time? Some new excitement? What shall it be? A bus trip to the national park? A cruise in the South Seas? The new novel everybody's talking about? A new boy friend? After all, you belong to the younger generation, and I'm only a silly old woman with old-fashioned ideas. One must keep up with the times, Nana, unless one wants to become just a back number. (*Goose*) Still unsatisfied? What about some fresh green peas, then? (*Goose grunts*) Oh—sulky! Then, a pretty little mountain primrose? (*Goose grunts*) It's a shame that you're kept shut up in a wire coop when every girl nowadays has a latchkey and goes to college and knows how babies are born. The young have a right to a good time. Are you jealous? Would you like to go down to the village hall one evening and play with all the other boys and girls? I'm sure they'd be delighted, and they wouldn't mind your being a goose a bit. The young are so tolerant. They'd think you just too cute. You'd be the belle of the evening.

And what would you think of them, Nana? Would you think them wonderful, the heroes of a new age, the brilliant freethinkers, the great lovers? No, even a goose wouldn't take long to see through the noise and nonsense to their frightened barren little hearts and heads. Even you would soon discover that, for all their pretence, they think love disgusting. To read about it and photograph it, to talk and titter is one thing; but to touch a real live person—ugh!

Only soap and bath salts and shaving creams and face creams and skin tonics and hair tonics and breath sweeteners and perspiration removers and nail files and eyebrow tweezers can make it bearable. And even then it must be just the right hour and the right room and the right clothes and the right sofa and the right temperature and the right moon and the right music and the right liquor and the right words. Oh, but it was otherwise, Nana, when I was born. Then love was a god who drove men mad. Girls kept it a secret, for it was danger and death; and many died, drowned in streams or stoned or burnt or buried alive. No one spoke of freedom then on this farm. There was no radio or magazines or movies or romantic novels or picnics or drives or dances. And mother watched every movement I made, afraid that father's passionate blood would appear in his daughter.

For the god of love was father's friend—yes, and mine. Mine also. It was the god that helped me defeat my mother and made her blind and never betrayed me. For he came to me in secret on soft feet; like the wind through the keyhole he came to my chamber; he came at his will through windows and walls, and the watching eyes were ignorant of his presence. In the yard or the kitchen, cooking or washing or feeding the hens or helping in the field, he was suddenly at my side, and I shook with joy—for his arms were about me and my beauty his. He never spoke nor said "I love you" nor told me his name; but I knew he was noble, with the blood of a prince and a prince's favor, clear-eyed as an eagle though he hid his face. And when he went away the world was empty. He kissed me farewell. I watched him stride up the mountain valley and vanish forever, and all clocks stopped as the clouds hid him.

SOUND.—*Goose grunts . . . airplane fades in overhead.*

WOMAN.—Look up, Nana, look up. There he goes. Do you see him? The new man in his new machine. Applaud him, Nana.

SOUND.—*Claps hands . . . Goose honks derisively.*

WOMAN.—If you're lucky, he might even wave at you. Yes, sure enough, he is waving.

SOUND.—*Goose noise.*

WOMAN.—Shout yourself hoarse. Show him that even the geese know he's the lord of creation, the master of matter whom the winds and waves obey. (*Honk-honk . . . plane up*) Think of it, Nana. Every evening at 6 o'clock, week in week out, winter or summer, storm or sunshine, that plane with its mail and its millionaires passes over this spot, punctual to the second. Think of that. What a triumph of organization. What a brain he must have, stuffed with wonderful plans for the future of humanity, for you and for me. For nothing's so small as to be beneath his notice, you know. He thinks of everybody. We're all free and equal, he says. We all have a right to do our share in the government by answering questions and filling up forms. All of us, even geese. Even your existence, Nana, is recognized in the capitol. Some official has you down on a file under "Geese, Domestic," along with gelatine, geldings, gems, gentians, gentlemen, geraniums, gerfalcons, Germans, germs, germicides, and geysers. As a statistic you exert immense influence. Professors use you in university courses; you help columnists and economists and political prophets; you win debates and defeat governments; you turn the scale for peace or war. Aren't you proud of yourself?

SOUND.—*A distant sound of hunting . . . horns and hounds.*

WOMAN.—But you mustn't think he's only a brain, a dreary bookworm, weedy, weary, and wan, who reads all day and never goes out of doors or takes any exercise. Oh dear, no, he's not like that at all. Can't you hear him down there in the forest, hunting the wild boar, with horns and hounds? (*Horns*) Nothing delights him so much as sleeping in log cabins or under canvas or cooking canned food on a campfire or saying woodgy-woodgy to his wife in a stony wilderness.

SOUND.—*Horns again.*

WOMAN.—But what do these hunters hope for, Nana, these sensitive lives from lighted cities? What shall the wilderness whisper in their ears; what secret do they seek in the shadows of the fir tree; what is it they ask of animals and stones, of the cold streams in the calm hills?

SOUND.—*Horns again.*

WOMAN.—What is it, Nana? They know nothing. They are only tame geese on a wild-goose chase. Listen to the lifeless longing for life, the lost and learned looking for their home. But nothing they run after shall they ever find. The lions leap aside in the valleys evading their vision; quickly into a quiet their quarry escapes; the unicorn wanders away; the treasure lies hidden under the stone; the precious gold is at peace in the rock; and echo will not answer when they ask for help. The clouds are gathering round the granite peaks; and the black storm broods above, preparing to loose its rain on a ruined race.

SOUND.—*Horns again.*

WOMAN.—For those horns are the howls of hunted creatures, the trumpets of a regiment retreating in rout, fleeing in panic through a perilous landscape with sinister shadows in pursuit behind them as they stumble through the darkness of a dreadful dream.

SOUND.—*Goose.*

WOMAN.—But why am I telling you all this, Nana? What can it matter to you what happens to the human race? What good can it do you if it lives or dies? You will die first.

SOUND.—*Goose hiss.*

WOMAN.—There, now, don't get alarmed. Of course, I don't mean anything personal. After all, you won't be the only one. I shall die, too. Whatever happens to us, there will still be tame geese and old women for a long time to come. At least we have to hope so.

SOUND.—*Patter of raindrops.*

WOMAN.—Oh dear, here comes the rain, and I'm afraid we shall have to interrupt our little chat. Old women aren't like geese, you know. If they get wet, they catch cold and die, and then who would look after poor Nana? So I must go indoors. Never mind. It's only going to be a shower this time. I'll be back as soon as it's over. By then I ought to be about ready. Yes, Nana, soon it will be your turn. (*During the song she goes indoors and busies herself in the kitchen as she sings*)

(*Fade in*) Lady weeping at the crossroads,
Watch you meet your love
In the twilight with his greyhounds
And the hawk on his glove?

SOUND.—*Steps on wooden floor . . . kitchen clock, utensils, etc., etc.*

WOMAN.—(*Sings*) Cross the silent empty ballroom,
Doubt and danger past.
Blow the cobwebs from the mirror.
See yourself at last.

SOUND.—*Steps on wooden floor.*

WOMAN.—(*Sings*) Put your hand behind the wainscot.
You have done your part.
Find the penknife there and plunge it
Into your false heart.

SOUND.—*Clock strikes . . . Board fade . . . Wind . . . Door opening and shutting . . . Goose fades in.*

WOMAN.—Yes, Nana, I'm coming. And how did my dear Nana enjoy the shower? Freshened you up a bit, eh? Still, it's nice to have got it over. Look, the sun's coming out over the valley. We shall have a fine evening after all. The day is going to end well for all of us. But now I warn you, Nana, this grindstone is going to make a horrid noise.

SOUND.—*Grindstone.*

WOMAN.—I'm sorry, but it has to be done. Life can't always be pleasant, can it? Geese have to hatch eggs and grow fat. And old women have to sharpen knives. What for? Why? You may well ask, but who knows? Why are we alive? Why don't we die?

SOUND.—*Distant church bells.*

WOMAN.—It's Sunday evening, Nana. Time for all respectable people to take their prayer books and go to church with their charming children, kneel in pews and murmur responses, sing hymns to the organ and hear a sermon and be gently assured that, somehow or other, all things for the righteous shall come right in the end. (*Pause*) The minister is modern and well mannered and mild and well read in evolution and the latest theories of physics and astronomy and is tolerance itself. The flames of hell are an old-fashioned idea, for his God is a mathematician and much like a man and understands perfectly and expects little. For business is business, and boys will be boys, and lust is a natural need like eating, and the search for the gold of grace is a grueling voyage.

SOUND.—*Coop opens . . . goose.*

WOMAN.—And he will forgive them if they go astray or are lazy and look for light no longer. (*Coop*) For the All-Father is proud of his pretty world and takes her on his knees, Nana, as I take you now, and strokes her back, smiling, till she squirms with pleasure and feels with his fingers in her feathery neck and calls her his daughter and his dear darling, his treasure, his princess, his precious goose; and she looks into his eyes and is ever so happy for the sunset is beautiful and the bells are ringing, though she wonders a little why his loving hands are gripping so tightly that she gasps for air. "Father, why—what is the matter? What have I done? Father, why are you looking so fierce? Father, don't you remember, I'm the world you made. Father, I'm so young and white, I don't want to die. Father . . . "

SOUND.—*Church bells up and fade.*

ANNOUNCER.—You have been listening to the Columbia Workshop's presentation of "The Dark Valley" by W. H. Auden. Dame May Whitty spoke the lines of the old woman. The entire production was directed by Brewster Morgan. Special music was composed by Benjamin Britten and conducted by Bernard Herrmann. (*Pause*)

Beginning next Sunday, the Workshop will be heard over many of these stations from 8 to 8:30 P.M. EDST. Next week's drama will be called "No Complications," by Louis Estes, a writer whose work is new to the Columbia Workshop.

For Richer—for Richer

by TRUE BOARDMAN

LAST year I included a Silver Theatre Show, written by True Boardman, which had to do with insanity. This year I am including another of his originals; and although it may deal with something akin to insanity—a superb pose of a superbly indifferent Clark Gable—this piece is not hard going. It's a good, gay comedy that plays fast and reads fast and lives happily ever after. It is called "For Richer—for Richer" and was heard over CBS Sunday afternoon, December 10, 1939.

For Richer—for Richer

Music.—*Opening signature.*

Joy.—International Silver Company presents the Silver Theatre!

Music.—*Musical progression.*

Joy.—Starring Clark Gable in "For Richer—for Richer"—directed by Conrad Nagel.

Music.—*Musical progression.*

Joy.—Brought to you on behalf of two of the greatest names in silverware, International Sterling, world-famous solid silver, and 1847 Rogers Brothers, America's finest silver plate!

Music.—*Theme . . . fade to background.*

Joy.—We welcome you to the tenth program in the new Silver Theatre series. And here is our director, Conrad Nagel, who has a few words regarding our play.

Nagel.—Ladies and gentlemen, the original comedy drama, in which Mr. Gable is starring today, was written especially for Silver Theatre by True Boardman. In future weeks our stars will include Kay Francis, George Brent, Margaret Lindsay, Madeleine Carroll, and many others equally famous. Shortly after the final curtain, I'll give you the news about next week's production and our next star.

But now for today's play:

Music.—*Curtain raiser.*

Nagel.—The house lights dim, and the Silver Curtain rises on the first act of "For Richer—for Richer," starring Clark Gable as Chris Morgan, with Mary Taylor as Peggy Turner.

Music.—*Segue to scoring behind narration.*

Nagel.—In a particularly luxurious bedroom of the altogether luxurious Turner mansion, Susan Turner is pacing the floor. In fact, Susan *has* been pacing the floor since 11 o'clock. And now it's nearly midnight. But suddenly . . .

SOUND.—*Over end of above . . . brief knock on door . . . door opens.*

PEGGY.—Susan. Are you feeling better? I left the dance early, because I thought . . .

SUSAN.—(*Blithely*) Oh, hello, Peggy.

PEGGY.—(*Astonished*) Susan, what are you doing up and dressed and with a bag packed?

SUSAN.—I'm eloping. Isn't it wonderful?

PEGGY.—Eloping? Susan! With Freddie?

SUSAN.—Freddie? Don't be silly. I've been engaged to Freddie for 2 years. Why should I run away and marry a man I'm engaged to. It doesn't make sense.

PEGGY.—Well, then, who?

SUSAN.—Chris Morgan.

PEGGY.—Chris Morgan? But we hardly know the man. Who is he? What about his family?

SUSAN.—Oh, I asked him about that. His family's just as good as ours. In fact one of his ancestors was a knight.

PEGGY.—A knight?

SUSAN.—Sir Henry Morgan.

PEGGY.—Look, sister darling, *for your information*, Sir Henry Morgan was a pirate.

SUSAN.—That's what I mean. Isn't it marvelous?

PEGGY.—(*Genuinely disturbed*) Susan, listen to me. You can't do this, not without telling dad.

SUSAN.—Peggy, you may just as well save your breath. (*She sighs*) Chris simply swept me off my feet.

PEGGY.—Does he love you?

SUSAN.—Well, he hasn't said so, but he's been awfully indifferent.

CHRIS.—*Over above . . . well off-mike . . . whistles . . . "Hail, Hail, the Gang's All Here."*

SUSAN.—Listen. He's here! (*She fades slightly . . . calls in a hoarse whisper*) I'm all ready. Be right down. (*Whispering*) Oh, Peggy. I'm so excited. Where's my bag?

PEGGY.—How are you going to get down from the window? Float?

SUSAN.—Oh, no. There's a ladder. I put it there myself. Chris said that would save him trouble.

PEGGY.—Hm. Apparently Chris thinks of everything.

SUSAN.—Everything. Well, good-by, darling. Wish me luck.

PEGGY.—(*Then . . . a new idea*) Susan, wait. If you must do this mad thing, at least be sensible about it. Take a warm coat. It's awfully bad form to catch pneumonia on your honeymoon.

SUSAN.—Maybe you're right. My fur coat . . .

PEGGY.—It's here in your closet. (*Sound . . . door opens*) Better get it.

SUSAN.—(*Fading slightly*) Yes, I'll . . .

SOUND.—*Door slams . . . key turns.*

SUSAN.—*Cries out ad lib from behind door, "Let me out of here. What are you going to do?" etc., etc., etc.*

CHRIS.—*Whistles again in the distance.*

PEGGY.—(*Calling*) I'm coming. (*Then to herself*) Elope with *my* kid sister, will you, you son of Henry Morgan. I'll show you.

MUSIC AND SOUND.—*Starting with above speech . . . clambering over window sill . . . special effect of descending ladder over above . . . footsteps on gravel . . . fade in sound of idling motor.*

CHRIS.—Hello.

PEGGY.—Hello.

CHRIS.—No bag?

PEGGY.—No bag? Oh, no. No bag.

CHRIS.—Then get in the car.

PEGGY.—(*Taken aback*) Get in?

CHRIS.—(*Yawning*) Yeah. Let's get this over and done with. I want to get some sleep.

SOUND.—*Car door closes . . . then another . . . car starts off . . . a moment's pause, and Chris speaks . . . yawning again.*

CHRIS.—I'm late.

PEGGY.—Oh, that's quite all right. Your apology is accepted.

CHRIS.—Who's apologizing? Don't jump at conclusions.

PEGGY.—Oh, excuse me. (*Pause*) I suppose it wouldn't be the thing for me to ask where we're going?

CHRIS.—We're going to get married. Where do people usually go when they elope?

PEGGY.—Hm. *How charming.* Well, this may be somewhat of a shock to you, Mr. Morgan, but I'd suggest that you look at me again, a little more closely this time.

CHRIS.—Why should I?

PEGGY.—It just happens that I'm *not* Susan Turner. I'm Peggy, her sister. Surprise!

CHRIS.—Yeah, I know. What difference does that make?

PEGGY.—What difference?

CHRIS.—Sure, I'm not marrying the girl, I'm marrying the 3 million. (*Pause*)

PEGGY.—(*Floored . . . Trying to laugh it off*) You're joking.

CHRIS.—I never joke after midnight.

PEGGY.—Well! So the change in brides makes no difference to you?

CHRIS.—Sure, it makes a difference. Your sister's younger than you are.

PEGGY.—Only a year and a half!

CHRIS.—She's got nicer hair, bluer eyes, and better teeth.

PEGGY.—Well, thank you.

CHRIS.—(*Reluctantly*) Maybe I'm wrong about the teeth.

PEGGY.—(*Icily*) If you'll forgive me for reminding you, you are *not* buying a horse, Mr. Morgan.

CHRIS.—Not much difference.

PEGGY.—Oh, isn't there?

CHRIS.—Come to think of it, there is. You can always sell a horse.

PEGGY.—(*A slight pause . . . then realizing*) This car. It's Susan's, isn't it?

CHRIS.—Sure. I took it out of the garage. Mine was low on gas.

PEGGY.—You were eloping with my sister in *her* car?

CHRIS.—Why not? It's her wedding. Or it was going to be. If I'd known you were coming, I'd have brought yours instead.

PEGGY.—(*A very slight pause*) Mr. Morgan, before this goes any further, there's one thing you really ought to know, as a confirmed fortune hunter, I mean. You are a confirmed fortune hunter, I take it?

CHRIS.—(*Agreeing*) You take it.

PEGGY.—Well, it so happens that if either Susan or I marry without father's consent we're automatically disinherited.

CHRIS.—Yeah?

PEGGY.—Yeah.

CHRIS.—Your nose is shiny. Fix it. (*Slight pause*) And you're a liar!

PEGGY.—What? Don't you talk to me like that!

CHRIS.—Both of you inherited 3 million apiece from your grandmother. Your old man hasn't anything to say about it.

PEGGY.—(*Sore because he's right*) Well! You certainly haven't left any stones unturned.

CHRIS.—Can't afford to. I only intend to get married once, so I want to be sure it's the right proposition.

PEGGY.—Proposition?

CHRIS.—What do you call it? Marriage is a business, pure and simple.

PEGGY.—I see. And that little element called love?

CHRIS.—Look at the people who married for love. Where do they end up? In the divorce courts.

PEGGY.—But how about the marriages that last? Some do, you know.

CHRIS.—Economic, practically every one of them. Two people meet, like you and me, say. They see it's to their mutual advantage to go into a business partnership.

PEGGY.—Hm. But in *your* case, why should you plan only one "partnership," as you call it? There are lots of girls with money. And there's always Reno.

CHRIS.—(*Sore*) What do you think I am, a chiseler?

PEGGY.—(*Grinning*) You're asking me?

CHRIS.—What are you kicking about? I've got every qualification you need in a husband. I can play bridge. I can juggle a teacup. I can dance, fence, ride, swim, bowl, ski, play tennis, badminton, and Chinese checkers. I can fly a plane, drive a car, and sail a boat. What more can you ask, for 3 million?

PEGGY.—I might ask if you ever work.

CHRIS.—Work?

PEGGY.—Yes. You've heard of the word, perhaps. It's an old custom, especially among self-respecting men.

CHRIS.—Do *you* work?

PEGGY.—Of course not!

CHRIS.—Well, the women in China are hod carriers. And in certain native tribes of Africa, the woman who even lets her husband lift his hand in manual labor has her ears lopped off.

PEGGY.—But this isn't Africa, Mr. Morgan.

CHRIS.—No. But we can learn.

PEGGY.—Then after this wedding tonight, you have no plans except, of course, to live on my money?

CHRIS.—Why not? That's what you're doing.

PEGGY.—I suppose the fact that it's mine has nothing to do with it.

CHRIS.—Whaddayamean, yours? Did you ever work for it?

SOUND.—*The car is slowed to a stop . . . anticipate.*

CHRIS.—Here we are. Justice of the peace.

PEGGY.—The lights are on. He's up.

CHRIS.—Sure, and waiting. I believe in having things organized. Come on, let's go in and get this over. I told you before, I want to get some sleep.

MUSIC.—*Brief transition.*

JUSTICE.—Yep, stand right here, please. Now, as soon as we make out this license. Your name, Miss.

CHRIS.—Her name's Turner, Peggy Turner.

PEGGY.—(*With a touch of sarcasm*) I can tell him my *own* name, "darling." Do you mind? My name is Margaret Evelyn Turner, and I live at Shore Beach.

JUSTICE.—(*Impressed*) Turner? Well! Well! Not *the* Turners?

CHRIS.—(*Irascibly*) Let's go.

JUSTICE.—Oh, sure, sure. Occupation, *Miss Turner?*

PEGGY.—Just put down "saving Susan."

JUSTICE.—What's that?

CHRIS.—Leave it blank.

JUSTICE.—Now you, mister . . .

CHRIS.—I'm Christopher Morgan. Address, the *Jezebel*, New York.

PEGGY.—(*A take*) The *Jezebel!* You would live in a hotel with a name like that!

CHRIS.—Oh, would I? Well, it just happens, the *Jezebel* is a boat.

JUSTICE.—A boat, eh? Well, let's get on with it. Occupation, mister?

PEGGY.—(*Quickly*) Fortune hunter.

JUSTICE.—Huh?

CHRIS.—She called it.

JUSTICE.—Hm. Well, things are bad all over. Let's go then. (*Calling*) Ma! Emmy! stick your heads out here and witness this.

WOMAN.—(*Sighing . . . yawning off*) All right, pa, we're witnessin'.

JUSTICE.—Join hands. Do you, Christopher Morgan, take this woman to be your lawful wedded wife?

CHRIS.—I do.

JUSTICE.—Hm. And do you, Margaret Evelyn Turner, take this man to be your lawful wedded husband?

PEGGY.—(*Matter of factly*) I do not.

JUSTICE.—Then by the power vested in me . . . (*Double take*) What'd you say?

PEGGY.—(*Very positively*) I said "I do not"!

JUSTICE.—That's what I thought you said. Well, certainly can't marry you folks. (*Sighing*) Go back to bed, ma.

SOUND.—*Door slams . . . off.*

CHRIS.—Wait a minute! (*To Peggy*) What's the idea?

PEGGY.—(*Accusingly*) You would have done it! You actually would have gone through with the marriage!

CHRIS.—Certainly I would. Why not?

PEGGY.—You weren't joking? You really are everything you said you were!

CHRIS.—Sure I am.

PEGGY.—(*Almost speechless*) Oh! Of all the arrogant, conceited, self-centered, weak-kneed excuses *for a man!* Marry you? Why, I wouldn't marry you, if . . .

CHRIS.—If I were the last man on earth. I know the line. Now look! Cut out the dramatics.

PEGGY.—Let go of me!

CHRIS.—Quit it, I said!

JUSTICE.—Look here, mister. You're not gonna hit nobody in this house. I'll . . .

CHRIS.—Do I look like a guy who'd hit a woman before I was married to her?

JUSTICE.—(*Very slight pause*) But, Mr. Morgan . . .

CHRIS.—Get out of here! You heard me! Beat it!

JUSTICE.—(*Meekly*) I heard you.

SOUND.—*Door closes . . . off.*

PEGGY.—(*Furious*) You let go of me!

CHRIS.—What's the idea, jilting me at the altar? I suppose you think I'll stand for that!

PEGGY.—Jilting you? I never said I'd marry you. You never even asked me! And I won't! I won't! I won't!

CHRIS.—(*Suddenly*) All right. You won't. Then come on.

PEGGY.—Where are we going?

CHRIS.—To get your sister.

PEGGY.—(*Unbelieving*) You wouldn't! You wouldn't still marry her tonight, after . . . after . . .

CHRIS.—Certainly I would. Why not? Don't argue. Let's go.

SOUND.—*Door opens and closes . . . light traffic noises low in background.*

PEGGY.—(*Protesting vainly*) But—but, the man in there. The license. You didn't pay him.

CHRIS.—Why should I? We didn't use it.

PEGGY.—That doesn't matter, Chris Morgan. I still refuse to be a party to cheating an old man out of $2. I know! You wait in the car. I'll be right out. (*Concerned*) You *will* wait? You won't go without me?

CHRIS.—Maybe I will, maybe I won't. But you'll never find out just standing there in the door. Go on!

PEGGY.—(*Angrily*) Oh . . .

SOUND.—*Door slams.*

CHRIS.—*Laughs.*

MUSIC.—*Transition.*

SOUND.—*Car running.*

CHRIS.—You took long enough. Another 2 minutes and I wouldn't have waited.

PEGGY.—The man had to wake his wife to get change. I only had a $20 bill.

CHRIS.—(*Snorts disapprovingly*) Huh!

PEGGY.—(*Bridling*) What did you say?

CHRIS.—I said "huh"! Any objections? Why did you have to mix up in this, anyway? Except for you, whatshername and I would be married now.

PEGGY.—Her name is Susan! And you'll only marry her over my dead body.

CHRIS.—Sounds a little messy to me for a wedding ceremony, but any way you say.

SOUND.—*Over above . . . a siren fades in in the distance.*

PEGGY.—Listen, Chris Morgan! You needn't think . . . (*She breaks off as she hears the siren*)

CHRIS.—(*Smiling grimly*) I'm listening.

SOUND.—*Car speed increases.*

PEGGY.—(*Beginning to be scared . . . laughing feebly*) You're, er, going pretty fast.

CHRIS.—Only the beginning.

SOUND.—*Car veers around curve . . . tires skid.*

PEGGY.—(*Stifles a scream*) Look! Don't you hear a siren behind us?

CHRIS.—I do.

PEGGY.—It couldn't be a motorcycle cop?

CHRIS.—It could, and it is. Two of them.

SOUND.—*Car running faster . . . another tire screams turn . . . more sirens.*

PEGGY.—(*Scared*) Oh, please, please, Chris! Don't drive so fast. We'll . . .

CHRIS.—Haven't really opened up yet. Never open up till there are at least six cops on my tail. Ah, now there are four.

PEGGY.—(*A moan of fright*) Ohhhh!

CHRIS.—(*Over the sound of the motor*) What did you say?

PEGGY.—I said you're a lunatic!

CHRIS.—(*Enjoying this*) So you wanted to pay the old man his $2? You really went back to phone, didn't you? Who to? Your father, or straight to the police?

PEGGY.—I don't know what you're talking about!

SOUND.—*There are now more sirens in the distance.*

CHRIS.—Well! Two more of our friends. That makes the six. Now we'll *really* travel.

SOUND.—*Car opens up full.*

PEGGY.—(*Terrified*) No! No, Chris! You can't go faster! Please! You'll . . . Chris! Ahead there! The road's blocked!

CHRIS.—Jeepers creepers! Ambushed!

SOUND.—*Tires scream as car careens to stop.*

CHRIS.—(*Angry*) A fine sense of sportsmanship those cops have. Incidentally, Miss Turner, you're going to be sorry you started this.

PEGGY.—Oh, am I?

SOUND.—*Through these speeches . . . sirens coming up to stop, etc.*

OFFICER.—(*Coming in hurriedly*) Is that you, Miss Turner? And are you all right?

CHRIS.—Look here, officer! What's the idea of . . .

PEGGY.—(*Interrupting*) Yes, officer, I *am* all right, now that you've caught up with "Killer Morgan" here.

OFFICER.—(*Astonished*) Killer Morgan!!!

CHRIS.—(*Even more astonished*) Killer Morgan?

PEGGY.—(*Quickly and positively*) Killer Morgan. Alias *Chris the Crook*, alias *Morgan the Mugg*, alias *Slugface Benedict*, Those are his names. He told me so!

CHRIS.—(*Grinning*) Oh, I told you that, did I?

OFFICER.—Never mind the lip, Morgan. You're comin' along with us. Miss Turner, what's the charge?

CHRIS.—(*Challenging*) Yes, Miss Turner, what is the charge?

PEGGY.—The charge? Well, officer, I do want you to go easy on him—but he *was* guilty of speeding—and reckless driving—and I don't think he has a license. He's *obviously* drunk—he stole this car—and—oh, yes—I almost forgot—*he kidnaped me!*

MUSIC.—*First act curtain. Applause.*

NAGEL.—Ladies and gentlemen, I'm sure you're all looking forward to the second act of our story tonight; but before the Silver Curtain rises again, may I ask you to look *backward* with me to a New England Christmas 92 years ago! There's new fallen snow on the ground outside, and inside, the house is fragrant with fresh-picked pine and laurel and spruce. There's a log roaring in the fireplace, and children's plump Christmas stockings hang from the mantelpiece. There are gifts under the Christmas tree for everybody from grandmother down, and for the young bride-to-be, a case of 12 *silver spoons* that are the envy and admiration of the whole household! And *this is why!*

JOY.—You see, ladies and gentlemen, those 12 silver spoons came from the brand-new house of 1847 Rogers Brothers! They possessed a beauty of design that surpassed any silver plate yet made, a perfection of craftsmanship that was to make the silversmiths who created them the most famous craftsmen in America! And you'll find that today, 92 years later, silver plate that bears the name 1847 Rogers Brothers is still the grandest gift of all for Christmas! This is especially true since the creation of their new and lovely "Adoration" pattern. For "Adoration" has the look of *solid silver!* Its ornament is more deeply etched, more highly raised than ever before in silver plate! Yes, "Adoration" is as exquisite as the first star at night! And it has a *lasting* loveliness that will gleam as gloriously many years from now as it does on Christmas morning! So *see* it . . . and *choose* it . . . this latest and greatest of silver-plate patterns . . . 1847 Rogers Brothers. "*Adoration*"!

MUSIC.—*Second act curtain raiser.*

NAGEL.—Again the house lights dim, and the Silver Curtain rises on the concluding act of "For Richer—for Richer," starring Clark Gable as Chris Morgan, with Mary Taylor as Peggy Turner.

MUSIC.—*Segue to narration background . . . jail theme.*

NAGEL.—Four days have passed since the would-be elopement. But since Peggy has failed to sign a formal complaint, Chris is still star boarder in the local county jail. At the moment he's playing cribbage through the bars of his cell with Jeff Barnes, his more than sympathetic jailor . . .

CHRIS.—(*Counting*) Fifteen-two, fifteen-four, fifteen-six.

JEFF.—Beats me what a guy with your luck is doin' in jail, Chris.

CHRIS.—Politics, Jeff, my boy! Politics!

PEGGY.—(*Slightly off . . . sarcastically*) Is that so!

JEFF.—Miss Turner! Gee whillikens!

PEGGY.—Sheriff, I'd like to speak to your prisoner.

JEFF.—Sure . . . (*Fading*) Go right ahead. I'll be seein' about dinner, Chris.

SOUND.—*Door closes off.*

PEGGY.—Well!

CHRIS.—Very well, thank you. How about you? (*Little pause*) Care to play a hand? Name your game. Penny ante, black-jack, pinochle, fan-tan, Russian bank or, oh, I have it! Old maid!

PEGGY.—(*A little mocking laugh*) Very amusing, Mr. Morgan. (*Sighs*) I wish you could see the charming picture you make through those bars.

CHRIS.—That's the Slugface Benedict in me.

PEGGY.—(*Coolly*) Mr. Morgan, I've come today to give you a final offer. At least you can't say I'm not generous.

CHRIS.—Can't I?

PEGGY.—(*Going on*) If you will promise to forget this whole idea.

CHRIS.—You mean marrying whatshername?

PEGGY.—(*Annoyed*) Her name is Susan! If you'll swear never even to see her again, I'll dismiss all charges against you.

CHRIS.—Couldn't be interested.

PEGGY.—Oh, you couldn't? Do you realize that if I press those charges you'll probably go to jail for 10 years? Kidnaping is . . .

CHRIS.—Kidnaping is exactly what I *want* you to charge me with. Remember, Miss Turner, we got a license from that justice. That's proof that you *went there* intending to marry me.

PEGGY.—I did not!

CHRIS.—Try to tell a court that. You go right ahead with your charges. They'll laugh the case out of court. Then I'll sue you for half a million for false arrest, illegal restraint of liberty, and defamation of my character.

PEGGY.—(*Furious . . . realizing he's got her*) You! You haven't got any character!

CHRIS.—I haven't much, have I? Isn't it unfortunate? Come to think of it, I could sue now. Who's a good lawyer?

PEGGY.—I can't believe you're as much of a heel as you're making yourself out to be.

CHRIS.—You'll find out when I bring suit.

PEGGY.—But you can't! I mean, you mustn't! Please!

CHRIS.—(*Generously*) Well, suppose I got big-hearted and dropped the suit; how about my going ahead and marrying whatshername?

PEGGY.—Her name is Susan.

CHRIS.—That's it. Susan.

PEGGY.—(*Troubled*) Well, before you do, won't you at least come and talk to my father? He's a very reasonable man. Maybe between you, you can work something out. Please, Chris—I mean Mr. Morgan.

CHRIS.—(*Reluctantly*) Okay. Okay. But I'm getting a little fed up with all this bother. As far as I can see, no woman is worth it.

MUSIC.—*Brief transition.*

TURNER.—Er, sit down, Mr. Morgan.

CHRIS.—Thanks, Mr. Turner.

TURNER.—(*Slight pause*) I understand you want to marry my daughter.

CHRIS.—That's right.

TURNER.—Which one?

CHRIS.—Any one you say. You know them better than I do. Which one would you recommend?

TURNER.—(*Laughs*) Very funny. Peggy told me you were quite a character.

CHRIS.—Oh, she did? She told *me* I didn't have any!

TURNER.—Now, let's quit this nonsense. You want to marry Susan.

CHRIS.—Have it your way.

TURNER.—What are your prospects?

CHRIS.—Excellent. I'm about to come into 3 millions.

TURNER.—Really. A relative?

CHRIS.—Yes. A wife.

TURNER.—Now, see here, young man.

CHRIS.—Suppose you see here. This meeting wasn't my idea. Your daughter thought talking to you might straighten this thing out.

TURNER.—Susan suggested it?

CHRIS.—Who said anything about Susan? I'm talking about Peggy!

TURNER.—But you said you wanted to marry Susan.

CHRIS.—(*Disgusted*) Of all the guys for putting words in somebody's mouth. *You* said I wanted to marry Susan. Personally, I don't care which one it is. I just want somebody to make up his mind.

TURNER.—(*Taken back*) Now wait a minute, Mr. Morgan. Are you admitting you want to marry into my family for—for money?

CHRIS.—Can you think of a better reason?

TURNER.—My daughters have had lots of men after their money, but you're the first one who ever admitted it. Such honesty deserves appreciation.

CHRIS.—Glad you look at it that way.

TURNER.—(*Almost apologetically*) But, er, there are still appearances. Maybe I can find a place for you, as a—as a vice-president in charge of something.

CHRIS.—(*Sore*) No you don't. I've got to draw the line *somewhere.* Nobody's gonna make me a vice-president!

TURNER.—Hmm. Well, some kind of a *managership*, then?

CHRIS.—(*Shrugging*) Sorry! Wouldn't work out.

TURNER.—You wouldn't take a job?

CHRIS.—Nope!

TURNER.—Just my money.

CHRIS.—That's all.

TURNER.—And my daughter.

CHRIS.—I can't help that part of it. Well, how about it?

TURNER.—You seem in pretty much of a hurry.

CHRIS.—Sure, I am. The eighteenth is the dead line.

TURNER.—The dead line?

CHRIS.—Yeah. For the kids.

TURNER.—The kids? Now, look here, young man. I thought at least you were single.

CHRIS.—No! The kids at Morgan Memorial. You've heard of the Morgan Memorial Hospital, haven't you?

TURNER.—Why, of course. Then . . . ?

CHRIS.—My family has been endowing the place for generations. But I've been traveling lately; and when I got back last month I found the hospital all ready to fold up. The investment securities went bust. So I had to figure out some way to keep it going.

TURNER.—I see.

CHRIS.—I tried every other angle I knew to raise the dough, even selling my boat.

TURNER.—But why couldn't you get someone else to endow the hospital. I'd even help myself. If 50 thousand or so would . . .

CHRIS.—You will not! Morgans have kept that hospital running for 92 years, and they're not stopping now.

PEGGY.—(*Suddenly fading in*) Of course they're not! He's right, dad.

TURNER.—(*Accusingly*) Peggy, you've been listening!

PEGGY.—Certainly I have! And I found out what I wanted to know. I'm sorry I backed out of the wedding, Mr. Morgan. But I'll make up for it now.

CHRIS.—You will, huh? And this time you mean it?

PEGGY.—This time I mean it.

CHRIS.—Strictly a business proposition?

PEGGY.—Strictly and absolutely.

CHRIS.—When?

PEGGY.—Would tomorrow do?

CHRIS.—Why not?

PEGGY.—Good! And if you'll stay for dinner we can talk over the, er, business arrangements.

CHRIS.—Guess I can make it.

TURNER.—Well, maybe I'm old-fashioned (*fade*), but all this is too much for me.

SOUND.—*Door slams off.*

PEGGY.—Poor dad. He still thinks being in love should have something to do with marriage. Isn't that absurd?

CHRIS.—Sure it is. Did I say it wasn't?

MUSIC.—*Transition.*

SOUND.—*Dissolve in night garden sounds.*

PEGGY.—And you really should see this garden. It's the loveliest part of the whole place.

CHRIS.—Yeah. Not bad.

MUSIC.—*Comes in low in background with "You and the Night and the Music" . . . filter.*

PEGGY.—(*On cue*) Oh, do you mind the radio? I can go back in and turn it off.

CHRIS.—No. It's Okay.

PEGGY.—(*Hesitantly*) I—I hope you enjoyed dinner. If not, we can get a new cook after the—the wedding.

CHRIS.—The dinner was all right.

PEGGY.—That's good. (*A little pause*)

CHRIS.—What's that song?

PEGGY.—"You and the Night and the Music."

CHRIS.—(*He snorts disapprovingly*) Huh. Don't like it.

PEGGY.—Don't you? (*Little pause*) I—I'm glad everything's all set. Dad turns over $200,000 to you on the day we're married. Right?

CHRIS.—Right.

PEGGY.—And then?

CHRIS.—Then?

PEGGY.—I was wondering where we might go on our honeymoon.

CHRIS.—Look. We won't talk about that now.

PEGGY.—All right. (*Little pause*) Nice night.

CHRIS.—Huh! (*Grunts*)

PEGGY.—Do you like my hair this way, Chris? I remembered you said you liked Susan's better, so I tried doing mine just like hers. (*Remembering*) Oh, about Susan, I didn't tell you. She's going to marry Freddie after all.

CHRIS.—Am I supposed to cheer?

PEGGY.—Funny, when she found out you were a fortune hunter, she was almost angry with you. But then Susan's like dad, a conservative. (*Little pause*) I'm sorry. Maybe—maybe you still would *prefer* Susan. Would you, Chris?

CHRIS.—(*Sharply . . . almost angrily*) No!

PEGGY.—Chris?

CHRIS.—I wouldn't prefer anyone! (*A little pause . . . he goes on softly*) And I'll *tell* you where we're going on our honeymoon. There's an island in the Indies, south of Java, an island so small you'd never find it on a map. But I've been there. And I promised myself that someday I'd go back, but not alone.

PEGGY.—(*In his tone*) Chris! Chris, tell me about it.

CHRIS.—Tell you? No one could do that. You'll have to see it yourself. (*He visualizes it again as he describes it*) See the waves breaking far out on a reef and rolling up to a beach that's whiter than snow. You'll have to steer a boat at night by the Southern Cross and smell the ginger blossoms on the trade winds. You'll have to . . . (*He breaks off*)

PEGGY.—(*Astonished at this quality in him*) Chris! Oh, Chris, darling.

CHRIS.—(*Low*) Peggy! You're a fool to marry me.

PEGGY.—Maybe I am, but I don't care. Oh, Chris! (*There is a pause*)

CHRIS.—(*Abruptly, sore*) Hey! What's the matter with us?

PEGGY.—What's wrong?

CHRIS.—Wrong? Everything's wrong. The whole business is messed up now.

PEGGY.—But it's all set, the wedding, everything.

CHRIS.—The wedding's off. And don't ask me why. I said it's off. And I'm leaving! (*Fades*) Good-by!

MUSIC.—*Transition.*

SOUND.—*Dissolve in harbor noises.*

CHRIS.—(*Calling*) Cap! Cap Norback!

CAPTAIN.—(*Slight Swedish accent . . . fading in*) Yah, hello, Chris. You come aboard the *Jezebel* at last, huh?

CHRIS.—All right, Cap. Get her underweigh.

CAPTAIN.—Yah, Chris. I get your message, but it ain't true. You ain't sold the *Jezebel.*

CHRIS.—(*Grimly*) No? We deliver her to the new owners in Norfolk tomorrow. I'll be in my cabin.

CAPTAIN.—(*Slightly off*) Chris?

CHRIS.—Yeah?

CAPTAIN.—I'm mighty sorry you lose the *Jezebel*. No foolin'.

CHRIS.—Maybe you think *I'm* cheering. Thanks, Cap. Let's get going.

CAPTAIN.—(*Fading*) Yah. Sure. (*He shouts orders in the distance . . . "Cast off, there. Up anchor," etc. . . . ad libs*)

SOUND.—*Footsteps along deck . . . cabin door opens . . . closes.*

PEGGY.—(*Blithely*) Hello, Chris.

CHRIS.—Peggy! (*His first impulse was to take her in his arms . . . now he suddenly remembers he's sore*) What are you doing here?

PEGGY.—Waiting for Christopher Morgan, a man who claims to be allergic to work. Funny. This doesn't say that at all.

CHRIS.—What are you talking about?

PEGGY.—This clipping. From "Who's Who." Listen! (*She reads*) "Morgan, Christopher, Jr.: oceanologist and explorer, owner of the motor ship *Jezebel*, most complete floating marine laboratory under American registry. In the past few years Mr. Morgan has devoted much of his personal fortune to exploring little known sea lanes of the globe." (*Little pause*) Well, don't look at *me*. That's what it says, Chris.

CHRIS.—You get back ashore.

SOUND.—*Motor ship's air horn.*

PEGGY.—(*Sighing*) It's too late. Hear that? We've started already. I guess I'm just a Jezebel aboard the *Jezebel*.

CHRIS.—Don't talk like a fool. We'll put about and land you.

PEGGY.—Why? Why can't I go along?

CHRIS.—Because—because women are bad luck on a ship.

PEGGY.—Any worse than on shore?

CHRIS.—Besides, I don't own the *Jezebel* any more.

PEGGY.—(*Surprised*) You sold your ship? Chris! Who bought her?

CHRIS.—How do I know? Somebody named Renrut.

PEGGY.—For how much?

CHRIS.—Two hundred thousand. (*A slight pause . . . Peggy starts to laugh*) Say, what is this? What are you laughing at?

PEGGY.—You!

CHRIS.—Me?

PEGGY.—Uh huh. You're such a dope.

CHRIS.—A dope? Me?

PEGGY.—(*Still laughing*) You look at everything backwards except the one thing you should see that way.

CHRIS.—Backwards?

PEGGY.—Renrut, Chris. Did you ever think of that in reverse?

CHRIS.—Reverse? R-E-N-R-U-T. T-U-R-N-E-R. Turner. Wait a minute!

PEGGY.—Don't be angry, Chris. Please. But when I found out you were selling the boat, well, I knew you needed the money for the hospital, and, well (*a note of desperation*) . . . Maybe . . . maybe I wanted to explore a few unknown sea lanes of the globe, too. (*A pause . . . he doesn't answer*) Why did you run away the other night, Chris?

CHRIS.—You know why. It messes everything up just as I said it did.

PEGGY.—What does?

CHRIS.—Love, that's what! I'm in love with you. How could I marry a girl I'm in love with? It's against my principles.

PEGGY.—Your ancestor didn't worry about things like that. Principles never bothered him in the least.

CHRIS.—My ancestor?

PEGGY.—*Henry* Morgan, the pirate. What he wanted, he took, principles or no principles. (*A little deprecating laugh*) But then maybe the Morgans today aren't what they used to be.

CHRIS.—(*Belligerently*) Oh, they're not, huh? Come here!

PEGGY.—(*Surprised*) Chris!

CHRIS.—Come here!

PEGGY.—(*Happily*) Oh, Chris. (*A pause for a kiss*) Oh, darling, I was wrong. And even if she is better looking than I am, I'm so glad you didn't marry (*Groping for the name*) uh, whatshername?

CHRIS.—Whatshername? Her name's *Susan!*

MUSIC.—*Curtain.* (*Applause*)

NAGEL.—Ladies and gentlemen, Clark Gable will be back for a friendly word for you in just a moment. During that moment, *we* have a friendly *invitation* for you. (*Three second pause for cut-in*) All right, Dick.

JOY.—It's an invitation to go to your silverware dealer's tomorrow, Monday, ladies and gentlemen. Visit his silverware department and *just see* the many wonderful silver-plate gifts he has, all bearing the proud name 1847 Rogers Brothers! There's a service for 8, 62 thrillingly beautiful pieces in a luster-walnut cabinet, that costs only 59 dollars and 75 cents! There's a *thirty-six* piece set for only $39.75. And there are smaller and larger services, priced to fit almost any purse! Many of the sets are created in the glorious "Adoration" pattern, that newest and greatest triumph of the house of 1847 Rogers Brothers, which brings the miracle of *sterling silver* craftsmanship to finest silver *plate!* See them all. Learn from your silverware dealer what easy, convenient payment terms can be arranged, and make your selection. Then, on that day of days, watch her face when she opens your package, when she sees the exquisite loveliness of that Adoration pattern, when she realizes that here is silver plate with the design prestige of America's first great craftsmen—1847 *Rogers Brothers!*

MUSIC.—*Theme sneak in and tag.*

NAGEL.—Thanks, Dick. And now, the star of our Silver Theatre, Clark Gable!

SOUND.—*Applause.*

NAGEL.—Clark, as usual you did a grand job. And thanks.

GABLE.—Thank *you*, Conrad.

NAGEL.—Tell me, what's the latest on "Gone with the Wind"?

GABLE.—Well, it opens this Friday in Atlanta, Georgia, and I'm going to fly down to be there.

NAGEL.—And I'll certainly be on hand when it opens in Hollywood. I hear the picture's packed with action and with romance, too.

GABLE.—Yes, it is. But there's bound to be plenty of romance in almost any story of the '50's and '60's.

NAGEL.—Ah, there was plenty of romance in the *forties*, too, Clark. Don't forget, it was in 1847 that Rogers Brothers started making 1847 silver plate. And the story of how *they* started is *really* a romantic one.

GABLE.—No doubt, Conrad. But it would be pretty tough for me to handle the part of a silversmith. I'm much more at home playing the Rhett Butler type, I hope.

NAGEL.—Don't worry, Clark, the Hollywood grapevine says that David Selznick has really produced a terrific picture, and that your performance is tops!

GABLE.—Before I start getting embarrassed, I'd better beat it. So long, Conrad.

NAGEL.—So long. (*Applause*) Clark Gable appeared on Silver Theatre through the courtesy of Metro-Goldwyn-Mayer.

MUSIC.—*Theme.*

NAGEL.—And now for that news about next Sunday's Silver Theatre production. Our star will be Kay Francis, who will be supported by a great cast in the unusual drama "Pot Luck."

I'll be waiting to welcome you. And so, good friends, this is Conrad Nagel, saying good evening and thank you. See you next Sunday.

JOY.—In the meantime, if you want *solid* silver, you want International Sterling. If you want silver *plate*, you want 1847 Rogers Brothers, both proudly created by International Silver Company.

MUSIC.—*Theme.*

JOY.—Today's radio play, "For Richer—for Richer," was written especially for Silver Theatre by True Boardman. Original music was scored and conducted by Felix Mills. Dick Joy speaking.

MUSIC.—*Theme . . . if needed.*

HOWELL.—(*On cue*) All names and designations of persons and of organizations used in the dramatic portions of this broadcast are entirely fictitious, and no actual organization or living person is thereby designated. Silver Theatre originates at Columbia Square in Hollywood.

This is the Columbia Broadcasting System.

MUSIC.—*Theme to fill.*

This Lonely Heart

by Arch Oboler

Fifty-three consecutive weekly radio plays, all of them originals, brought the name of Arch Oboler into great prominence last year. The series was appropriately called Arch Oboler's Plays. They were all dark, humorless, disturbed pieces, fraught with many varieties of anguish and anxiety, written with overpowering sincerity, very well acted and produced, feelingly directed by the author himself. They were not literary, and they were not mature; but they were terrifically popular, and they deserved all the attention they received. Here is Good Gulf's Screen Guild Theater version of Mr. Oboler's intriguing production of the bleak romance of Tchaikovsky's withered but persistent angel. "This Lonely Heart" was heard on January 14, 1940.

This Lonely Heart

Music.—*Two bars of "Romeo and Juliet" theme.*

Conte.—The Gulf Screen Guild Theatre!

Music.—*Repeat two bars of theme in different key.*

Conte.—Your neighborhood Good Gulf dealer and the Gulf Oil companies welcome you to the Gulf Theatre, the one place where you meet all your favorite stars! Tonight, we bring you the brilliant and charming twice winner of the Motion Picture Academy Award Bette Davis, supported by one of the finest and largest radio casts ever assembled. And Oscar Bradley and his Gulf orchestra! And now, here is the director of the Gulf Theatre, and your host, Roger Pryor! (*Applause*)

Pryor.—Good evening, everybody. I am especially proud to be the director of the Gulf Theatre tonight, because I sincerely believe I am about to present a play that will long be remembered. Bette Davis, her supporting players, the author Arch Oboler, and Oscar Bradley and his augmented Gulf orchestra have spent many long hours in rehearsal to bring to perfection one of the strangest, almost unbelievable love stories ever told; the great and undying romance of Nadejdo Phila Retovna and Piotr Tchaikovsky, the same Tchaikovsky who was the composer of the lyric "Romeo and Juliet" overture that has been the theme of the Gulf Screen Guild Theatre since the curtain first rose a year ago this month.

Music.—*Theme . . . "Romeo and Juliet" . . . then fade.*

Pryor.—On our first broadcast, just as today, spokesman for your neighborhood Good Gulf dealer was John Conte, who has something worth speaking about right now. John Conte!

Music.—*Out here.*

Conte.—Thank you, Roger. Forty years ago, ladies and gentlemen, travel by airplane was an inventor's dream. Twenty years ago it was still something of an adventure. Today it's a practical, everyday affair, thanks to experts whose experience has taught them exactly what various planes and motors can do and what various gasolines and motor oils can do, also, which is what makes it news to you as a motorist when Captain Eddie Rickenbacker and his engineers at the famous Eastern Air Lines announce . . .

MAN.—This year Eastern Air Lines has again selected for use throughout *all* its entire system, the same gasoline and motor oil that have already been used exclusively for more than 5 years—*Gulf* gasoline and *Gulf* motor oil!

CONTE.—Yes, Eastern Air Line planes operating between New York and Miami, New York and Brownsville, Texas and Chicago, and both coasts of Florida have now flown the astonishing total of 300 million passenger revenue miles using Gulf gas and motor oil and have hung up a record for safety and efficiency that's the envy of the industry! More mileage, complete dependability, top performance, the same things you want for your car, are what led Eastern Air Lines to select Gulf products for the air, just as millions of motorists select them for the highway. So next time, why not take a tip from Captain Rickenbacker and his experts, and stop at the Sign of the Orange Disc for Gulf Quality gasoline and motor oil?

MUSIC.—*"None but the Lonely Heart" down and continuing far behind.*

PRYOR.—In a darkened room sits a woman, an old woman. She sits very quietly, white hands motionless. This is a room in a fashionable house in a city of the Imperial Russia of 1893, the Russia of great poverty and great riches, of great ignorance and great art. (*Music out*) The old woman sits, motionless, listening, listening to the thoughts in her mind.

MUSIC.—*Strings of second movement "Concerto Number One, B Flat Minor" andantino semplice.*

NADEJDA.—(*Cue from Bradley*) Piotr, Piotr, why are you in my mind? Why do I think of you now? Why is your song with me here in the darkness? Why today, Piotr? I had put you away from me. Why have you come back today, Piotr?

RUBINSTEIN.—(*Fade-in*) Madame, it is of the utmost importance that you listen to me!

NADEJDA.—Who is it said that to me?

RUBINSTEIN.—(*Fade-out*) Madame, it is of the utmost importance that you listen to me!

NADEJDA.—(*Over fade*) Ah, yes. I remember now! Sixteen years ago, it was you, Nikolay Rubinstein. You have been dead so long, and yet I remember what you said that day. How strange I should remember.

MUSIC.—*Fades out behind above . . . out at "How strange."*

RUBINSTEIN.—(*Cue . . . fade-in*) Nadejda Phila Retovna, my mission here is of the utmost importance.

NADEJDA.—(*Middle-aged . . . vigorous*) Really, Nikolay?

RUBINSTEIN.—There is a young man in my music school of great poverty and pride and shyness.

NADEJDA.—I am very busy today.

RUBINSTEIN.—There is one more quality this young man possesses which *may* interest you, his ability! (*Fade*) Listen, listen closely!

NADEJDA.—Nikolay! I have neither the time nor the inclination for music now! I . . .

RUBINSTEIN.—*Strikes a chord on the pianoforte, then begins to play Tchaikovsky's "Concerto Number One, B Flat Minor," first movement, fading after a few seconds and continuing back behind.*

NADEJDA.—(*Cue from Bradley*) What music was this? What music was this you began to play, Nikolay Rubinstein? So many years, and yet I hear it! Music and yet not music! A voice, a man's voice, singing to me!

MUSIC.—*Swells . . . pianoforte playing alone . . . then full orchestra behind.*

NADEJDA.—(*Cue from Bradley*) Saying, "You are tired, Nadejda? I tell you there will be no weariness! You are old, Nadejda? I tell you you will be young! You will have life again, a glorious, singing life! I tell you this, Nadejda! I tell you this! I tell you this!"

MUSIC.—*Fades slowly.*

NADEJDA.—(*On last note*) When you had finished, Nikolay, I remember I said (*back, up*), "Nikolay! Tell me! Whose . . . whose is that"?

RUBINSTEIN.—His name? No one you've heard of! Piotr Ilich Tchaikovsky.

MUSIC.—*Strings at beginning of second movement of Concerto, down behind.*

NADEJDA.—(*Cue from Bradley*) So I heard your name for the first time, Piotr.

MUSIC.—*Concerto . . . fade with above fade, then, on cue, pianoforte far back playing concerto, fading out slowly, then string strains of concerto.*

NADEJDA.—(*Cue from Bradley*) Would *I* help you, Piotr? No, would *you* help *me?*

MUSIC.—*Out.*

VOICE 1.—(*Graham on cue . . . whispering*) The wealthy widow Nadejda von Meck!

VOICE 2.—(*Max*) Private railroads!

SOUND.—*Clinking of money out behind.*

VOICE 3.—(*Whispering*) Good investments!

VOICE 1.—(*Quickly*) Town house!

VOICE 2.—Country house!

VOICE 3.—In the Ukraine!

VOICE 1.—On the Riviera!

NADEJDA.—Yes, yes, I had those!

VOICES OF HER CHILDREN.—Milochka.
George.
(*Fade*) Julia.
Vladimar.
Anya.
Leonya.

NADEJDA.—(*On cue through above fade*) Yes, yes, my children! I had them, but . . .

VOICE 1.—(*Whispering*) Nothing!

NADEJDA.—Yes, nothing for *me!* How could I explain to Nikolay, to anyone? To run a house, to count my money . . . was this enough a life for *me?* I wanted, I wanted . . .

MUSIC.—*Opening movement of "Concerto Number One in B Flat Minor," fading behind.*

NADEJDA.—(*Cue from Bradley*) Yes, you said what I wanted, Piotr! Help you? Yes, always! (*Quickly*) In a moment my pen was in my hand! I would write you, yes, yes! I was a woman past middle age; my husband was dead, and my children were growing in their own lives, and I had nothing, and I must have something! You, Piotr, you, the music in you, if I could give it life and reality, my life. No!

SOUND.—*Reedy pen thrown on table.*

NADEJDA.—I threw the pen from me! What madness had come over me? I didn't need man nor God! I would pay you for your music and have done with you! Yes! (*Down*) And then, at the concert that very night, your music, when it was over . . .

RUBINSTEIN.—Unimportant! All of it definitely unimportant!

NADEJDA.—Oh, no! No!

MUSIC.—*Lyrical strains of "Romeo and Juliet" theme.*

NADEJDA.—The night was singing with your song, Piotr, and I walked in the dark along the boulevard to my home, the soft flakes of snow wet in my face; and with every step there was a singing in my heart that said . . .

PIOTR.—(*Fade-in*) Help me! I need your help, Nadejda! They torture me with their indifference! I have written so much, and it has meant so little! (*Fade*) I am weary unto death. Help me! Help me!

MUSIC.—*Fades with above fade . . . cross fade wind which comes up with above fade . . . fading out slowly.*

NADEJDA.—(*After slight pause*) I told myself, yes, I would always help you, Piotr. Do you remember your next letter?

PIOTR.—(*Fade in fast*) "Dear Nadejda Phila Retovna: Thank you for your sweet, kind, and friendly letter and your wonderful and kind generosity. I have finished the outline of my new symphony, the fourth."

NADEJDA.—A symphony!

PIOTR.—I want very much to dedicate it to you.

NADEJDA.—A symphony, dedicated to me! How the days ran then, Piotr! I, an elderly woman, a symphony dedicated to *me!*

MUSIC.—*Up, then fade and continue behind.*

SOUND.—*Fade in Nadejda laughing.*

JULIA.—Oh, mother, it's so good to hear you laughing!

BOY.—You're very pretty when you laugh, mother!

OLDER BOY.—Oh, we're so happy that you're happy, mother dearest! (*Fade*) So happy! (*Fade laughter and music with above fade*)

NADEJDA.—And then three months, Piotr! Three months and not a word from you! What had happened to you, my friend? What?

VOICES 1, 2, 3.—(*Whispering in close*) He is ill! Sick! Dying! Accident! Cholera! Fever! Ill! Sick! Dying! (*Building slowing behind*)

NADEJDA.—No, that couldn't be true! But with every day the voices in my head grew louder and louder. No, no, stop saying that! Not Piotr! He couldn't. (*Voices out clean with blasts of postman's whistle, back*)

NADEJDA.—The postman! A letter! Your handwriting, Piotr!

SOUND.—*Tearing paper, rattle of paper.*

PIOTR.—(*Fade in fast*) "Dear Nadejda Phila Retovna, you must forgive me for not writing before. I am now . . . "

NADEJDA.—What was that word?

PIOTR.—(*Softly*) Married!

NADEJDA.—No! I must have read it wrong, I told myself! I held the letter close to my eyes!

PIOTR.—(*In a little closer*) Married!

NADEJDA.—Oh, no!

PIOTR.—(*Up*) Married! (*Echo chamber*) Married!

NADEJDA.—(*Cries out*) Oh, no! (*Down, tensely*) Oh, no!

MUSIC.—*Strings at second movement . . . "Concerto B Flat Minor" continuing behind.*

NADEJDA.—(*Cue from Bradley*) You never knew I cried that day, did you, Piotr? Yes, I cried, as a woman cries, in my heart. And when I stopped crying, I dipped my pen in my tears, and I wrote you . . .

SOUND.—*Scratching of pen behind.*

NADEJDA.—(*Brokenly*) "With all my heart, I congratulate you, my dear friend. Who should be happy if not you, the giver of such great joy to others? From my heart, I press your hand. (*Music out*) Do not forget one devoted with all her soul."

MUSIC.—"*Francesca da Rimini*" *. . . down and continuing behind.*

NADEJDA.—(*Cue from Bradley*) The days after that? Like the days after someone who—someone who was close to you has gone away forever. Everything is just the same, and yet nothing is the same. Who was she, this woman who had taken your heart?

ANTONINA.—*Happy laughter of young woman, back.*

NADEJDA.—Was she very young?

ANTONINA.—(*In close, softly, lovingly*) I love you, my husband.

NADEJDA.—Would she understand you? Would she respect your shyness, suffer your angers when fires of music blazed in you, humor your child ways, strengthen your uncertainties, respect your greatness? I asked myself all this a thousand thousand times in the days that crawled on. Would she do all these things for you, Piotr, that . . .

MUSIC.—*Out cold.*

NADEJDA.—That anyone who truly loved you would do . . .

MUSIC.—*Again.*

NADEJDA.—(*As orchestra continues*) How could there be an answer? No, this was my destiny—to watch the days and the years spin around nothing, into nothing, always nothing—to need no one and to have no one who needed me. (*Music out*) How strange the night I remember now, Piotr.

CHILDREN.—(*Fading*) Good night, mother! Sleep well, mother!

SOUND.—*Door back.*

NADEJDA.—I lay down on my bed. (*Music in*) Sleep, yes, sleep and forget.

SOUND.—*Rushing water, back, behind.*

NADEJDA.—(*In wonder*) That sound! What! The river! A dream, why should I dream this dream?

PIOTR.—(*Far back, calling*) Nadejda!

NADEJDA.—(*In puzzlement*) My name? Had someone called my name?

PIOTR.—(*Calling, in a little closer*) Nadejda!

NADEJDA.—Yes, again! Who was it? In my dream I wanted to see, I *had* to see! A man, in the water, his arms lifted toward me. I saw! Piotr! You!

PIOTR.—(*Fading in close . . . his voice full of supplication*) Nadejda!

NADEJDA.—*Screams.*

MUSIC.—*Out knife-clean with above scream.*

SOUND.—*Fade in murmur of voices as children rush in room.*

NADEJDA.—The children, servants, in the room!

JULIA.—Oh, mother, what is it? (*In great surprise*) Mother! You're awake and smiling!

MUSIC.—*Andantino semplice . . . first concerto.*

NADEJDA.—(*Cue from Bradley*) Yes, Piotr! Somehow I knew then you still needed me.

MUSIC.—*Out completely.*

NADEJDA.—I sent for Rubinstein.
(*Fade-in*)

RUBINSTEIN.—This I can say with certainty, if he stays with that wife Antonina of his, Tchaikovsky will end his life either in an asylum or in the river!

MUSIC.—"*Francesca da Rimini.*"

NADEJDA.—The river! Piotr, when he said that word, my heart died in me. But I said nothing, Piotr, afraid he would laugh at me, say:

RUBINSTEIN.—(*Whispering*) Old woman, are you coming between a husband and his bride?

NADEJDA.—So I waited for you to turn to me, Piotr, waited.

MUSIC.—*Fades quickly.*

SOUND.—*Murmur of voices, down, continuing far back behind.*

NADEJDA.—Rumors, I began to hear rumors!

SOUND.—*Unintelligible murmur of many voices up for a few seconds, then down behind.*

NADEJDA.—And from what they said I began to see the whole horrible picture of her.

ANTONINA.—Why are you doing that, Piotr? Where are you going, Piotr? What are you writing, Piotr? Will you make much money, Piotr? (*Fade*) Will you buy me something pretty, Piotr? Do you like me every minute, Piotr? What are you thinking, Piotr? What are you doing, Piotr? What are you writing, Piotr? You don't love me! You hate me! You don't think about me! (*Etc. . . . ad lib far back*)

NADEJDA.—(*On cue through above*) So this was the woman my friend had taken! Yes, this was Antonina! How clearly I saw her! Grinding his heart away with her miserable "why this," and, "do this," and "don't that!" Put an end!

ANTONINA.—*Ad lib out clean.*

NADEJDA.—An end to this leech in your veins, Piotr! I said it! I would, I would! And I *did.*

RUBINSTEIN.—(*Fade-in*) He has gone off to Italy, of all places, this unpredictable Piotr Ilich! To Italy. (*Chuckles*) Without that new wife of his and to write a new symphony, no less! I wonder where he got the money!

NADEJDA.—Clever Nikolay Rubinstein! I think he knew, Piotr. Ah, what did it matter? You were free, free to work. And as you worked you would live. And as you lived. Piotr, I lived!

MUSIC.—*Piano far back playing opening bars of "Fourth Symphony."*

NADEJDA.—At last the day!

VOICE 1.—(*Softly*) The twenty-second of February.

NADEJDA.—The day, yes.

SOUND.—*Murmur of concert crowd, down, behind.*

NADEJDA.—The Conservatory! So many lights! So many people! (*Applause . . . far, far back . . . applause takes out voices*) The conductor bowed to the right and to the left. The baton up, down!

MUSIC.—*Opening movement of "Fourth Symphony."*

NADEJDA.—(*On cue from Bradley*) Oh, Piotr! (*On cue*) Mine!

MUSIC.—*Fading slowly . . . and continuing far, far back.*

NADEJDA.—(*On cue through above fade*) Yes, my own, out of the mind and out of the heart of you for me!

MUSIC.—*Fades out behind.*

NADEJDA.—I sat there; yet I was with you, Piotr! Yes, with you, for the first time even in thought, alone with you, as young as you.

SOUND.—*Murmur of concert crowd.*

NADEJDA.—Over! No, not over!

SOUND.—*Murmur of concert crowd leaving auditorium back behind . . . shuffling feet.*

NADEJDA.—Someone thrust a program into my hand.

VOICE 2.—Don't you want a souvenir of the evening? (*Crowd effects out*)

NADEJDA.—I looked at the paper. The words, I could hardly see. "Fourth Symphony of Piotr Ilich Tchaikovsky, dedicated . . . "

PIOTR.—(*Whispering*) To my beloved friend.

NADEJDA.—Oh, Piotr. if the rest of my life could have been as at that moment!

MUSIC.—*Part one . . . "Sleeping Beauty Suite" . . . Opus sixty-six.*

NADEJDA.—(*Slight pause*) And yet, only your letters talking to me. Oh, Piotr (*building with music*) walking in the night I was lonely! I wanted your footsteps echoing mine. I wanted your voice answering mine. I wanted—I wanted (*down, tensely*) to see you, Piotr! Yes, why not? Why not? The thoughts in you were as my thoughts! The dreams in you were as my dreams! The music in you, mine; you'd written that to me a hundred times! Then why shouldn't I—why shouldn't I see you? (*Down with music*) The want in me was so great, did the heavens take pity?

MUSIC.—*Fades out.*

SOUND.—*Fade in sound of horses and carriage moving slowly along country road . . . down and continuing back behind.*

MILOCHKA.—Mother!

NADEJDA.—Yes, Milochka?

MILOCHKA.—Mother, look! The other carriage. It's stopped!

NADEJDA.—(*Up*) Driver! Stop! Stop at once!

SOUND.—*Dim out with above.*

NADEJDA.—I looked up. My heart began to beat so strongly I could feel the pulse of it in my throat, the sound of it in my ears.

MUSIC.—*Strings of concerto behind.*

NADEJDA.—(*Cue from Bradley*) You, Piotr! You! Older than your photograph, but you! My heart beat louder and louder! I wanted to . . . (*Music out clean*) Your eyes! In a quick moment I saw what you were thinking.

PIOTR.—(*In close, intensely*) Nadejda Phila Retovna, I beg you, do not speak! Your wealth has given me solitude, and in this solitude is my music! Speak, and you destroy the silence which brings me my music! Speak, and you destroy the wordless perfection of our friendship!

MUSIC.—*Strings of first concerto continuing behind.*

NADEJDA.—And so I did not speak, Piotr. How could I speak? What answer can there be when a young man says to an older woman, "*This* is our friendship. Dare to change it and you destroy it!" And so I did not speak, Piotr. Through all the years I did not speak.

MUSIC.—"*Capriccio Italienne,*" *opus forty-five, part four, continuing behind.*

NADEJDA.—(*Cue from Bradley*) But your music, always the wonder of your music!

SOUND.—*Applause over the music, fading quickly behind.*

NADEJDA.—How they begin to applaud you!

VOICE 1.—I always said the man's a genius!

VOICE 2.—(*Fade*) A medal from the Czar himself!

VOICE 3.—Our leading composer!

VOICE 1.—(*Fading*) You must invite him!

VOICE 2.—One of Europe's greatest!

VOICE 3.—You must invite him!

NADEJDA.—(*Through above*) Yes, yes, let them pat you on the back with the quick flattery of their useless hands! It didn't matter! As long as you wrote your music, Piotr, for me! For me!

MUSIC.—*Into rollicking strains.*

NADEJDA.—Happy years, busy years. There was no weariness. I had life again, a glorious, singing life. And you gave it to me, Piotr, you, you, you! And it would last forever. Your need of me was as great as my need of you; so all of it would last as long as we lived, and I was young again, and life was good, Piotr, everlastingly good! Everlastingly.

MUSIC.—*Cuts knife-clean with last word in above "everlastingly."*

NADEJDA.—No! There was my son!

DOCTOR.—(*Off slightly*) He is dying, Madame.

NADEJDA.—My son, dying?

DOCTOR.—He has been working beyond his strength. The illness caught him quite weakened. (*Fade*) He is dying, Madame.

NADEJDA.—(*Softly, tensely*) Working beyond his strength. For what? For me! For the money I—oh, Piotr, the thought is a knife in my heart!

SOUND.—*Door opening and closing softly.*

NADEJDA.—I went into the room.

SOUND.—*Fade in sound of dying man breathing with effort, continuing behind.*

NADEJDA.—Was this Vladimar? My first-born, my dearest.

VLADIMAR.—(*With effort*) M-mother.

NADEJDA.—(*Whispering*) Vladimar.

VLADIMAR.—M-mother, help me. (*Fade*) Help me, help me.

NADEJDA.—"Help me, help me"—whose words? Ah! You, Piotr. Yes, for 13 years forgotten children and home. Only you, my every waking thought you and the help of you! And now those same words from my son!

VLADIMAR.—(*Back*) Help me, mother, help me.

MUSIC.—"*Pathétique*," *first movement . . . open with* "*Fate*" *chord.*

NADEJDA.—(*Cue from Bradley*) *Yes!* For 13 years I had sinned against him, but now I would help him! At his bedside I said it! Not a prayer. Who was I to pray? (*Up . . . bitterly*) "You, up there, whoever and whatever you are, listen to me! Let him live, my son. Let him live even a little longer, and I will give up all else but my children! Let him live, my son"! And so the compact was made, Piotr, between God and me. And all these years I have kept it. My son lived a little longer. And I died when I wrote you that letter, that letter full of the bitterness of lies telling you it was ended between us. But all lies, Piotr, for now I tell you the truth. I love you, Piotr! There! I've said it! At last I've said "I love you, Piotr"! As a woman loves a man! A young woman! Young! Young!

MUSIC.—*Cuts clean after* "*a young woman*" *in above.*

NADEJDA.—(*Down . . . wearily*) Oh, Piotr, Piotr. Why have I told you now? You're so far away, and yet why have I spoken after all these years what I have never dared even think? Why?

SOUND.—*Church bells tolling far, far back.*

NADEJDA.—The church bells! Why do they ring so late at night? (*Gasps*) Ah! Oh, Piotr, I remember! They told me, and my poor old head had forgotten! Yesterday they carried you through the streets, thousands of them mourning, carried you and put you to rest.

MUSIC.—*Strings of first movement of first concerto.*

NADEJDA.—Piotr, Piotr, why are you in my mind? Why have I thought of you now? Why was your song with me here in the darkness? Why today? I had put you away from me. Why have you come back today, Piotr? To talk to me as I have talked to you?

MUSIC.—*Fading out behind next sentence.*

PIOTR.—(*Fade-in*) Dear friend, be assured I shall remember you and bless you until my last breath.

NADEJDA.—Ah! Your last letter to me!

PIOTR.—Probably you yourself do not realize the extent of what you have done for me. Never for one moment have I forgotten you, nor will I forget you, because every thought I have concerning myself concerns you also. I kiss your hand (*fade*) with all the warmth my heart contains.

NADEJDA.—(*Repeats softly, wearily*) I kiss your hand with all the warmth my heart contains. Oh, Piotr, Piotr, I am so weary. I want to rest. (*Very sleepily*) Sing me to sleep now, beloved friend . . .

MUSIC.—*Fade in finale of "None but the Lonely Heart" to finish.* (*Applause*)

PRYOR.—(*Over applause . . . on cue*) Thank you, thank you, Bette Davis. Congratulations on a beautiful performance. And thanks to you, Arch Oboler, for a magnificent play, and to you, Oscar Bradley, for your superb scoring and conducting.

And, ladies and gentlemen, you never saw a more excited audience in all your life. Photographers' flashlights are still going off. And all around me things are happening. Men are busy setting up newsreel cameras because in just a moment Bette Davis is going to receive another award, Yes, *another* award to add to the two "Oscars" she's already received from the Academy of Motion Picture Arts and Science. This is truly a great night here in the Gulf Theatre and one I'll never forget. How do you feel about it, Johnny?

CONTE.—The same way you do, Rog. Say, who's going to give the award to Bette?

PRYOR.—Mr. Douglas Churchill of *Redbook* magazine. Look, Johnny, will you take over for a minute? I'll check and see if the newsreel cameramen, Mr. Churchill, and Miss Davis are ready.

CONTE.—Okay, Roger, I'll follow through and check something with all the motorists listening in. When you go out for a walk in winter, the chances are you look first to see that you have your gloves, or perhaps your overshoes and a scarf, to be *sure* that you have *everything* that you need. Well, in somewhat the same way, when you start off in your car, it's a good idea to use a *gasoline* that *has everything* you need. During winter especially, it's not enough for a gasoline to be good in just one way; it should be good in every way. Knowing this, Gulf engineers are *constantly* at work to step up the *all-round quality* of that Good Gulf gasoline and Gulf No-Nox gasoline, each in its own class. As a result, your good Gulf dealer gives you even *better* gasoline today than 6 months ago. Just as 6 months ago he delivered a *better* gasoline than the year before. For instance, take the important matter of anti-knock rating. You may own a 1940 model or an older car; you may want hill climbing or smooth quick acceleration in traffic. Whatever your needs, you'll be *delighted* with the smooth-running performance of Gulf Gasolines. And you'll be *just as pleased* with the *quick* cold weather starts and the high mileage, even on winter roads.

Yes, folks, for high anti-knock and high quality on all other points, too, look *ahead* when you buy gasoline. Look ahead for the Sign of the Gulf Orange Disc!

PRYOR.—Thanks, John. Ladies and gentlemen, *Redbook* magazine has chosen the Gulf Theatre to make its first award because *this* is the star's own theatre. Every cent that Gulf would ordinarily pay the stars who appear here is given instead to help meet the needs of the motion picture relief fund. Douglas W. Churchill, motion picture editor of *Redbook*, is here to present *Redbook*'s first annual award to Miss Bette Davis, who they consider has done the most during the year for the artistic advancement of the screen in any of its branches. Mr. Churchill.

CHURCHILL.—Thank you, Mr. Pryor. Miss Davis, we of *Redbook* know very little of what goes on behind the scenes in Hollywood because *Redbook* is not a fan magazine; but I and my editors are thankful to you for aiding in making going to the movies a pleasurable experience. During 1939 you made four of the year's finest films for Warner Brothers: "Dark Victory," "Juarez," "The Old Maid," and "The Private Lives of Elizabeth and Essex." *Redbook* is happy that we selected three of them as our picture of the month.

DAVIS.—I'm indebted to *Redbook* for one of those stories, "The Old Maid." And in the current issue is the beginning of Somerset Maugham's "The Villa on the Hill," which I will do for Warner Brothers when we finish "All This and Heaven, Too."

CHURCHILL.—We're proud of that. Now, Miss Davis, here in the Gulf Theatre, it is my pleasure to give you this cup on behalf of our editors and our 4 million readers, for your distinguished contribution to the art of the motion picture during 1939.

DAVIS.—Thank you, Mr. Churchill. In accepting it I am conscious again of the great debt I owe to press and public, both of which have accepted my efforts in a most kind and friendly manner. To Mr. Edwin Balmer, the editor of *Redbook*, to Mr. Voldemar Vetulguin, and to you, my sincere thanks. To my radio audience I wish I could say, like the delighted woman that I am, "See what I got!" (*Applause*)

MUSIC.—*Theme.*

PRYOR.—(*Over applause*) Thank you, Bette Davis and Mr. Churchill. Listen to the Gulf Theatre next week, when we bring you Roy D'Arcy, Paulette Goddard, Douglas Fairbanks, Jr., Frank Morgan, and Margot Stevenson. Listen in, won't you?

This is Roger Pryor saying good night for your neighborhood Good Gulf dealer.

ANNOUNCER.—This is the *Columbia Broadcasting System.*

BEST SCRIPT BY A NEW WRITER

The Clinic

by TED KEY

ONE of the greatest pleasures that an editor and his readers enjoy is the discovery of unheralded talent. On March 28, 1940, a Mrs. Key arrived at NBC and announced to the page at the reception desk that she had a manuscript, the work of her husband, that she would like to submit.

It was taken from her and, in the usual routine, read by one of the readers, in this case Miss Barbara Frank. She recommended it as possessing "good mature writing, excellent dialogue, ably drawn characterizations." Miss Frank's opinion was concurred in by Lewis Titterton, manager of NBC's script division, and Wilfred Roberts, manager of NBC's production division, who also agreed with Miss Frank that certain changes would improve the script.

Mr. Titterton asked Mr. Key to come in and discuss the matter, which he did. He made the revisions suggested, and the play went on the air in the form in which it is printed in this book.

It was produced by NBC's Radio Guild over the Blue Network on June 8, 1940.

The Clinic

Music.—*Up full . . . hold . . . drop under announcer, then up full again and come to an abrupt stop.*

Opening Announcement.—It's time for the Radio Guild once again, and, as has been our pleasure for the last week or so, we bring you a new play by a new writer. The author is Ted Key, and his play is called "The Clinic." Listen as John Libbey approaches the desk in a hospital.

Clerk.—(*Feminine*) Let me have your slip please.

Libbey.—I was here about a year ago. They said downstairs you had my record.

Clerk.—John Libbey. What month?

Libbey.—April.

Clerk.—April—yes. Doris, type this for me a moment. You had an operation.

Libbey.—Yes.

Sound.—*Typing in background.*

Clerk.—I remember you. Remember him, Doris? He was in the clinic last year.

Doris.—(*Typing stops*) Sure, I remember him. How you feeling?

Libbey.—Not so well.

Sound.—*Typing continues in background.*

Clerk.—Wait in there, Mr. Libbey.

Libbey.—(*Fading*) All right.

Clerk.—He's married.

Doris.—He's the one who chewed gum all the time.

Clerk.—Orderly, give Dr. Fineman this chart. This man's been here before.

ORDERLY.—(*Fading*) Dr. Fineman's on a cystoscopy.

CLERK.—Dr. Bethume—he'll know about it! You can't tell that guy anything. Where's Libbey? Libbey!

LIBBEY.—(*Toward mike*) Yes?

CLERK.—Did they see you downstairs about charges?

LIBBEY.—Well, I saw them, and they said to come up here . . .

CLERK.—About finances, though . . .

LIBBEY.—I can't afford any more than I could last time. (*Typing stops*)

CLERK.—I'm no prophet, what do they expect me to go on?

LIBBEY.—Shall I see them now?

CLERK.—Wait till the examination. What's the matter with you?

LIBBEY.—I don't know, I just have these aches sometimes on this side.

CLERK.—Adhesions, probably.

LIBBEY.—Adhesions should be on the other side. This side wasn't operated on.

CLERK.—Well, you'd better sit down and wait till the doctor's ready.

LIBBEY.—(*Fading*) All right.

CLERK.—How old do you think he is?

DORIS.—I dunno, how old? Forty?

CLERK.—He's thirty-eight.

DORIS.—He looks more'n forty.

CLERK.—He's thirty-eight.

ORDERLY.—(*Coming toward mike*) Dr. Bethume can see him now.

CLERK.—Mr. Libbey!

LIBBEY.—(*Coming toward mike*) Yes?

CLERK.—You want to follow the orderly? Take your hat and coat with you.

ORDERLY.—This way, please. Dr. Bethume wants to see you.

LIBBEY.—Bethume?

ORDERLY.—Step in here.

SOUND.—*Door closing.*

ORDERLY.—(*Turning from mike*) The doctor's reading your chart.

LIBBEY.—Thank you.

SOUND.—*Door opening and closing.*

DR. PHIL SEIDEL.—(*Muffled, behind door and some distance away*) Now still, hold your breath.
Silence for 3 *seconds . . . the single note of the X-ray bell far off-mike*)

SEIDEL.—(*Muffled, far off*) Breathe again . . .

SOUND.—*Door opening and closing.*

DR. BETHUME.—Are you Mr. Libbey?

LIBBEY.—Yes, doctor.

BETHUME.—What seems to be the trouble?

LIBBEY.—I don't know, doctor, on this side every so often I have aches. Feels like something's wrong.

BETHUME.—Take off your shirt.

LIBBEY.—Yes, sir.

BETHUME.—How often do you have these pains? Undershirt, too.

LIBBEY.—I don't know, just recently, every so often. I was in the hospital last year.

BETHUME.—Do you want to stand up straight, please—that's fine—fine.

LIBBEY.—My heart's all right, I think.

BETHUME.—Lean your head just slightly—that's it—want to look at your eyes. (*Silence*) Open your mouth. Open your mouth, please. (*Silence*) Your right arm—just for blood pressure . . .

LIBBEY.—I'm scared it might be something serious on the other side. I wouldn't want that, doctor.

BETHUME.—Don't you worry about it too much.

SOUND.—*Rubber bulb of blood pressure instrument.*

BETHUME.—That's fine. Okay. Now when I ask you to cough—cough. Cough.

SOUND.—*Cough.*

BETHUME.—Again.

SOUND.—*Cough.*

BETHUME.—Again.

SOUND.—*Cough.*

BETHUME.—Again.

SOUND.—*Cough.*

BETHUME.—Sit up on the table.

LIBBEY.—How am I, doctor?

BETHUME.—Lungs all right. Blood pressure up a little but nothing to worry about. Over more. Lie back.

LIBBEY.—You going to X-ray me?

BETHUME.—I think so. The only way to tell anything. You'll have to lie still, Mr. Libbey.

SOUND.—*Door opening.*

BETHUME.—All right, nurse; come in, close the door.

SOUND.—*Door closing.*

BETHUME.—We're not going to try anything fancy on you. Mr. Libbey. You've had intravenous before.

LIBBEY.—Sure.

BETHUME.—Did you call Dr. Seidel?

NURSE 1.—He's coming, doctor.

BETHUME.—It's not going to hurt. Clench your fist. Let's see if we can find a vein here . . . fine . . . Okay, nurse . . .

LIBBEY.—How much dye you using?

BETHUME.—20 cc.'s.

LIBBEY.—Isn't that a lot?

SOUND.—*Door opening and closing.*

SEIDEL.—This the man?

BETHUME.—Intravenous, Phil.

SEIDEL.—He's not hurting, is he?

LIBBEY.—No, I've had these before. As long as it's not a cystoscopy. (*Phil laughs*)

BETHUME.—That's all.

SEIDEL.—I'm going to move you a little, Libbey. That's it. We've got to get you in line here.

LIBBEY.—That stuff gets down fast enough, doesn't it?

SEIDEL.—Sure does. I want you to take two deep breaths. Breathe through your mouth. I'll tell you when to hold it. Then lie perfectly still. I want you to lie perfectly still.

LIBBEY.—Okay.

SEIDEL.—(*Off-mike*) Inhale.

SOUND.—*Inhaling.*

SEIDEL.—Exhale.

SOUND.—*Exhaling.*

SEIDEL.—Inhale.

SOUND.—*Inhaling.*

SEIDEL.—(*Still off-mike*) Hold it! (*Silence for 3 seconds*)

SOUND.—*Off-mike, the chime of the bell . . . followed immediately by the tinkle of a typewriter bell and the usual patter of typing . . . phone rings off-mike . . . Harry speaks into it, and sound of typing drops under.*

HARRY.—Hub Auto Finance. Just one minute, please. (*To stenographer*) Make a little more noise, Molly, I'm talking on the telephone. (*Typing stops*) Will you repeat that again; there was a little disturbance . . . oh, Mrs. Libbey, sure, sure, how are you Mrs. Libbey? That's fine, I'll call him for you. Your wife, John!

LIBBEY.—(*Fading in*) She insists on calling at the office. (*Into phone*) Hello, Stella.

STELLA.—(*Filter mike*) John, darling, what did they say at the hospital?

LIBBEY.—I'll tell you when I get home, Stella.

STELLA.—(*Filter mike*) Tell me if it's serious, that's all.

LIBBEY.—I'll tell you when I get home. Mr. C-A-R-L-I-N is in the office. He doesn't like pleasure on a business phone.

STELLA.—I'm so worried. I been worried all day.

LIBBEY.—There's no use worrying, Stella.

STELLA.—Is it serious? At least you can tell me if it's serious.

LIBBEY.—It's serious.

STELLA.—Oh, God.

LIBBEY.—You asked me. I told you.

STELLA.—How serious? Who examined you, John?

LIBBEY.—The regular doctors.

STELLA.—The same you had last time?

LIBBEY.—Darling, I got work to do. Wait till I get home. Can you wait till I get home? I'll tell you all about it when I get home.

SOUND.—*Stella sobbing on filter mike.*

LIBBEY.—Are you crying, Stella?

SOUND.—*Click of receiver as Stella hangs up . . . silence . . . click of receiver as John hangs up.*

HARRY.—I heard a good one last night. Charlie tell you, John? About this chorus girl who has a vaccination on her . . .

MOLLY.—Who was that lady I seen you with? Yeh, yeh, yeh!

HARRY.—A great sense of humor, Molly, like an ox. Do you mind me tellin' John a joke? Like she never heard a joke in her life.

LIBBEY.—I been thinking I'll take a vacation before I go to the hospital, Harry.

HARRY.—That's a good idea. Listen to this, John. This gal . . .

LIBBEY.—Just for maybe 2 weeks. You think he'll mind?

HARRY.—If he minds or doesn't mind, take a vacation. Take it, and then tell him. If it was me, I'd take 4 weeks and with pay.

MOLLY.—All your big ideas you give to other people.

HARRY.—Listen now, Molly.

LIBBEY.—Has he eaten?

HARRY.—He's eatin'. You know what you gotta say to him, John? Like you was givin' *him* orders, not vice versa. Don't stand for a negative answer. And if he tries to say something, speak first.

LIBBEY.—I deserve a vacation.

HARRY.—Sure you do. I deserve one myself.

LIBBEY.—I have a week coming to me from last year I didn't take. So it's only an extra week.

MOLLY.—Who's gonna keep the books?

HARRY.—You'll keep the books.

MOLLY.—Ho! Listen to him, *me* keep the books. You think he wants to come back and find a mess a figures upside down and every which way? I'm not messin' John's books.

LIBBEY.—I'm not coming back, so you don't have to worry about my books, Molly.

HARRY.—Not coming back, what d'ye mean? You quitting?

LIBBEY.—I don't think I'll come back, that's all.

HARRY.—(*It dawns on him*) John, you're absolutely crazy! Get it out of your head once an' for all. Don't talk yourself into it! Are you crazy? That's no mental condition to be in! How you like it, a guy with his brains lettin' himself go like that. Why there's millions a guys with operations every day an' what happens to 'em. You think they have that attitude?! Where would they be if they had that attitude! Okay, you're feelin' bad; you just come from the doctor's; now you take a nice long rest . . .

MOLLY.—Don't think such things, John. You mustn't think such things.

HARRY.—He's all right, Molly, don't worry. And when he comes out, I'm gonna throw him a party. Get your mind off the whole business, John. Don't take it so serious. Ask him for a vacation. Have a good time. Molly will take care of the books while you're gone.

MOLLY.—I'll take care the books, John.

LIBBEY.—(*Fading*) I'll see what he says.

HARRY.—You understand me, don't you, John? (*Silence*) How you like the guy? (*Fading*) Operations are three-fourths mental condition an' how you like *him?*

SOUND.—*Soft rapping on door.*

CARLIN.—(*Muffled as if from behind door*) Come in.

SOUND.—*Door opening.*

CARLIN.—Come in, John. What is it?

SOUND.—*Door closing.*

LIBBEY.—I'd like to speak to you a minute if you're not busy, Mr. Carlin.

CARLIN.—Well, I'm always busy, John, but sit down. I understand you went to the hospital this morning.

LIBBEY.—I had these aches in my side and . . .

CARLIN.—Oh now, John, you needn't apologize for going. A thing like that must be seen to and the sooner you do it the better for all concerned.

LIBBEY.—That's true.

CARLIN.—I don't believe in tampering with nature; nature has her own laws. But a thing like yours . . . well, I want my people healthy. Health first, I say. Health first, always, never stint on health. You've been with us 15 years, you know how I feel about that.

LIBBEY.—Sixteen years.

CARLIN.—Sixteen years should tell you that, John. If there's anything we can do for you, I want you to say it.

LIBBEY.—Well, you can do something for me, Mr. Carlin.

CARLIN.—All right, John?

LIBBEY.—I'd like to have my vacation now.

CARLIN.—Then later you're having this operation, is that it?

LIBBEY.—Yes, Mr. Carlin.

CARLIN.—How long do you think it will take, John, speaking conservatively, say.

LIBBEY.—Oh, I don't know. These things you can't tell. Depends on what they do, Mr. Carlin.

CARLIN.—Last year you were out about 5 weeks weren't you, John?

LIBBEY.—Yes, sir.

CARLIN.—You understand why we didn't allow the vacation you speak of. Under normal circumstances you would have had your vacation like the rest of them.

LIBBEY.—I know that, sir, but usually there's 1 week with pay.

CARLIN.—John, weren't you *paid?*

LIBBEY.—No, sir.

CARLIN.—How did that happen. You were never paid?

LIBBEY.—No, sir.

CARLIN.—Oh, now, there must be some mistake. There must be some mistake. That's never happened here before has it, John?

LIBBEY.—I don't believe so.

CARLIN.—I'm sure it hasn't. Well! Well! Suppose you take your 2 weeks' vacation, John, and we'll see about that pay business when you return. How is that? Suppose we do that, John; and meanwhile you take good care of yourself, and let's have you back with us soon.

LIBBEY.—All right, Mr. Carlin. Thanks.

CARLIN.—Good luck, John, and take good care of yourself.

LIBBEY.—Yes, sir. Good-by, Mr. Carlin.

CARLIN.—Yes. Good-by, John.

SOUND.—*Door opening and closing . . . dead air . . . key turning in keyhole . . . door opening and closing.*

STELLA.—(*Far off-mike*) John?

LIBBEY.—(*Wearily*) Yes.

STELLA.—(*Fading in*) Give me your things.

LIBBEY.—I'll put them away, Stella.

STELLA.—I have some hot tea for you. Dinner's on the stove. Give me your things.

LIBBEY.—I'm all right.

STELLA.—(*Fading*) Go in, dear, and sit by the table now.

LIBBEY.—You don't have to baby me, Stella. I don't need babying.

STELLA.—(*Fading in*) Sit down now, sit down.

LIBBEY.—Well, Stella, this has been a long day.

STELLA.—Yes, of course it has. The tea is hot and I'll give you some lemon.

SOUND.—*Tea pouring into cups behind voices.*

STELLA.—Tea is nice no matter how you feel.

LIBBEY.—I have to have another operation, Stella.

STELLA.—(*After a time*) Cut me a piece of lemon with the knife, John . . .

LIBBEY.—Don't get nervous, and don't cry, Stella. I don't want you to cry. It's nothing to cry about.

STELLA.—I'm not crying, John.

LIBBEY.—Let's talk sensibly like two human beings. I don't like crying.

STELLA.—I know you don't, John.

LIBBEY.—They showed me the plates. I took X rays, and there were two white spots in the right kidney. That's the only good side left, Stella.

STELLA.—Maybe they'll dissolve.

LIBBEY.—They won't. They're too big.

STELLA.—Is that what they said?

LIBBEY.—I saw them myself. They're too big.

STELLA.—Maybe they're not stones, John.

LIBBEY.—They're stones.

STELLA.—You feel all right now?

LIBBEY.—I feel Okay. They wanted me immediately, tomorrow or Thursday, but I said no. I think I'll wait a couple weeks. They have to give me a cystoscope and more X rays for further examination. So I'll go in on a Tuesday, and they'll operate on a Thursday or Friday.

STELLA.—You're not afraid, are you, John?

LIBBEY.—Yes, I am, Stella.

STELLA.—I'm afraid too, John. I'm afraid. (*Fading*) Something's in the kitchen.

LIBBEY.—(*Off-mike*) Smells good.

SOUND.—*Frying in background.*

STELLA.—(*Full*) Your specialty with onions.

LIBBEY.—(*Fading in*) I spoke to Mr. Carlin; and he's giving me 2 weeks off, so we'll have a vacation before I go.

STELLA.—That's good, John. A vacation won't hurt you.

LIBBEY.—Don't make the onions so brown.

STELLA.—You need a rest.

LIBBEY.—I don't need a rest. That's all I been doing. I been resting. I been dieting. I been following all their instructions. So what, now I'm sick again.

STELLA.—We'll go someplace where there's fresh air, and then afterwards, when it's over, you'll get better quickly.

SOUND.—*Frying ceases.*

LIBBEY.—Should I slice the bread?

STELLA.—Dinner's ready. Sit down; I'll slice it.

LIBBEY.—(*Off-mike*) Any mail today, Stella?

STELLA.—No mail, dear. Sit down.

SOUND.—*Dishes being placed on the table.*

STELLA.—Don't stare at me that way, John.

LIBBEY.—I didn't mean to stare, Stella. Was I staring?

STELLA.—Eat the beets. They're good for you.

LIBBEY.—I checked up on the insurance policy today. It's all right.

STELLA.—I don't wanna hear about the insurance policy.

LIBBEY.—Those things have to be checked on and it's all right. There's $5,000 coming, and it's in order. These things have to be talked about.

STELLA.—All right, we talked about it.

LIBBEY.—All right. It just had to be said. When the time comes, you know where it is. (*Silence*) It's fortunate I . . .

STELLA.—I don't wanna hear about the insurance policy!

LIBBEY.—Okay. I didn't say a word. Okay.

STELLA.—Like you were gonna die, don't talk like that. (*Silence*)

LIBBEY.—I am going to die, Stella.

STELLA.—John, no, John, you're not. You're not. You mustn't say it when you're not.

LIBBEY.—(*Stella sobs behind his voice*) Please, Stella. (*Hardly audible*) You mustn't even think about it. Sure, you think I don't know how you feel, but I know very well, Stella. I got ten times the pain thinking about it as from the pain itself.

STELLA.—No, John, no, John.

LIBBEY.—Well, I'm no different from anybody else, I realize that.

STELLA.—You're not going to leave me. I'll be all alone. You won't leave me, will you, John?

LIBBEY.—I don't wanna die.

STELLA.—I'll die, too.

LIBBEY.—Let's not talk about it. There's lots pleasanter things to talk about.

STELLA.—John, you won't, will you? You won't?

LIBBEY.—How can I say, Stella . . .

STELLA.—Say, you're not gonna die. Tell me like you meant it. (*Pause*)

LIBBEY.—Here's my wallet, Stella. Open it, and take what you see there.

STELLA.—Why don't you answer me? There's ten $100 bills and two $500 bills. $2,000.
What is it? Where did you get the money, John?

LIBBEY.—Pick it up, Stella. Have you ever seen a $500 bill before?

STELLA.—Where did you get it, John?

LIBBEY.—We're spending it on ourselves. I decided for both of us. Anything you see or want, we'll buy. Like you always wanted to go to the opera. We'll go to the opera. We'll buy some clothes, and we'll go to the opera, and we'll do everything we've always wanted to do. That's what the money's for.

STELLA.—We never had $2,000 in our life.

LIBBEY.—I borrowed it from Mr. Carlin.

STELLA.—He gave it to you?

LIBBEY.—I didn't ask him.

STELLA.—How—you took it?

LIBBEY.—He'll get it back.

STELLA.—Get it back? How's he getting it back if you're spending it?

LIBBEY.—The money you're getting from the insurance, Stella. You'll pay him back. Don't look like that, Stella. It's no crime.

STELLA.—There won't be any insurance.

LIBBEY.—You'll have $5,000; and after you pay Mr. Carlin, you'll have $3,000 left. Why say there won't be any?

STELLA.—So you're already figuring on it. Your mind's made up.

LIBBEY.—Stella, all my life I've been broke. I never had a dime that wasn't somebody's soon's I got it. What's wrong then? Just because I'm doing what I always had a mind to? And now I can do it. I'm borrowing from you, but there'll be lots left. You won't feel sorry for the pleasure, Stella. We'll have that together, Stella.

STELLA.—You coulda borrowed off the insurance, John.

LIBBEY.—How long we had the policy—5 years. What is there to borrow?

STELLA.—Like money was the only thing in the world. Like it was the only . . .

LIBBEY.—It's not the only thing in the world. I know it's not. I want some fun, Stella, that's all. Isn't that what we've always been talking about? Someday, we said. If we can't afford it now, when, then? When, then? Answer me. We've been living in this same place, this same apartment for years.

STELLA.—I don't mind that.

LIBBEY.—I mind it. I'm sick of it. Why don't you say you're sick of it, you are. I get $35 a week so's you can wash and cook and take care of the home day after day, listen to the radio, and look at the furniture day after day after day, and that's not all. Don't tell me how you feel, Stella.

STELLA.—I haven't complained about it.

LIBBEY.—And I'm sick of your not complaining about it.

STELLA.—What did you want me to do? I tried to make the best of things, didn't I, John?

LIBBEY.—Making the best of things, all the time being brave. Denying and scrimping and saving and making ends meet, it adds up to nothing. That's what it adds up to, Stella, nothing.

STELLA.—(*A moment . . . then*) Put the money away, John, I'll give you some more tea.

LIBBEY.—We'll use it then?

STELLA.—We'll use it.

LIBBEY.—You're not feeling bad. Please don't feel bad. That's not why I took it.

STELLA.—I'm all right, John.

LIBBEY.—Show me by smiling. See? It s not stealing. It's nothing like stealing, Stella. He'll get it back soon. We'll be very happy.

STELLA.—The tea is still hot, John. If you'll pour me some, and you haven't eaten much, John.

LIBBEY.—I'm full just thinking. I can't eat.

STELLA.—You have to eat something.

LIBBEY.—(*Silence . . . then*) What are you thinking about? About me? And what about me?

STELLA.—I'm not thinking anything at all, John.

LIBBEY.—Do you hate me?

STELLA.—I love you, John.

LIBBEY.—Maybe afterwards you'd hate me?

STELLA.—If I love you now, what's the sense of hating you later? I could ask you to change your mind, but you won't do that; for it's made up, and I can't argue things like that away. That's all I don't like about it, your scaring me and your thinking of what's coming and the fact maybe it's true.

MUSIC.—*Tread of descriptive music . . . hold . . . then drop into background for this sequence.*

BARBER.—Anything else besides the haircut?

LIBBEY.—A shampoo and a scalp massage and tell the boy I want a shine. And put some of that smelly stuff on my hair and whatever else you can think of. Give me whatever you can think of.

MUSIC.—*Same thread of music swells in . . . then drops behind.*

B. P. OPERATOR.—The manicurist will be with you in a jiffy.

STELLA.—(*Listlessly*) How long does this take? I'd like my hair washed and after the facial maybe a marcel.

MUSIC.—*Swells in . . . then drops behind.*

LIBBEY.—Look all right, Stella?

STELLA.—It fits all right.

LIBBEY.—How is it in the back? Is it all right there?

STELLA.—How's it supposed to be? You never bought a suit with tails before. They just hang. They hang all right.

MUSIC.—*Swells in . . . then drops under.*

STELLA.—Well, John?

LIBBEY.—I like it.

STELLA.—Yes, but should I take it?

LIBBEY.—I'd take it. It's the prettiest dress I ever seen on you, Stella.

MUSIC.—*Swells in . . . mix into operatic aria, as if played by orchestra in the pit far off-mike and sung by soprano voice far off-mike . . . mix into descriptive music . . . hold . . . mix into the roar of a fight crowd . . . hold . . . roar subsides and stays under as we hear*

VOICE.—(*Far off-mike*) The winner and still heavyweight champion of the world, *Joe Louis!!*

SOUND.—*Roar of acclaim sweeps in . . . hold . . . mix into descriptive music . . . hold . . . mix into the whirl of the roulette wheel, the hum of voices in the background, the whirling ball as it rolls to a stop.*

CROUPIER.—Eighteen on the red.

SOUND.—*Chips . . . the whirl of the roulette wheel.*

CROUPIER.—Bets, please.

SOUND.—*The ball coming to a stop.*

CROUPIER.—Twenty-two on the black.

SOUND.—*Chips . . . whirling wheel . . . descriptive music swells in . . . music mixes into typical melody played by hand organ . . . hold . . . then keep in background for*

LIBBEY.—An organ-grinder, Stella.

STELLA.—John, let him have something. Have you something?

ORGAN-GRINDER.—(*After silence, far off-mike*) Grazias, grazias, signor, grazias!

STELLA.—How much did you give him, John?

LIBBEY.—Five dollars.

MUSIC.—*Descriptive music swells in . . . hold . . . mix into duet singing popular love song to each other with orchestral accompaniment, all this far off-mike as if coming from a musical comedy stage . . . applause of audience as it ends . . . hold . . . mix into the roar of an airplane . . . hold . . . then drop roar under for*

STELLA.—John, you see it? Look 'way down there, see?

LIBBEY.—A boat. It's about the size of . . . we must be going ten times as fast. Twenty times.

STELLA.—How long will we stay in Florida? Long, John?

LIBBEY.—As long as we feel like. Let's see what it's all about first. We'll stay as long as we feel like.

MUSIC.—*Descriptive music swells in . . . hold . . . fades as sound of ocean waves sweeping on beach comes up strong . . . hold . . . then subdue behind.*

STELLA.—I could just lay here and lay here, the sand's so warm.

LIBBEY.—We'll take one more swim tomorrow before we go. Listen to the ocean. You like the sound of the ocean?

STELLA.—The sun's good for you, John. You've got a tan.

LIBBEY.—Have I? So have you. Your face and your shoulders.

STELLA.—I don't feel like going back. I'd like to stay here, John.

LIBBEY.—Kiss me.

SOUND.—*Soft kiss.*

STELLA.—Do we have to go back, John?

MUSIC.—*Descriptive music swells in . . . hold . . . mixes with the street noises of New York City and finally fades out altogether, and we hear only the street noises . . . hold . . . then drop under voices and fade out . . . cricket-like sound of elevator captain off mike.*

ELEVATOR CAPTAIN.—(*Off-mike*) Those going to the tower take the elevator to the right.

SOUND.—*Patter of feet, voices, all behind voice of*

ELEVATOR BOY.—Going up. Step back, please.

SOUND.—*Elevator door closing . . . hum of rising elevator as it rises swiftly . . . fade-out . . . fade-in . . . stops . . . elevator door opening.*

ELDERLY LADY.—Is this still the tallest building in the world, young man?

ELEVATOR BOY.—Yes ma'am. All out.

SOUND.—*Voices of passengers up . . . then drop under and fade completely out.*

STELLA.—You want to sign the book, John? Here's a book.

LIBBEY.—Let's just look around. Where? We might as well sign first.

SOUND.—*Scratching of pen . . . hold . . . then drop under.*

LIBBEY.—John Libbey, New York City. What's the date? Never mind, I see it, Stella. (*Scratching stops*) You sign.

SOUND.—*Pen scratching behind her voice.*

STELLA.—Mrs. John Libbey—ditto.

LIBBEY.—It's windy.

STELLA.—Button up your coat, John.

LIBBEY.—See everything from here—I'm all right, Stella. Don't button me.

STELLA.—It's windy.

LIBBEY.—There's the perisphere and trylon, see?

STELLA.—Over there.

LIBBEY.—It's sure high up. Look straight down, Stella.

STELLA.—They look like ants.

LIBBEY.—Can you see where we live?

STELLA.—Over there.

LIBBEY.—Can't see it. There's buildings in the way. Pretty, isn't it Stella. Big and far away. It gives me a funny feeling inside. We had a good time, didn't we, Stella?

STELLA.—Yes, John.

LIBBEY.—It's the prettiest scenery I ever seen.

STELLA.—I'm not sorry, John.

LIBBEY.—I have to be in the hospital by four. (*A moment . . . then*) You were good to me all the time, Stella.

STELLA.—(*Warmly, softly*) John.

LIBBEY.—I'd better get rid of the nickels. Got the duffel-bag?

STELLA.—Must you, John?

LIBBEY.—I just wanna see what happens. We're too high up (*Fading*). Let's go down to the tenth floor . . . (*Dead air*)

SOUND.—*Muffled street noises . . . window opening and the street noises come up full . . . hold . . . then keep behind.*

LIBBEY.—Nobody will get hurt from here. You hand me the nickels, and I'll throw them out. Open the bag.

STELLA.—Someone may see you.

LIBBEY.—Hand them fast. There's only $50 worth. Unwrap them first, Stella. Anybody looking?

STELLA.—Nobody's looking.

SOUND.—*Jingling nickels.*

LIBBEY.—Here goes.

STELLA.—I can't see the sense to it, John.

LIBBEY.—There isn't any sense to it.

STELLA.—Throw them out fast.

SOUND.—*Jingling nickels.*

LIBBEY.—All my life I been making sense. Look at the people.

SOUND.—*Jingling nickels.*

LIBBEY.—People everywhere. Look at the people, Stella.

STELLA.—Maybe they'll see you.

LIBBEY.—I'm standing on the side here. They can't see me. Give me the rest quick.

SOUND.—*Jingling nickels.*

LIBBEY.—Don't it give you a thrill, Stella? All those people, and we're making them run. It's power. We have power. When you can afford to spend, Stella, it's power.

STELLA.—We better go.

LIBBEY.—Look at them, look.

STELLA.—We better go, John.

LIBBEY.—I never seen anything like that in my life.

SOUND.—*Honking of car horns increases . . . other street noises become louder . . . hold . . . then fade out . . . fade in on sound of shuffling slippers on linoleum . . . hold . . . then stop as voice breaks in.*

BED 1 (*Off-mike*) Will you lower the blind a little while you're there?

BED 2.—This one?

SOUND.—*Adjusting blind . . . it stays under his voice.*

NURSE.—(*Fading in*) Here—what are we doing out of bed, Mr. Corroni?

BED 1.—(*Off-mike*) The light was in my eyes, nurse.

NURSE.—All right, we'll fix it. Back in bed, Mr. Corroni. Some orange juice for you, Mr. Libbey.

LIBBEY.—Thanks.

NURSE.—Sleep well last night?

LIBBEY.—Pretty well, thanks.

NURSE.—You'll sleep better tonight. It's hard the first night. Dr. Beems will be here in a minute.

LIBBEY.—The X rays done?

NURSE.—Oh sure. You're down for surgery tomorrow, aren't you? Bed high enough?

LIBBEY.—Yes.

NURSE.—(*Fading*) He'll be here in a minute.

BED 2.—(*Far off-mike*) See in the paper about all those nickels, Mr. Michaels?

BED 4.—(*Off-mike*) I didn't see the paper yet.

BED 2.—(*Far off-mike*) Someone threw a lot of nickels from the Empire State Building. They had a traffic jam a mile long.

BED 4.—(*Off-mike*) Nickels?

BED 2.—(*Far off-mike*) Two women fainted, and some guy had his fingers smashed.

DR. BEEMS. (*Far off-mike*) Be right there, nurse. (*Fading in*) Put on your bathrobe, and come with me, Mr. Libbey.

LIBBEY.—Yes, sir.

BEEMS.—Slip on anything.

SOUND.—*Shuffling slippers behind voices.*

LIBBEY.—The cystoscopy X rays, doctor?

BEEMS.—Yes. We can see them here. (*Shuffling stops*)

SOUND.—*Click of electric switch.*

BEEMS.—There. How does that look to you, Mr. Libbey?

LIBBEY.—I can't tell. What do you mean?

BEEMS.—There's nothing the matter with you, nothing that we can see, Mr. Libbey. I'm going to give you a discharge. Have your wife call for you.

LIBBEY.—But the other X rays there was something wrong.

BEEMS.—Intravenous is not always dependable. The dye sometimes upsets the diagnosis. You're all right, Mr. Libbey. Go home whenever you feel like it. Have Mr. Libbey's clothes brought up, nurse.

NURSE.—Yes, doctor.

BEEMS.—The dressings in 10G for Baker?

NURSE.—Yes, doctor.

BEEMS.—(*Fading*) Bring me his chart. (*Off-mike and constant*) Ask Dr. Collins if I can see him. (*A little further off-mike and constant*) You're a very lucky man, Mr. Libbey.

MUSIC.—*Very soft . . . hold . . . volume remains constant under announcer's voice.*

CLOSING ANNOUNCEMENT.—The Radio Guild of the National Broadcasting Company has brought you a first play by Ted Key called "The Clinic."

BEST COMEDIES

Jack Benny*

Here is Jack Benny, master comedian of them all. The Jack Benny show has been the top-ranking comedy program for years, and the man himself has brought without question more laughs to more people than any entertainer who ever lived. His instinctive sense of the ridiculous; his immediate response to a "take"; his perfect timing; his frenetic excursions into the regions of self-improvement and self-realization; his smashed but blobby ego; his flabby, self-asserting manhood; his loud bark and his edentate bite; his confusion, hurry, and perpetual opportunism; all these dizzy unpredictables are knocked around the studio in a frantic free-for-all, with primitive latrations from Rochester, boos from the band, surgical asides from Mary Livingston, and a peculiar sprinkling of acidulous holy water from Dennis Day. Don Wilson and Phil Harris punish the poor man whenever he gets in range, and, from time to time, a menagerie of birds and animals is let loose in the kitchen to multiply the miseries of his life.

Jack Benny stands in the midst of it all, beleaguered, resourceful, and stingy. Always depreciated, but always vainglorious, guyed, gulled, and tyrannized, but never completely routed, Benny swings and misses, ducks and stumbles but never goes down for the count. About him there seems to hang a protective philosophy of superiority. Confounded by circumstance and hounded by his friends, he keeps slugging away, oblivious to every argument but his own. One would need to be a student of celestial mechanics to measure the mound of Jell-O that rolls so pleasantly with all the punches. But one thing certainly can be said without qualification: The Jack Benny program is the fastest moving half hour in American radio.

* Permission to reprint the Jack Benny script of March 3, 1940, has been arranged with Jack Benny; General Foods Corporation, makers of Jell-O and Jell-O Puddings, the sponsors of the Jack Benny program; and Young and Rubicam, Inc. This script cannot be reproduced in whole or in part for any purpose whatsoever without the permission of the sponsor, Jack Benny, and Young and Rubicam, Inc.

Jack Benny

MUSIC.—*Jell-O signature.*

WILSON.—The Jell-O program, starring Jack Benny . . . with Mary Livingston, Phil Harris, Dennis Day, and "Yours Truly" Don Wilson.

The orchestra opens the program with "Little Girl."

MUSIC.—*Segue into number . . . "Little Girl."*

WILSON.—One way to define an ideal dessert, ladies and gentlemen, is to say it's something you look *forward* to with eagerness and look *back* upon with satisfaction. Yes, that's one way. But an even better way is simply to say, *Jell-O.* Because Jell-O is really tops for topping off a meal. It's a grand-looking dessert, one that sets off a table in first-rate style, a gay, glistening dessert, radiant with jewellike colors, the most tempting and attractive treat you ever laid eyes on. And what a *swell taste*, a top-notch, tantalizing flavor, extra-rich, as inviting as the juicy, ripe fruit itself.

So tomorrow, friends, try a delightful Jell-O dessert in any one of Jell-O's six famous flavors. Ask your grocer for *Jell-O* by name. For Jell-O is a trade-mark, the property of General Foods. And those big red letters on the box are your assurance of the highest quality and that delicious Jell-O flavor.

That was "Little Girl" played by the orchestra and now, ladies and gentlemen, we are back in Hollywood after enjoying the winter sports in Yosemite. So without further ado, we bring you our master of ceremonies, that outdoor man with an indoor body, Jack Benny. (*Applause*)

JACK.—Jell-O again, this is Jack Benny talking. And, Don, if you're referring to that little incident when I hurt my leg skiing in Yosemite, you're not being very fair. I'm a very good skier,—but after all, accidents *will* happen.

WILSON.—Well, Jack, if you're such a good skier, how come the very first day you started down the hill you had your skis on backwards?

JACK.—Don, did you ever hear that expression, "doing it the hard way"? Anybody can go down a hill frontwards.

WILSON.—Oh, I must have misunderstood the whole thing. I thought that you made a mistake and didn't know what you were doing.

JACK.—Oh, no, Don, no.

WILSON.—Then I'm sorry, Jack. I apologize.

JACK.—That's all right, Don. That's all right.

MARY.—I *object!*

JACK.—Well, if it isn't Livingston, the D.A. What are you objecting to, Mary?

MARY.—I object to that big fib you just told Don Wilson. If you're such an expert skier, how come you didn't even know how to stop?

JACK.—Well . . .

MARY.—Why, the very first thing you did, was crash right through the ski house.

JACK.—It coulda been a publicity stunt, you know.

MARY.—Go on, you don't know any more about skiing than you do about spending money.

JACK.—Spending money?

MARY.—You do that the hard way, too.

JACK.—All right Mary, all right. My skiing accident is over. I lived through it, so let's forget it.

PHIL.—Now listen, Jackson, I don't want to butt in, but that accident was nobody's fault but your own. You had no business getting on a pair of skis in the first place.

JACK.—Do ah hear a voice from the cornfield? What was that, Phil?

PHIL.—I said the whole thing was your own fault.

JACK.—Oh, it was!

PHIL.—Certainly. It never would have happened, if you weren't such a show-off.

JACK.—*I'm* a show-off! Listen, Phil, your calling me a show-off is equivalent to Guy Kibbee telling Edgar Kennedy to buy hair tonic. And furthermore, I'm not interested in your diagnosis of my accident. Oh, hello, Dennis.

DENNIS.—Hello, Mr. Benny. How's your leg?

JACK.—It's much better, thanks, but it still hurts a little. Every once in a while I feel a twitch of pain there.

MARY.—How can you tell where your accident stops and the rheumatism begins?

JACK.—Now, wait a minute, Mary. If I've got rheumatism, how is it I'm such a good skier?

MARY.—I'm not going through that again!

JACK.—You bet you won't. Well, Dennis, are you glad to be back home?

DENNIS.—Yeah, I'm as happy as a lark.

MARY.—Oh, he's always happy.

JACK.—Well I regard that as a virtue. I'm glad that somebody is contented around here.

PHIL.—There's nothing wrong with me that a raise wouldn't cure.

JACK.—There he goes with that raise again. All that guy thinks of is money, women and money.

PHIL.—I don't know of a better parlay, do you?

JACK.—Phil, let's forget it. Well, tell me, Dennis, did you enjoy our little vacation at Yosemite?

DENNIS.—I sure did, Mr. Benny. And I want to thank you very much for treating us to the trip.

JACK.—That's all right, Dennis.

WILSON.—Yes, Jack, it was a grand gesture on your part.

JACK.—That's Okay, Don. It was a pleasure. You and Dennis have acted like gentlemen, and you've always spoken very nicely of me. Therefore I was glad to pay for your trip.

PHIL.—I'm sincere, so I get hooked.

JACK.—Hooked?

PHIL.—Yes, and I think it was a pretty cheap trick for you to pay everybody else's expenses and leave me out.

JACK.—Oh, you do!

PHIL.—Sure. That vacation cost me over a hundred bucks!

JACK.—All right, Phil, I'll tell you what I'll do. Just give me an itemized bill of all your expenses in Yosemite, food, room and everything, and I'll be only too happy to reimburse you.

PHIL.—Oh, Jackson, you're kidding.

JACK.—If I'm not may the roof fall on me! You've got a nerve expecting me to pay your expenses after the way you acted. There I was flat on my back in bed, and you were out every day with my nurse.

PHIL.—Well, she was a cute kid.

JACK.—*I don't care if she was Ann Sheridan. She was supposed to rub my back.*

DENNIS.—Gee, Mr. Benny, would Ann Sheridan rub your back?

JACK.—I wish I knew. And pay attention! I was talking about Miss Kelly, my alleged nurse.

MARY.—I think she did pretty well, considering that she had to work 24 hours a day.

WILSON.—24 hours a day? Didn't he have a night nurse?

MARY.—No! Jack hired a girl with insomnia.

JACK.—Well, she certainly wasn't on the job in the daytime. She was out with Phil Harris every minute.

PHIL.—By the way, Jackson, I had a letter from her this morning.

JACK.—Really? Well, I'm glad you finally met a girl that can write. Did she say anything about *me?*

PHIL.—Yeah, she told me to be sure and say hello to "Grapes of Wrath."

JACK.—Well, that's very clever, and Phil, when you answer her letter, be sure to give her my regards. And tell her that as a nurse she doesn't know an aspirin tablet from a manhole cover. I wouldn't recommend her to my worst enemy.

WILSON.—Your worst enemy, who's that, Jack?

JACK.—Well, Don, take the name Edgar Allan Poe. Remove the Edgar and the Poe, add Fred, and boil for 10 minutes. Now look, fellows, we've got other things to do tonight, so let's settle down and eliminate all references to our vacation. How about a song, Dennis? Are you all set?

DENNIS.—Yeah, I got a swell number, Mr. Benny, called "Make Love with a Guitar."

JACK.—Oh, yes, that's a very good song, "Make Love with a Guitar." You know, when I was a young fellow, I used to serenade the girls myself; only instead of playing a guitar I played my violin.

MARY.—And instead of girls you got pennies from heaven!

JACK.—Is that so? Well, all I know, Mary, everybody in Waukegan used to call me the "Sheik."

MARY.—Sure. You lived in a tent.

JACK.—*I lived in a house.* Go ahead with your song, Dennis.

DENNIS.—Okay.

WILSON.—By the way, Jack, I knew I had something to ask you. Did you go to the Motion Picture Academy Award dinner Thursday night?

JACK.—Yes, Don, Mary and I attended, and it was a grand affair. Go ahead, Dennis.

WILSON.—Well, Jack, weren't you disappointed that you didn't get the award for the outstanding performance?

JACK.—Disappointed? Why, no, Don. Go ahead with your song, Dennis.

PHIL.—Now come on, Jackson. Weren't you just a little bit jealous?

JACK.—Me jealous? What are you talking about?

MARY.—He's talking about the Academy Award dinner Thursday night. You shoulda seen him, fellows.

JACK.—*Dennis, are you going to sing or not?*

MARY.—Boy, was Jackson burned up. He nearly . . .

JACK.—*Dennis, what are you waiting for? Sing!*

MARY.—Jack was so mad, I thought he was going to . . .

JACK.—*Sing, Dennis, for heaven's sake!*

DENNIS.—Okay, Mr. Benny.

JACK.—Come here a minute, young lady. I want to talk to you.

DENNIS DAY AND ORCHESTRA.—*Segue into number* . . . "*Make Love with a Guitar.*"

JACK.—That was "Make Love with a Guitar," sung by Dennis Day. And very good, Dennis. That was one of your best numbers. And now, ladies and gentlemen, as a special offering and for the feature attraction of our program, *tonight* we are going to present one of the . . .

MARY.—*Giggles.*

JACK.—Mary, I warned you. *Tonight* we are going to present one of the outstanding plays of the . . .

PHIL.—All right, Jackson, come clean. What happened Thursday night at the banquet?

JACK.—Phil. I'm trying to introduce our play. This, ladies and gentlemen, is one of the outstanding . . .

WILSON.—I'm curious, too, Jack. What happened, Mary?

MARY.—Well, fellows, it was like this.

JACK.—Oh . . .

MARY.—Jack took me to the Academy Award dinner; and on the way over he was so nervous and fidgety, he nearly drove me crazy.

JACK.—Of course I was nervous. We were late.

MARY.—Late? We got there so early, the head waiter gave Jack a box of silverware and told him to set the tables.

JACK.—I didn't do it, did I? Anyway, getting back to our play . . .

WILSON.—What were you so nervous about, Jack?

MARY.—I'm coming to that.

JACK.—He asked *me*.

MARY.—Well, fellows, you know Jack. As usual, he thought he was gonna win the Academy Award.

PHIL.—For what, *acting?*

JACK.—Don't be so surprised.

PHIL.—Why, that's silly, Jackson. Even before the banquet, everybody knew it was a toss-up between Jimmy Stewart and Robert Donat.

JACK.—All right, Phil, didn't you ever hear of a dark horse? Didn't you?

PHIL.—Oh, Rochester! That's different!

JACK.—I don't mean Rochester. I mean *me*, Tough Luck Benny, that's who I mean.

MARY.—Well, anyway . . .

JACK.—(*Mocking*) Well, anyway, anyway.

MARY.—Anyway, all the stars got there, and during the dinner Jack ran around like a regular politician, shaking hands with everybody and passing out cigars.

JACK.—There's nothing wrong with passing out cigars.

MARY.—You didn't have to give one to Bette Davis.

JACK.—Well, I was excited.

MARY.—Sure you were excited. *And here's the pay-off, fellows*

JACK.—Oh . . .

MARY.—When the dinner was over and they announced that Robert Donat was the winner, Jack got up and yelled, "*You can't do that to me!*"

JACK.—Well, I told you I was nervous. Anyway, I sat right down, didn't I?

MARY.—Not until someone hit you in the face with an artichoke.

JACK.—That was a Brussels sprout, and I didn't even feel it. Artichoke! You have to exaggerate everything. Anyway, folks, as I started to announce . . .

WILSON.—But, Jack, getting back to the award, I can't understand why you objected to the decision.

JACK.—Because I don't think Robert Donat deserves that statue as much as I do.

PHIL.—What are you talking about? Did you see "Good-bye, Mr. Chips"?

JACK.—Yes, but I don't remember *him* in it.

MARY.—You don't?

JACK.—No!

MARY.—You're the kind of a guy that would visit the Grand Canyon and not remember the hole!

JACK.—Well, let me tell you something about "Good-bye, Mr. Chips," Mary. I just wish *I* had a chance to play that kind of a role, that's all.

DENNIS.—Say, Mr. Benny, I didn't see that picture. Would the part really fit you?

JACK.—Like a glove. You know, Dennis, it's a story about an English schoolmaster, and we follow his career. First, he's young, then middle-aged; then he gradually becomes older and older and older. And finally he's a white-haired, wrinkled old man, sitting by the fireplace.

MARY.—That's where the glove fits.

JACK.—All right. Now listen, fellows, let's change the subject and forget about this year's Academy Award. First thing you know, people will think it's a case of sour grapes on *my* part. Now getting back to our play.

WILSON.—Pardon me, Jack. Ladies and gentlemen, speaking of sour grapes, I would like to announce that Jell-O does *not* come in that particular flavor.

JACK.—*Well.*

WILSON.—However, it does come in six *other* flavors, and you will find each one of them tempting, economical, and easy to make. So go to your neighborhood grocer and insist on genuine Jell-O. Look for the big red letters on the box!

JACK.—Very good, Don. Allow me to congratulate you. That was not only brilliant, but obvious. And now, ladies and gentlemen, getting back to our play, *tonight* we are going to present something entirely different and away from our usual sketches. However, before we begin, I'd like to explain . . .

SOUND.—*Loud knock on door.*

JACK.—Oh, who is it? Come in.

SOUND.—*Door opens.*

JACK.—Well, look who's here, fellows!

ANDY.—Hi yuh, Buck. Remember me?

JACK.—Andy Devine! (*Applause*)

GANG.—*Ad lib greetings to Andy.*

JACK.—Well, Andy, it's about time you showed up. Gosh, you've been away a long time.

ANDY.—Yup, about 2 months. Had a lot of fun, though.

JACK—Oh, that's right, you were out playing vaudeville. How did you do, Andy? How was business?

ANDY.—Swell, Buck. I was the biggest thing since Powers' elephants. (*Andy laughs*)

JACK.—Well, I'm glad to hear that, Andy, because I'd like to go back on the road again myself, and play those good old four-a-days.

MARY.—I got a great idea for your act, Jack.

JACK.—What?

MARY.—You start out as a young man, and the audience gets older and older and older.

JACK.—Don't worry. *I'd* entertain 'em. Well, tell me, Andy, what sort of a routine did *you* do?

ANDY.—I sang songs and told some jokes, all sophisticated stuff.

JACK.—I'll bet.

ANDY.—Then for a wind-up *maw, paw, and me* would come out and do our adagio act.

JACK.—Well, that sounds exciting. You mean to say you and your paw would throw your maw around in the air?

ANDY.—Not only that, he'd catch her blindfolded.

JACK.—Blindfolded?

ANDY.—Yeah, he couldn't stand the sight of her in them pink tights.

JACK.—Oh! Well, I'd like to have seen that myself. Say, that musta been pretty dangerous for your maw. Didn't your paw ever miss her?

ANDY.—Every show, Buck. That was our big finish.

JACK.—Say, that musta been sure-fire, and I'm glad you did so well. Well, stick around, Andy. We're going to put on a little play right after Phil's number. Maybe we can find a part for you in it.

ANDY.—Sorry, Buck, I gotta run along now. I got a *blonde* and a *brunette* waiting for me down in the car.

JACK.—Oh, two girls, eh?

ANDY.—No, *just one*. And you oughta see her. (*Laughs*)

JACK.—I'd like to. Well, so long, Andy.

ANDY.—So long, everybody.

GANG.—*Ad lib "Good-by" . . . "So long, Andy."*

SOUND.—*Door slams . . . Applause.*

JACK.—Dawggone, Andy sure gets a kick out of life. Well, Phil, now that I feel good again, let's hear a number, and we'll do our play right after it.

PHIL.—Okay, Jackson. Is there anything special you'd like from our large repertoire?

JACK.—Large repertoire? Phil, you never played anything that was over 3 feet away from "Dipsy Doodle," so get in the groove.

SOUND.—*Knock on door.*

JACK.—Hold it a minute. Come in.

SOUND.—*Door opens.*

BALDWIN.—Telegram for Jack Benny.

JACK.—Take it, Mary. Hey, buddy, got change for a half?

BALDWIN.—Only two quarters. That won't help *you.*

SOUND.—*Door slams.*

JACK.—Hm! Well, I'm glad he finally got a job. Who's the wire from, Mary?

MARY.—It's from your father in Miami Beach.

JACK.—From dad, eh? What does he say?

MARY.—"My dear son Jack, Received your letter saying you were gonna win the Academy Award. The newspapers here got it all wrong."

JACK.—Poor dad, he'll be so disappointed.

MARY.—Wait, there's more.

JACK.—Oh.

MARY.—"Congratulations, and I am very anxious to see your new picture 'Mr. Chips Rides Again.'"

JACK.—He means Buck Benny. Let me have that, Mary, I'll answer it. Play, Phil. Gosh, how will I ever tell dad?

MUSIC.—*Segue into number . . . "I've Got My Eyes on You."*

JACK.—That was "I've Got My Eyes on You," played by Phil Harris and his orchestra. And, Phil, that number was vaguely familiar. Didn't you play it a few weeks ago?

PHIL.—I dunno. Hey, Eddie, did we ever play that number before?

BELOIN.—I dunno. Hey, Bill, did we ever play that number before?

MORROW.—I dunno. Hey, Sam.

JACK.—Never mind, I was just asking. No use going through the whole band. It's not that important. I think, Phil, you ought to be a little bit careful about repeating band numbers so soon, that's all. And now, ladies and gentlemen.

PHIL.—Well, I don't remember whether we played it before or not. It bothers me.

BELOIN.—Me, too!

MORROW.—Me, too!

JACK.—Cut it out. You know, Phil, if your boys would worry more about their music ahead of time instead of spending all week at the Santa Anita race track, we'd be a lot better off.

PHIL.—What do you mean?

JACK.—I mean I went out to the track yesterday, and there they were, every one of 'em, including your guitar player. What a pest he is!

PHIL.—Who, Frankie? He useta be a tout.

JACK.—*Useta* be? He's got more information now than Clifton Fadiman. Every race he'd come around and say, "Play this horse," "Play that horse."

PHIL.—Well, you know how Frankie is. He gets enthusiastic, that's all.

JACK.—Phil, I don't object to enthusiasm, but those tips he hands out. Yesterday in the big race he insisted that I play Heel Fly. He said "I'm so sure of that horse that if he don't win I'll kill myself."

PHIL.—Well, what about it.

JACK.—I lost $2, and I don't see any lily in his hand. I can't stand a welcher. No, sir.

WILSON.—Well, Jack, you certainly don't expect a fellow to kill himself just because he gave you a bad tip, do you?

JACK.—No, but he could cut his finger or something and show he was sincere—*some* little gesture.

MARY.—You know, Jack, a guy like you should stay away from the races. You don't have any fun there.

JACK.—Listen, Mary, there's nobody that enjoys a hot dog and a little fresh air more than I do.

MARY.—I mean you can't stand to lose.

JACK.—Well, naturally, six races in a row is just a little too much.

WILSON.—No kiddin', Jack, did you really lose six straight races yesterday?

JACK.—Yeah.

MARY.—(*Giggles*) Jack was so mad that, instead of tearing up his tickets at the track, he took 'em home and ran 'em through the meat grinder.

JACK.—You're darn right I did. Well, so much for Santa Anita. And now, ladies and gentleman, as I started to announce, for our feature attraction this evening we are going to present, if possible, a dramatic version of one of the outstanding . . .

SOUND.—*Knock on door.*

JACK.—Well, I give up. Come in.

SOUND.—*Door opens.*

GRACIE.—Hello.

JACK.—Hello. Look, miss, I'm very busy and I . . .

MARY.—Oh, hello, Gracie. Jack, it's Gracie Allen!

JACK.—Oh. (*Applause*)

GRACIE.—Hello, Mary. Hello, Jack.

JACK.—Hello.

GRACIE.—Hello, Dennis. Hello, Don.

DENNIS and WILSON.—Hello.

GRACIE.—Hello, beautiful.

PHIL.—Hello, Gracie.

JACK.—Oh, fine. Gracie, you're the only one in the world that thinks Phil Harris is beautiful.

GRACIE.—Yes, so do I.

JACK.—Oh. Well, Gracie, it was nice of you to drop in; but we have a play to do, and we haven't much time. What brought you up here tonight?

GRACIE.—I dunno. When I hitchhike, I never ask their names.

JACK.—I see. Well, if you'll excuse me, I'll . . .

GRACIE.—Say, did you know I'm running for President?

JACK.—President? Oh, yes, I heard about it. Where's George?

GRACIE.—He's out digging up worms so I can go fishing.

JACK.—Oh. Well, look, Gracie, I'll be through in a few minutes, so if you'll just . . .

GRACIE.—I came up here to ask you if you'll vote for me.

JACK.—Well, are you nominated?

GRACIE.—No, I just drink to be sociable.

JACK.—Well, that I don't understand at all. Now if you don't mind, Gracie . . .

GRACIE.—How about you, Mary? Will you vote for me, Don?

JACK.—What's she talking about?

MARY.—I'll be glad to.

WILSON.—Me, too. So you've thrown your hat in the ring, eh, Gracie?

GRACIE.—Yes, and it was adorable. I paid thirty-seven fifty for it at Bullocks' Wilshire.

MARY.—No, did you really? I think the hats they're wearing this year are much better than last year, don't you, Gracie?

GRACIE.—Yes, I like the hat I got on even better than my head.

MARY.—Well, it's more becoming.

GRACIE.—Yeah, isn't it?

JACK.—Look, girls, you can discuss . . .

GRACIE.—I got this dress there, too. Feel the material.

MARY.—Gee, Gracie, it's stunning.

GRACIE.—Oh, it's just a little thing I'm gonna wear around the White House.

JACK.—Look, girls, you can discuss all this later. We're very busy.

PHIL.—Hey, Jackson, come to think of it, we *did* play that number 3 weeks ago!

BELOIN.—That's right!

MORROW.—That's right!

GRACIE.—That's right!

JACK.—Forget about it. Now look, Gracie, I'm glad you're running for President, and we'll be very happy to vote for you, but right now . . .

GRACIE.—You know I've got my own party, the Surprise Party. and I was thinking that maybe you could get me a lot of votes from your home town Waukegan.

JACK.—Waukegan? Why, I haven't lived in Waukegan for 10 years.

GRACIE.—Then maybe they'd be glad to do *you* a favor.

JACK.—Gracie, listen to me, will you? The election isn't until fall, and we'll all vote for you. Now don't annoy us any more. We've got our own show to do. Good-by.

GRACIE.—Good-by.

JACK.—And give my regards to George.

GRACIE.—I will. You know, George will be pretty busy after I'm President!

JACK.—You mean between writing a column and flying to Seattle. I know.

MARY.—Imagine "My Day" by George Burns.

JACK.—Yes, that oughta be something. Well, so long, Gracie. Good-by.

GRACIE.—Good-by. Well, if I'm gonna be elected, I got to run along now and make some speeches.

JACK.—And perhaps kiss babies.

GRACIE.—That's not a bad idea. *Come here, Phil.* (*And they kiss*)

JACK.—*Wait a minute!*

GRACIE.—*That's my baby! Good-by.*

SOUND.—*Door slams . . . applause.*

JACK.—That's about the silliest thing I ever heard, Gracie Allen running for President.

MARY.—Wouldn't it be funny if she *were* elected President next year?

JACK.—It sure would.

MARY.—And you won the Academy Award?

JACK.—Oh, quiet. And now, ladies and gentlemen, I have a little announcement to make. This evening, for our feature attraction, we were going to do "Mr. Smith Goes to Washington." But inasmuch as we only have a few minutes left, we will change it to "Mr. Smith Goes to Glendale." Now in this abbreviated version, I will play the part of . . .

SOUND.—*Telephone rings.*

JACK.—*Aw, nuts!* Let it ring. In our abbreviated version, I will play the part of . . .

SOUND.—*Telephone rings again.*

JACK.—Oh!

MARY.—Answer it, Jack. Mr. Smith went to bed.

JACK.—He might as well. (*Click*) You try to do something high-class and . . . *Hello!*

ROCHESTER.—Hello, Mr. Benny. This is Rochester.

JACK.—Well, you'll have to call me later! We only got a short time left, and we have a play to do.

ROCHESTER.—Okay, boss, but they're at it again, hot and heavy. So long.

JACK.—Wait a minute. You mean to say Carmichael and Trudy are having another scrap?

ROCHESTER.—A-huh.

JACK.—My goodness, Rochester, I told you to keep that polar bear and ostrich separated. Is it much of a fight?

ROCHESTER.—Tune in; we're broadcastin' it.

JACK.—It's nothing to get funny about. Now tell me exactly what happened.

ROCHESTER.—Well, I was in the kitchen when I heard a noise, and I ran into the livin' room.

JACK.—Yes.

ROCHESTER.—And *apparently* Carmichael had run the vacuum cleaner over Trudy.

JACK.—Apparently? What do you mean, *apparently?*

ROCHESTER.—Well, the bag is full of feathers, and she *ain't!*

JACK.—For heaven's sake, Rochester, why didn't you take the vacuum cleaner away from Carmichael?

ROCHESTER.—I ain't the finance company.

JACK.—I don't mean that. Anyway, the whole thing is your own fault. In the first place, Carmichael is supposed to be locked up in the garage. What was he doing in the house?

ROCHESTER.—I brought him in to help me wipe the dishes.

JACK.—Are you crazy? The last time you did that, he broke four plates.

ROCHESTER.—Well, he established *a new high* today.

JACK.—*What?*

ROCHESTER.—He broke everything but that big meat platter.

JACK.—Oh, my goodness!

SOUND.—*Loud crash.*

ROCHESTER.—He broke everything!

JACK.—Now look, Rochester, I've had just about enough. And you're gonna pay for all the damage that's been done in the living room and the kitchen. It's coming out of your salary.

ROCHESTER.—That old refrain!

JACK.—Never mind! Now you separate those animals and keep them quiet. I'll be home in a little while. Good-by.

ROCHESTER.—Good-by. Oh, say, boss!

JACK.—What?

ROCHESTER.—I see where Robert Donat won the Academy Award this year.

JACK.—I know, I know.

ROCHESTER.—Should I go out and buy a statue for that shelf you built?

JACK.—Never mind, there's always another year. Good-by. (*Click of telephone*) Hm, I'll perhaps find a nice-looking mess when I get home. Oh, well. And now, ladies and gentlemen, getting back to our feature attraction, *tonight*, we are going to . . .

SOUND.—*Loud knock on door.*

JACK.—*Oh, the heck with it! Play, Phil.*

MUSIC.—*Segue into number . . . "Where Was I"?*

WILSON.—And now, folks, here's something that's really extra-special, truly a *mealtime masterpiece. Jell-O Apricot Mold,* a swell new Jell-O dessert that's sure to prove one of the best you've ever tasted. It's a gay, sunny combination of delicious, golden apricots and clear, shimmering lemon Jell-O. And it's so easy and simple that you can make it in a jiffy.

First, dissolve one package of lemon Jell-O in 1 pint of hot water and apricot syrup. Chill until slightly thickened. Fold in 2½ cups of apricots. Then mold, and you've got a grand, intriguing dessert or salad that's simply sunshine itself, bright with color and brimful of rare, delightful goodness.

So tomorrow, friends, for a real thrill, try this new Jell-O creation, *Jell-O Apricot Mold,* a marvelous blend of golden, tangy apricots and *rich, tempting lemon Jell-O.*

JACK.—This is the last number of the twenty-second program in the current Jell-O series, and we will be with you again next

Sunday night at the same time, when we will present a play which will be *my* challenge to Robert Donat.

MARY.—Oh, Jack, Robert Donat is in England, otherwise you wouldn't make a crack like that.

JACK.—I wouldn't, eh? What about all those things I said about Spencer Tracy and Paul Muni and the rest of those guys that won Academy Awards? *And I'll tell you another thing, Mary . . .*

MARY.—Oh, good night, folks.

JACK.—*Good night nothing. If you think that I'm going. . . .*
Signature

WILSON.—And here's *more* fun and enjoyment for you. Tune in every Tuesday night for another swell half hour of Jell-O entertainment, the famous Aldrich family. See your local paper or movie and radio guide for time and station.

Fred Allen

HERE is Fred Allen again. One of the satisfactory features of the Fred Allen shows is that they read almost as well as they play. This is not true of many other comedy programs. Delivery, accent, pause, pronunciation, volume, inflection, and thirty other things more subtle often represent the difference between good and bad comedy over the air—the method and manner of delivery and the man or woman delivering often being as important as the material. The show reprinted here is, to be quite honest, a hybrid, the Rochester spot and the Information Please burlesque not having been performed on the same program. I think that they were a week apart. They are both typical and both excellent, and I have secured the necessary permission to telescope them in this way. The travesty of Canada Dry's quiz show was perhaps radio's most hilarious and ingenious ten minutes of fun during the past year. It was beautiful burlesquing, deadly accurate, utterly nonsensical, and mechanically so exact that even such refinements as what show precedes "Information Please" were observed and burlesqued. " . . . only meat balls that contain helium," as the selling feature for the product, was an inspired new high in incongruities and was typical of the quality of fun they had at the expense of the three wizards of pin-point carbonation.

It is a great, good-natured show, materially assisted by a good band, a performing band leader, and the Merry Macs, the best trained and most perfectly balanced rhythm and harmony unit on the air.

In last year's anthology I neglected to mention the importance of two very finished and inventive writers who are responsible for much of the comedy writing on the Fred Allen show. These men are Arnold Auerbach and Herman Wouk. They met each other at Columbia College, did not like each other's looks but approved of each other's talents, and immediately began an intensive and productive collaboration that brought their efforts to undergraduate fruition in two of the university's varsity shows. They also worked together on humorous material for college publications, Wouk finally becoming editor of the *Columbia Jester*. Auerbach graduated first and landed a job with the late Dave Freedman. Wouk joined the combination as soon as he was graduated from Columbia, and they worked together for a year. Dave Freedman died, leaving behind him the largest library of old jokes (and a few good ones) in the world. He also left behind him the distinction of being radio's only legendary character so far. Auerbach and Wouk work constantly on the Fred Allen show every week and have done so for the past five years steadily. Don Johnson is another writer who is on the regular staff, and Bill Schorr directs the shows. I mention these items to correct an oversight of which I was guilty last year and to give credit where it belongs. Most of the credit, however, still belongs to Fred Allen.

Here are the best spots from the programs for April 24 and May 1, 1940:

Fred Allen

MUSIC.—*Fanfare.*

VON ZELL.—The Fred Allen Show! (*Fanfare*) Brought to you by Ipana tooth paste for the smile of beauty! Sal Hepatica for the smile of health!

MUSIC.—"*Smile, Darn Ya*" . . . *up and under billboard.*

VON ZELL.—An hour of smiles with Fred Allen, folks, 3,600 seconds of fun and music; fun with our star comedian Fred Allen; with our guest, Carmichael's playmate, Rochester; music with Peter Van Steeden, the Merry Macs, and Wynn Murray. The time has come. It's the Fred Allen Show! (*applause*)
And now the auditorium darkens. A hush falls over the throng. Maestro Van Steeden raises his baton. And overture is "You Little Heartbreaker, You."

ORCHESTRA AND MERRY MACS.—"*You Little Heartbreaker, You.*"

VON ZELL.—And now, ladies and gentlemen, we bring you a young man who this week celebrates his thirtieth anniversary as an entertainer of his majesty, the great American public. Meet . . . Fred Allen in person. (*applause*)

ALLEN.—Thank you. Thank you. And good evening, ladies and gentlemen. Say, Harry, I wish you hadn't brought up my anniversary. You make me feel like an old man. I'm not creeping around the microphone here, am I?

VON ZELL.—Well, you're not exactly hounding around like a gazelle, Fred.

ALLEN.—I am not here for an adagio audition, Harry. When the occasion warrants, I can give vent to the fawn in me and frisk about like a centaur.

VON ZELL.—What's a centaur?

ALLEN.—A centaur is a fabled monster who has the body of a man from the waist up. From the waist down the centaur is a horse. Is the picture clear?

VON ZELL.—Yes. You're a centaur, all right.

ALLEN.—Look. If I was a real centaur and I walked up to you, you wouldn't know whether to shake hands or put $2 on me.

VON ZELL.—Well, never mind the centaurs. Is this really your thirtieth anniversary, Fred?

ALLEN.—Yes, Harry. I made my first stage appearance doing a juggling act in 1910. By the time I picked up all the things I dropped that first show, it was 1912.

VON ZELL.—Things must have been a lot different back in 1910, Fred.

ALLEN.—No. They were just about the same, Harry. In 1910 Mr. Hughes was appointed to the Supreme Court. He's still there, isn't he?

VON ZELL.—That's right.

ALLEN.—In 1910 Woolworth opened his first store in England. He's still in business, isn't he?

VON ZELL.—With that necktie you re wearing, you ought to know.

ALLEN.—In 1910 Glenn Curtiss flew from Albany to New York. Politicians are still flying out of Albany today.

VON ZELL.—That is correct.

ALLEN.—In 1910 the big song hit was "Come Josephine in My Flying Machine."

VON ZELL.—Why, the Merry Macs sang that song on the program a couple of weeks ago.

ALLEN.—That's what I mean, Harry. Everything is just the same as it was back in 1910. And that goes for me, too.

VON ZELL.—But in those days, Fred, you were an amateur.

PETE.—Yes, everything's the same as it was back in 1910, Harry.

ALLEN.—Everything but your salary, Mr. Van Steeden. And I shall attend to that tonight.

PETE.—You're going to split the atom, eh?

ALLEN.—Doggone you, Van Steeden, you do it every time. And now, since the merriment seems to have reached its little peak, let us turn to the latest news of the week.

MUSIC.—*Fanfare.*

ALLEN.—Ipana News presents the world in review!

MUSIC.—*Up . . . Fades.*

ALLEN.—Jamaica, New York. Jamaica race track opens with new pari-mutuel machines replacing bookmakers as result of recent state law. Pari-mutuels prove instantaneous success as 25,000 racing fans jam Jamaica track and bet over $800,000 on opening day. Ipana News visits the race track to get public's reaction to betting innovation. State Senator Bilbu Tweezer has some interesting statistics on prospective pari-mutuel returns. You have the figures, senator?

JOHN.—Yes. I've got them right here. Will you hand me the papers out of my back coat pocket?

ALLEN.—Yes, I'll be glad . . .

JOHN.—That's the worst of these swallow-tail coats. A man with short arms can't reach anything in his back pockets.

ALLEN.—I'll get them right . . .

JOHN.—Be careful of that bottle in there. It's whisky.

ALLEN.—Oh, you drink, do you?

JOHN.—As a duty. I'm cooperating with the mayor during the water shortage. I'm drinking whisky.

ALLEN.—But the water shortage is over.

JOHN.—Who asked you?

ALLEN.—I'm sorry. Ah. Here are your figures, senator.

JOHN.—Thank you. This Tweezer report on the pari-mutuel shows that everybody wins.

ALLEN.—How do you mean?

JOHN.—Well. During the racing season 100 million dollars will be wagered.

ALLEN.—But how does everybody win?

JOHN.—The state collects 50 million dollars in taxes. The state wins. Right?

ALLEN.—Right.

JOHN.—The race track collects 50 million dollars in revenues. The track wins. Right?

ALLEN.—Right.

JOHN.—The little man who bets $2 . . .

ALLEN.—The little man wins?

JOHN.—He loses.

ALLEN.—Ah. He loses.

JOHN.—Ahh. But he wins.

ALLEN.—Oh, now, wait a minute, senator. If the little man loses . . . how can he win?

JOHN.—He can't keep bettin' his $2 forever, can he?

ALLEN.—No.

JOHN.—He's gotta go broke sometime, ain't he?

ALLEN.—Yes.

JOHN.—That's where the little man wins.

ALLEN.—But, I . . .

JOHN.—What does the little man do when he's broke?

ALLEN.—I don't . . .

JOHN.—He applies to the state fer aid, don't he?

ALLEN.—Yes. I guess he . . .

JOHN.—The state gives him the money, don't it?

ALLEN.—Yes. As far . . .

JOHN.—Where does the state get the money to give the little man?

ALLEN.—You mean . . .

JOHN.—Right. From the 50 million little men like him who lost at the track in the first place.

ALLEN.—In other words . . .

JOHN.—It's a vicious circle. Everybody wins, including the horses.

ALLEN.—How do horses win? All a horse gets for running is a mess of oats.

JOHN.—That ain't hay, brother.

ALLEN.—You bet. And thank you, Senator Bilbo Tweezer. A bookmaker who points out the pari-mutuel shortcomings is "Hot-Horse Sam." Where *do* the pari-mutuels fall down, Sam?

VON ZELL.—Well, foist they ain't got no poisonality. A horse player don't get no kick outta beatin' no machine. With a bookmaker, he enjoys it.

ALLEN.—The horse player dislikes the bookmaker?

VON ZELL.—It's instinct, like Damon and Runyon.

ALLEN.—I see.

VON ZELL.—Anudder thing. With them machines the lowest you kin bet is $2.

ALLEN.—You took smaller bets?

VON ZELL.—If I seen a little gray-haired old lady sneakin' a buck outta her stockin', I'd tip me hat and say "What's on yer mind, ma? A seven horse parlay?"

ALLEN.—No machine will extend that courtesy.

VON ZELL.—You said it. If I seen a little boy with a dime in his hand runnin' fer a hot dog, I'd stop the boy and get him to put it on a horse. When he lost the dime, that taught him a lesson.

ALLEN.—And thanks to you bookmakers . . .

VON ZELL.—Old ladies and kids was gettin' action.

ALLEN.—Well, thanks. Say, what are you doing now, Sam?

VON ZELL.—I'm layin' low till them barry-neutrals blow over.

ALLEN.—You're not working?

VON ZELL.—Well, I got a little spot up in Poughkeepsie. I'm openin' a rabbit track.

ALLEN.—You mean a dog track with the mechanical rabbit.

VON ZELL.—No, I'm racin' rabbits. I woik it with an electric head of lettuce.

ALLEN.—Fine. Since you're an old horseman, Sam, tell me, who do you like in the Derby?

VON ZELL.—Al Smith.

ALLEN.—I'll play him across the board. And thank you Short-Odds Sam. A young lady who attended the track, opening day, was Miss Mavis Mildew. You were there, Mavis?

MIN.—Would you mind usin' me pen name? It's Beau Bell.

ALLEN.—Beau Belle? You're a newspaper woman, are you?

MIN.—I'm fashion editor on the *Racin' Form.*

ALLEN.—I see.

MIN.—When a goil writes on a newspaper, you don't use your real name. You gotta coin up a numb de plum.

ALLEN.—A numb de plum?

MIN.—Yeah. That's French fer don't give yer right name. So I'm Beau Belle.

ALLEN.—And you say you are fashion editor on the *Racing Form.*

MIN.—Yeah. And I'm also runnin' a dope column fer ladies under the name of "Feedbag Fanny."

ALLEN.—Feedbag Fanny? Do you play the horses yourself?

MIN.—Yeah. If I get a hot one, I'll go fer a couple of skins.

ALLEN.—Well, this is very interesting; but about the pari-mutuels, can you give us the woman's angle?

MIN.—Women around a race track is dopes.

ALLEN.—You've seen specific instances?

MIN.—Yeah! One dame hoid a horse was scratched. She run around to the paddock with Mercurochrome. Ha!

ALLEN.—Fancy.

MIN.—Somebody yelled, "They're at the post," 20 dames run out lookin' for Emily. Ahh! Them dowgers make me laugh.

ALLEN.—How do you mean?

MIN.—I hoid one old dame braggin' about her mink coat. She set it down.

ALLEN.—Yes.

MIN.—When the guy blew the bugle, the mink coat went to the post with six other horses.

ALLEN.—Tell me, Beau Belle, did you select the best dressed woman at Jamaica the opening day?

MIN.—Yeah. I give her four fetlocks in my column Tuesday.

ALLEN.—Four fetlocks. Who was the best dressed woman?

MIN.—Mrs. Divine Ledbetter of Tuxedo Junction. She was the best dressed woman comin' and goin'.

ALLEN.—Mrs. Ledbetter wore two different creations, did she?

MIN.—Yeah. She arrived at the track wearin' a gown by Schiaparelli, hat by Lucille, shoes by Janet, and furs by I. J. Fox.

ALLEN.—What did Mrs. Ledbetter wear leaving the track?

MIN.—A barrel by Ruppert.

ALLEN.—Thank you, Miss Mavis Mildew, alias "Beau Belle," alias "Feedbag Fanny," Minnehaha. A small horse player who feels quite strongly about the pari-mutuels is Tyler Vanz. What is your opinion of this new system of betting, Mr. Vanz?

CHAS.—The coise of the pari-mutuels is there's too many touts.

ALLEN.—By touts, you mean too many people giving a horse player unwanted advice?

CHAS.—Yeah. In the good old days every other guy at the track was a bookmaker.

ALLEN.—I see.

CHAS.—When you got a yen to play a horse, you could turn to the guy standin' next to you and make a bet.

ALLEN.—Oh. The pari-mutuels aren't as convenient.

CHAS.—You got a yen to play a horse. You gotta walk from where the yen hits you to a window.

ALLEN.—To bet your money?

CHAS.—Yeah. Between the yen and the window is where the tout comes in.

ALLEN.—And the tout talks you out of the bet you intended to make?

CHAS.—Every time. Lemme tell you what happened last Saturday.

ALLEN.—Using the pari-mutuels system?

CHAS.—Yeah. I go to the track. I got 10 bucks. In the first race I like Creole. I'm on my way to the 2-dollar window.

ALLEN.—Yes.

CHAS.—A tout sticks his thumb in my lapel. He says "I just seen Farley. He ain't talkin! It's a hunch. Play Silent Jim."

ALLEN.—You played Silent Jim instead of Creole?

CHAS.—Yeah.

ALLEN.—What happened?

CHAS.—He touts me offa Creole. Creole win. Paid seventeen-ten.

ALLEN.—What do you know!

CHAS.—The second race I'm on my way to play High Breeze. A tout gives me the leg. While he's helpin' me up, he says Gun Bearer. I go again.

ALLEN.—You bet Gun Bearer.

CHAS.—He touts me offa High Breeze. High Breeze win. Paid eleven-forty.

ALLEN.—And this went on all afternoon?

CHAS.—Every time I start for a window, I'm grabbed by a tout. He touts me off. Finally, I'm down to 60 cents. I gotta get home. I figure I'll buy my ticket back to New York.

ALLEN.—What happened?

CHAS.—I'm on my way to the railroad station.

ALLEN.—Yes.

CHAS.—A tout starts walkin' me over. I tell him I'm only buyin' a ticket to New York.

ALLEN.—Yes.

CHAS.—He touts me offa New York. I end up in New Rochelle.

ALLEN.—Before you go, Mr. Vanz, tell me, is there any sure way a person can beat the horses?

CHAS.—There's only one way you can beat the horses, and that's with a whip.

ALLEN.—Thank you, Tyler Vanz. Well, complaints may come and complaints may go. But the pari-mutuels are here to stay. The state can smile as it rakes in the tax money. The pari-mutuel officials can chuckle as they get theirs. The winners can be gay as they collect. But when you think of the thousands who lose their money at race tracks, the one who has the last laugh at the track is . . .

SOUND.—*Horse neighs and laughs.*

MUSIC.—*Up to finish.*

ALLEN.—And now, if you have a date with a beautiful girl and don't know where to go, the Merry Macs give you a little tip in song. The number—"Take Your Girlie to the Movies."

MUSIC.—(*Orchestra and* MERRY MACS). "*Take Your Girlie to the Movies.*" (*Applause*)

SOUND.—*Ad lib*, "*Thank you's.*"

ALLEN.—While our guest of the evening is being slowly unveiled, I'd like to ask all of you to remember one thing, ladies and gentlemen, remember *Ipana*, for the smile of beauty.

VON ZELL.—Oh, Fred, I hope you won't mind a suggestion, but I think that statement is unnecessarily *long*.

ALLEN.—Is it, Harry?

VON ZELL.—Well, look, Fred, Ipana is the largest selling tooth paste in America today. And when so many people are *using* it, that's certainly *proof* they're *remembering* it, isn't it?

ALLEN.—That's right, Harry. So I don't need the word "remember." This will do it. "Ladies and gentlemen, Ipana for the smile of beauty."

VON ZELL.—Well, when it comes right down to it, Fred, you don't even need "the smile of beauty."

ALLEN.—Don't I?

VON ZELL.—No. Fred. You see, a beautiful smile depends on clean, bright teeth and firm, healthy gums. And Ipana stands for both, because Ipana is especially designed not only to clean and brighten teeth but, when used with massage, to help give our gums the stimulation they need to help guard against gum trouble. So with healthier gums and brighter teeth, your smile's *bound* to be more beautiful, you see? So all you really have to say, Fred, is "Ipana."

ALLEN.—I see your point, Harry. Ladies and gentlemen—*Ipana.*

VON ZELL.—Oh, oh . . .

ALLEN.—What's the matter, Harry? *Still* too long?

VON ZELL.—No. Fred. This time I think it's just a little too *short.*

ALLEN.—Then, Harry, what *am* I going to say?

VON ZELL.—I've got it, Fred, and this should briefly cover everything. Just say, "Remember Ipana—for the smile of beauty!"

MUSIC.—"*San.*" *Applause.*

ALLEN.—Peter Van Steeden and his Scarsdale Serenaders have just played "San." And now, ladies and gentlemen, our guest tonight is a . . . Oh, hello, Portland. You're late.

PORTLAND.—Yes. There's such a crowd, I couldn't get through. The studio is packed.

ALLEN.—Yes. The man on the door told me this is the biggest crowd they've ever had in here.

PORTLAND.—But why should the studio suddenly be crowded tonight? There must be a reason.

ALLEN.—There is. Benny's picture opened at the Paramount today. And people have to go someplace.

PORTLAND.—Did you hear Jack's program Sunday night? Was he funny?

ALLEN.—Are you asking me? Or telling me?

PORTLAND.—Jack said . . .

ALLEN.—I heard him. He said I made people laugh with a pair of breakaway suspenders. According to Benny, my suspenders break away and gravity and my trousers commune.

PORTLAND.—Do your suspenders break away?

ALLEN.—Look, I've got on the same suspenders I wear every week. Look at this. (*Pulls suspenders*) Do these suspenders break away?

PORTLAND.—No.

ALLEN.—That debunks the Benny propaganda, I guess.

PORTLAND.—But Jack said you had applause written on your underwear, too.

ALLEN.—I'll debunk that underwear canard.

PORTLAND.—Mr. Allen, you're not going to take off . . .

ALLEN.—Don't worry, Portland. It's warm tonight. I took my underwear off before the show started. I've got it right here. (*Allen holds up union suit*) Do you folks see the word "applause" written on this union suit?

ALL.—No.

ALLEN.—There you are, Mr. Benny. Again we fling the lie in your teeth. A man who will stoop to underwear for libel fodder . . .

SOUND.—*Knock at door.*

ALLEN.—See who that is, will you, Harry?

VON ZELL.—Sure.

SOUND.—*Door opens.*

VON ZELL.—Oh, thanks. You'd better wait, son. There may be an answer.

SOUND.—*Door closes.*

ALLEN.—What is it?

VON ZELL.—It's a note, Fred. It's open.

ALLEN.—Read it, Harry.

HARRY.—It says "Dear Fred, How are you pal? The new cinema masterpiece 'Buck Benny Rides Again' is now playing at the Paramount Theater to tremendous business. Line forms at Ninth Avenue. Signed: Jack Benny. P.S. Mnaaaa!"

ALLEN.—Why, that Macy's basement cowboy. Who brought that commercial in here?

PORTLAND.—The boy's waiting for an answer, Mr. Allen.

ALLEN.—Bring him in here. I'll send Benny an answer. Why, that . . .

SOUND.—*Door opens.*

PORTLAND.—Come in, please.

EDDIE.—Thank you. Hello, Mr. Allen!

ALLEN.—Why, it's Rochester. *Applause*

EDDIE.—Thank you.

ALLEN.—So you brought that letter from Benny, Rochester?

EDDIE.—I cannot tell a lie. I did it with my little fetchit.

ALLEN.—Why didn't he mail it?

EDDIE.—It was 2 cents against the wear and tear on my feet. And here I am.

ALLEN.—How do you like that? Rochester, that boss of yours is the cheapest guy alive. I'm surprised he even brought you East with him on the train.

EDDIE.—What train?

ALLEN.—The train from Hollywood to New York.

EDDIE.—Is that train still runnin'?

ALLEN.—Of course it is.

EDDIE.—Well, I'll be doggoned! Mr. Benny told me they took that train off.

ALLEN.—Of all the . . .

EDDIE.—Mr. Benny said the engineer saved his money. He said the engineer stopped runnin' the train regular. He was free-lancin'.

ALLEN.—How did you get here?

EDDIE.—Mr. Benny took me down to the Lincoln Highway and handed me a compass.

ALLEN.—Yes.

EDDIE.—Then he said, "Rochester, you know what Horace Greeley said. Reverse it."

ALLEN.—And you had to thumb rides from Hollywood to New York.

EDDIE.—Only in the daytime. At night my thumb was a liability.

ALLEN.—Why, that's the cheapest trick I ever heard of. Confidentially, Rochester, have you ever seen anyone cheaper than Benny?

EDDIE.—Well, so long, Mr. Allen.

ALLEN.—No, you don't. While you're here I want to get the low-down on Benny.

EDDIE.—Uh-uh. I've got an option coming up.

ALLEN.—Look, we don't want any true confession, Rochester, just a short educational chat. You know, how you run the household, what your daily routine is.

EDDIE.—What you really want is "My Day."

ALLEN.—That's it.

EDDIE.—Well, all right. But don't let me say nothin' derogatory about Mr. Benny.

ALLEN.—You mean you are inclined to make an occasional slip.

EDDIE.—Sometimes my subconscious borrows my mouth.

ALLEN.—I'll watch it for you. Now, let's take an average day in the Benny household. What happens?

EDDIE.—Well, the first problem of the day is gettin' me up.

ALLEN.—Who does that?

EDDIE.—I've never been able to catch the party.

ALLEN.—Well, after you are thoroughly aroused, what is your initial chore?

EDDIE.—First, I wake up Mr. Benny. That takes a bit of doin'.

ALLEN.—You mean he's a heavy sleeper?

EDDIE.—He sure hates to break it up with Morpheus.

ALLEN.—I can imagine.

EDDIE.—When other people's eyes are open, they're awake. That don't mean a thing to Mr. Benny.

ALLEN.—He can still sleep with his eyes open?

EDDIE.—He sure can. He's got short eyelids or somethin'.

ALLEN.—After Benny is awake, what goes on?

EDDIE.—I run his tub and strap on his water wings.

ALLEN.—And after the master is bathed?

EDDIE.—I assemble him.

ALLEN.—You assemble him? Don't tell me you have to put Benny together every morning?

EDDIE.—Mr. Benny's teeth and hair don't spring into place when he whistles.

SOUND.—*Telephone rings.*

ALLEN.—Will you answer that phone, Harry?

VON ZELL.—Okay, Fred.

ALLEN.—Excuse me, Rochester.

SOUND.—*Receiver off.*

VON ZELL.—Hello. Just a minute, Mr. Benny. It's for you, Rochester.

EDDIE.—Uh-uh. CCC, here I come. (*Telephone*) Hello, boss. Now, take it easy, boss. No, sir. I won't spill another bean, Mr. Benny. Okay. Say, boss, you're all wrong about Mr. Allen. I been here 5 minutes, and I've still got my wallet. Yes, sir. I'll back out when I leave.

SOUND.—*Hangs up.*

EDDIE.—Well, the interview is over. (*Sings*) Good evening, friends.

ALLEN.—Wait a minute. That was Mr. Livingston, I presume.

EDDIE.—Yes. And the boss was pretty mad, too. He says he don't like me tellin' his private business to strangers.

ALLEN.—He didn't threaten you, did he?

EDDIE.—Mr. Benny's exact words were: quote, "Watch what you say, or else." Unquote.

ALLEN.—Or else what?

EDDIE.—Emancipation is havin' a revival.

ALLEN.—Don't worry about Benny. I'll handle him. Let's get on with this exposé. After you get Benny assembled, what happens?

EDDIE.—Mr. Benny tosses me for my breakfast.

ALLEN.—You lose, of course.

EDDIE.—With unceasin' regularity.

ALLEN.—Well, after you drive Benny over to Paramount and get back to the house, what's your next move?

EDDIE.—In the general direction of the icebox.

ALLEN.—You eat again?

EDDIE.—Again is superfluous.

ALLEN.—That's right, I forgot. This time you eat your fill. And when you finish . . .

EDDIE.—I put an I.O.U. in the icebox. Then I wash the dishes in the swimmin' pool, sweep out the house and the hurricane cellar.

ALLEN.—The hurricane cellar. You don't have hurricanes in Beverly Hills.

EDDIE.—No, sir. But we have bill collectors.

ALLEN.—I get it. When creditors come around, Benny hides in his hurricane cellar. Is that right? Is that right, Rochester?

EDDIE.—That ain't the phone ringin', is it?

ALLEN.—Forget about that guy. Benny can hide from his creditors, but he can't hide from those bills that come in by mail. What becomes of those?

EDDIE.—That ostrich has gotta eat somethin'.

ALLEN.—You mean Trudy depends on bills for her sustenance.

EDDIE.—That bird has eaten so many "Please remits" she's layin' eggs in her sister's name.

ALLEN.—Rochester old boy, say no more. Your word cameo of Benny is complete. Why, the man is a monument to avarice.

SOUND.—*Telephone rings.*

EDDIE.—Uh-uh! If that's for me, try the Savoy Ballroom.

ALLEN.—What can Benny do now? Go ahead, answer the phone.

EDDIE.—Okay. (*Receiver off*) Hello. Yes, boss. Now, take it easy, boss. Yes. I *know* what happened to Benedict Arnold. Don't fire me, boss. Yes. Yes. Okay, boss.

ALLEN.—What did he say?

EDDIE.—One more peep out of me, and I'm a migratory worker.

ALLEN.—Listen, Rochester, don't let that guy bully you. Why don't you quit that male Hetty Green and get a real job?

EDDIE.—Is that an offer?

ALLEN.—Yes. I can use a good man around the house.

EDDIE.—It won't take me 2 minutes to write my reference.

ALLEN.—How would you like to work for me?

EDDIE.—Define that word "work," Mr. Allen. Much depends on that.

ALLEN.—Well, there's nothing to do. You won't have much work around the house.

EDDIE.—That's what Mr. Benny said.

ALLEN.—You'll have Thursdays off, Sundays off, holidays off.

EDDIE.—Mr. Benny said that, too.

ALLEN.—Now, we come to your salary.

EDDIE.—That's where Mr. Benny stopped talkin'.

ALLEN.—Say, that reminds me. What *does* he pay you, Rochester?

EDDIE.—Well . . .

SOUND.—*Telephone rings.*

EDDIE.—Uh--uh. (*Telephone off*) Hello, boss. No, I ain't tellin', boss. I'm just as much ashamed of it as you are. All right. I won't take Mr. Allen's offer. Why do I listen to him? Well, I can dream, can't I? Okay, boss.

SOUND.—*Hangs up.*

ALLEN.—Well? Rochester, how about my offer?

EDDIE.—It's too late, Mr. Allen. Mr. Benny's taken up my option. I guess I'll stick to him.

ALLEN.—Well, I guess everything happens for the best. Without you Benny wouldn't be Benny. That would be an improvement. But I know you'd rather stay with him.

EDDIE.—Yes, sir. Mr. Benny may be frugal. But on him it looks good.

ALLEN.—All right, Rochester. I'm glad your boss let you come over tonight. I appreciate this visit. You're doing a swell job on Jack's program and in pictures. And we all wish you every success for the future.

EDDIE.—Thank you, Mr. Allen. Good night.

ALLEN.—Good night. And thank you, Rochester!
(*Billboard . . . Applause*)

MUSIC.—"*China Boy.*"
(*Applause*)

ALLEN.—That was "China Boy," the unbreakable version, played by Confucius Van Steeden and his Hong Kong Hotshots. Tonight, our guest is a most unusual . . . Oh, hello, Portland.

PORTLAND.—Hello. Am I late?

ALLEN.—I wouldn't know. Since daylight saving time came in I'm all mixed up.

PORTLAND.—Mama is, too. Every place Mama goes she's either an hour late or an hour early.

ALLEN.—Didn't she set her clock up an hour Saturday night.

PORTLAND.—Mama tried to, but it's an electric clock. Sparks kept coming out.

ALLEN.—What did she do?

PORTLAND.—Mama called up the powerhouse and asked them to shut down a minute till she moved up the clock.

ALLEN.—Did they?

PORTLAND.—No. The man said if he shut down the powerhouse, the lights would go out and Mama couldn't see to set the clock anyway.

ALLEN.—What is the solution?

PORTLAND.—Mama's home holding the hands on the clock for 11 hours till it's right again.

ALLEN.—When she gets through, I hope the clock will reciprocate.

PORTLAND.—Reciprocate?

ALLEN.—Yes. I hope the clock will hold your mother's hands until she's right again. But, tell me . . .

SOUND.—*Knock at door . . . door opens.*

ALLEN.—Hey! Just a minute, mister. I didn't say "Come in." did I?

CHARLES.—That's me all over. I couldn't wait. I'm the impulsive type.

PORTLAND.—Did you want something?

CHARLES.—Yes. Which one is Fred Allen?

ALLEN.—Look. I'm Allen. What is this?

CHARLES.—Mr. Allen! You're my favorite comedian. I hope I'm not intruding. I just had to tell you.

ALLEN.—Now, look!

CHARLES.—My wife and I never miss one of your programs.

ALLEN.—Wait a . . .

CHARLES.—I just go around our neighborhood screaming. I go from door to door yelling "That Fred Allen is the one." I'd yell it from the housetops, but I get dizzy up that high.

ALLEN.—Look . . .

CHARLES.—The neighbors twit me. They say "You and your long-pussed Fred Allen."

ALLEN.—Hold it, brother. What is your name again?

CHARLES.—Jerkfinkel. Logan Jerkfinkel.

PORTLAND.—Weren't you on Jack Benny's program last Sunday?

ALLEN.—Yes. And the Sunday before. You gave Benny and Don Wilson this same routine.

CHARLES.—Well, what if I did?

ALLEN.—First Benny was your favorite, then Don Wilson. Tonight, I am. Why don't you make up your mind?

CHARLES.—I'm fickle. Good-by.

SOUND.—*Door slams.*

ALLEN.—That guy don't know who he likes.

SOUND.—*Door opens.*

CHARLES.—My real favorite is Bob Hope. Minaah!

SOUND.—*Door slams.*

ALLEN.—I ought to give Benny this program and get another one.

PORTLAND.—Your two programs are getting mixed up all right. Rochester was with you last Wednesday.

ALLEN.—Van Steeden was on Benny's show Sunday night. He and Phil Harris made that program sound as though it was Benny on We, the People.

PORTLAND.—I thought Peter and Phil were very good.

ALLEN.—They sounded like an East Side Lum and Abner. Well, enough about the Waukegan Woollcott. What about our guest tonight?

PORTLAND.—His occupation is a most unusual one.

ALLEN.—Really?

PORTLAND.—Yes. This gentleman is one of the country's leading worm hunters.

ALLEN.—A worm hunter? Is that a business, bagging worms?

PORTLAND.—You'll have to ask our guest. Mr. Allen, meet Mr. Robert Bradley.

ALLEN.—Good evening, Mr. Bradley.

BRADLEY.—Good evening, Fred.

ALLEN.—Portland advises me, Mr. Bradley, that you are a worm Nimrod. That you have made a profession of snaring the elusive and legless invertebrate.

BRADLEY.—That is correct, Fred. Worms are my stock in trade.

ALLEN.—I don't know much about worms, Mr. Bradley. To me a worm is just a nudist caterpillar. Do you collect worms as a hobby surely?

BRADLEY.—No. Fred. I supply worms to private aquariums, hatcheries, and pet shops.

ALLEN.—Oh, as food for fish.

BRADLEY.—That's right.

ALLEN.—You are sort of a guppy chef. An Oscar of the fish bowl. How did you ever get started in this unique profession, Mr. Bradley?

BRADLEY.—Well, as a boy I liked to collect fish.

ALLEN.—But how did you digress from collecting fish to hunting worms?

BRADLEY.—Well, the fish I collected got hungry, and I had to provide their food.

ALLEN.—How can you tell when a fish is hungry, Mr. Bradley? When a fish is swimming around in a bowl, you can't tell if its mouth is watering, or can you?

BRADLEY.—Yes. It's very easy to tell. The fish looks anemic and lifeless.

ALLEN.—It's just fin and bones. Well, I guess when you've taken a fish away from its mother, you've got to supply the fodder. How did you cope with your problem?

BRADLEY.—Well, I experimented with various worms and water insects to find the best foods.

ALLEN.—And when you found them, you decided to go into business?

BRADLEY.—That's right. On the side I started raising and breeding tropical fish.

ALLEN.—What are a fish's favorite foods, Mr. Bradley? If Broadway was under water tonight and a goldfish came down off the Wrigley sign and swam into McGinnis's Cafe, what would tempt him on the bill of fare?

BRADLEY.—The goldfish would probably order *Chironomus larvae* or *Tubifex rivulorum.*

ALLEN.—*Chironomus larvae?*

BRADLEY.—Or *Tubifex rivulorum.*

ALLEN.—Those sound like the names you'd expect to find on a Greek Pullman car. What is this *Chironomus larvae?*

BRADLEY.—The *Chironomus larvae* is just a bloodworm.

ALLEN.—I see. What about the Chironomus's straight man, that *Kleenex rivoli* or whatever it is?

BRADLEY.—The Tubifex is about the same size as the Chironomus but thinner.

ALLEN.—Without the paunch and jowls, eh? Tell me, Mr. Bradley, how do you catch these worms? Do you lie down in Central Park and make a noise like a rotten apple? Do you have a decoy worm or a robin on your wrist as a falcon?

BRADLEY.—I'd be wasting my time in Central Park, Fred. Both of these worms are only found in muddy streams and ponds.

ALLEN.—Where do you have to go to stalk the digest reptile?

BRADLEY.—I cover swamps and marshes in upper New York state, Long Island, and New Jersey, Fred. Occasionally, I've had to go almost to Philadelphia.

ALLEN.—Why do you have to go so far? Are the worms around here getting wise to you?

BRADLEY.—No. The government projects have drained off most of the near-by swamps, and the worms go elsewhere.

ALLEN.—I guess to you WPA means "Pushing Worms Around."

BRADLEY.—I'm not complaining, Fred. But in my business mud is essential.

ALLEN.—I know. It's the same in politics. Well, after you've found a place where you think worms are putting on the bog, how can you tell if they're really there?

BRADLEY.—It's partly a matter of instinct, Fred.

ALLEN.—Say, if you can just look at mud and tell it has worms in it, you must be the Wizard of Ooze. How do you do it?

BRADLEY.—Sometimes I tell by color. Mud that contains worms has a slight greenish tinge.

ALLEN.—When you've located a worm preserve, how do you get the little quagmire cobra to come up? Do you go "psst" in the wormhole? And then when the worm looks out to see who it is, do you tie a knot in him so he can't get back down the hole again?

BRADLEY.—It's not that complicated, Fred. I just scoop up the mud and wash the worms out later.

ALLEN.—You wash the worms out? How?

BRADLEY.—I spread the mud out in trays and put a covering of sand over it.

ALLEN.—Why the sand?

BRADLEY.—As water is run gently through the mud, the worms crawl up through the sand. The sand cleans them off as they come up.

ALLEN.—Say, you have all the elements of a night club there, Mr. Bradley. A little dirt, a little liquid, a cover, and the customer comes out clean. After you get your stock ready for market, how do you dispose of them?

BRADLEY.—I don't have any trouble selling my worms, Fred. Thousands of people today are keeping fish as a hobby.

ALLEN.—Well, thanks a lot for all of the data you have given us about worms, Mr. Bradley. The future looks bright for you indeed. If you ever tire of your profession, you can always go to work for the Internal Revenue Department.

BRADLEY.—How do you mean, Fred?

ALLEN.—If the Income Tax Department wants any confidential information about people's tax figures, you can worm it out of them.

BRADLEY.—Good night, Fred.

ALLEN.—Good night. And thank you, Mr. Robert Bradley. (*Billboard . . . Applause*)

ALLEN.—And now, Miss Wynn Murray to sing for us "My Man."

MUSIC.—"*My Man.*" (*Orchestra and Wynn Murray*)

ALLEN.—(*Ad lib "thank you's"*) Tonight, ladies and gentlemen, following the popular trend in spring entertainment we have a slight questionnaire for you—in two parts. If you can answer "no," honestly and sincerely, to the questions in the *first* part, you will be excused from participation in the second part. Question number one!

MARK.—Do you ever wake up in the morning feeling grouchy and sluggish?

ALLEN.—Question number two!

MARK.—Does your morning's work seem such an awful task that you "fold up" in the afternoon?

ALLEN.—Number three!

MARK.—Do you feel "dragged out" by evening, too tired to romp with the children?

ALLEN.—Those of you who answered "no" to those questions may relax, the rest of you are invited to listen carefully to this next part.

VON ZELL.—If you're feeling under par, ladies and gentlemen, and need a laxative, a sparkling glass of Sal Hepatica quickly helps you feel your best again. It helps *faster* in *two* ways. First, as a laxative, Sal Hepatica is quick acting, yet it's exceptionally *gentle*. Second, and just as important, Sal Hepatica also helps counteract excess gastric acidity, which chases that sickish feeling fast. So get a bottle of Sal Hepatica at any drugstore, and see how quickly you feel more alert, more like your normal, buoyant self again when you take Sal Hepatica for a faster comeback.

MUSIC.—"*What's the Matter with Me.*"

VON ZELL.—(*Fade*) The Fred Allen hour continues after a brief pause for your station identification.

(*Station break . . . applause*)

ALLEN.—Peter Van Steeden and his Rhumba Rascals have just played "What's the Matter with Me." And now the Mighty Allen Art Players. Tonight they present a burlesque of one of radio's most popular programs. It's called Information Tease, or "The Guest Is Always Right Except on a Quiz Program." Music, Arturo!

MUSIC.—"*Kiss Me Again*" . . . *Wayne King tempo . . . fades.*

VON ZELL.—And so, to the soggy, saccharine strains of "Kiss Me Again," we bid adieu to Wayne Lefkowitz and his Overripe Melodies. Until this same time next week, Wayne Lefkowitz hopes you'll remember his slogan and keep "Waiting for Lefky." Good night.

SOUND.—*Burlesque chimes.*

JOHN.—This is station FOO, operating with a frequency that gets on your nerves. We now give you the correct time, through the courtesy of Bango, the exploding cigarette. Bangos are especially designed to discourage chiselers who borrow your cigarettes. When you hear the chiseler inhale his Bango, it will be exactly 9:48.

CHAS.—This is a Bang-up smoke, old man. (*Long inhale*)

SOUND.—*Firecracker explodes . . . loud pop.*

CHAS.—Ow! Where's my nose!

JOHN.—9:48, Bango Cigarette time! And now, station FOO presents!

MUSIC.—*Fanfare.*

VON ZELL.—Information Tease!

CHARLES.—*Rooster crow.*

VON ZELL.—Stop snoring, America! Time to stump the experts! As you know, ladies and gentlemen, Information Tease is entirely unrehearsed. You, the public, match wits with our board of experts. For every question used the sender gets $5.

If your question stumps the experts you receive $10, plus a complete unabridged set of the Farmer's Almanac. Yes, folks, $10 and a handsome set of Farmer's Almanacs, bound in burlap, will be sent to you by our sponsors, the makers of . . . (*Fanfare*) Mother Murphy's Meatballs!

JOHN.—(*Dignified*) Yes, folks! Mother Murphy's Meatballs! The only meatballs that contain helium. Your delicatessen man knows helium as yokeltate fornostrophide. Is a Mother Murphy Meatball just another meatball, a hamburger in pill form? No! Mother Murphy's Meatballs contain . . .

CHARLES.—Vitamin A, for strength.

VON ZELL.—Vitamin B, for blood.

ALLEN.—(*Low*) Vitamin B flat, for a laugh.

JOHN.—And Mother Murphy's Meatballs also contain a small quantity of liquid rubber. If you drop a Mother Murphy Meatball on the floor, don't be embarrassed. It will bounce back on your plate again. Have fun with your meatballs, folks. Play potsy with them. Dribble them up and down the table. Tie a meatball on your spaghetti and make a yo-yo. But buy them. Buy—spelled B-U-Y.

CHARLES.—And now Information Tease presents our master of ceremonies, the noted literary critic, Mr. Tifton Battiman. (*applause*)

ALLEN.—Good evening, ladies and gentlemen. On our board of experts tonight we have our three regulars. First, the celebrated newspaper columnist Franklin O. Baddams, better known to you as F.O.B.

VON ZELL.—(*Sour voice*) Hello, hoi polloi.

ALLEN.—Next, the famous sports writer and animated encyclopedia John Tieran.

CHARLES.—(*High*) Hello. A greeting in common usage. Hello is actually a corruption of the Latin gladiators salute *morituri te salutamus.*

ALLEN.—Don't show off, Mr. Tieran.

CHARLES.—I'm warming up.

ALLEN.—Oh, excuse me, Mr. Tieran, and shut up. Our next expert, the noted music authority and wit Mr. Oscar Bevant.

JOHN.—Hi, folks. As Beethoven said to Mozart, notes to you. Ha, ha, ha!

ALLEN.—Mr. Bevant is in a gay mood tonight. That is just a sample of the spontaneous, unrehearsed fun on our program, folks. And now, as our guest expert, may I present the famous Republican congressman, the author of the recent political exposé called "What Am I Getting out of Washington, Is It the Train." Meet the Republican representative Barnaby Fluke. (*Pause*) Don't you want to say something to the folks, congressman?

CHARLES.—(*Low dope*) Duh-duh. Hello. Duh. I think I got stage fright.

ALLEN.—Don't be silly, congressman. You were all right before the program.

CHARLES.—Yeah. But gettin' in wid all you highbrows. It's makin' me nervous.

ALLEN.—Buck up. All of our guests get an inferiority complex.

CHARLES.—Why can't I just go to the Union League Club and lay down?

ALLEN.—Never lie down at the Union League Club, congressman. They might bury you by mistake. Ha, ha, ha!

CHARLES.—Ha, ha, ha!

ALLEN.—Well, enough spontaneous, unrehearsed fun for now. It's time for our questions. And our first question tonight comes from Mrs. Ima Wack of Rat Falls, Arkansas. Mrs. Wack says there are three colors in the American flag. She wants you to name two of the colors. Mr. Tieran's hand is up. No, it's down again. All right, Mr. Baddams.

VON ZELL.—Blue?

ALLEN.—That is right. Blue is one of the colors in the American flag. Mr. Bevant!

JOHN.—White?

ALLEN.—White is right.

CHARLES.—(*High*) Red.

ALLEN.—Red is correct, Mr. Tieran. The three colors in the American flag are blue, white, and red. You were only asked to get two. You got three. Remarkable, gentlemen. Our next question comes from Harley Drab of Cheesecake, Ohio. Mr. Drab wants you to complete the following question. "I like coffee, I like tea, I like the girls. And the girls like . . ." Well?

JOHN.—Say, that's a tough one.

ALLEN.—Come! Get your thinking caps on, gentlemen. Ah. Mr. Baddums! Have you got your hand up?

VON ZELL.—No. I'm just wetting my cowlick.

ALLEN.—Oh, sorry, Mr. Baddums. Can anyone complete the rhyme?

JOHN.—Will you read the quotation again?

ALLEN.—Gladly, Mr. Bevant. "I like coffee, I like tea. I like the girls. And the girls like . . ." Can you finish it, congressman?

CHARLES.—Duh. I got stage fright. I'm stricken dumb.

ALLEN.—Buck up, congressman. For the last, gentlemen. "I like the girls. And the girls like . . ."

VON ZELL.—Gable?

ALLEN.—No! No! Mr. Bevant, who is the greatest musical genius in America today?

JOHN.—Me.

ALLEN.—That is correct. The girls like me. Absolutely correct!!

SOUND.—*Applause . . . cheers and whistling.*

ALLEN.—Gad! I don't know how they do it. Now this next question. Mr. Roquefort Fumes of Bedspread, Iowa, sends in a puzzler. It's a question on fish.

JOHN.—Is Mr. Fumes a good skate? No. That's the wrong answer. I'm sorry.

ALLEN.—We're all sorry, Mr. Bevant. Mr. Baddums is our expert on fish. Perhaps you'd like to try it, Mr. Baddums?

VON ZELL.—Fry it. Ha! Ha!

ALLEN.—Ha! Ha! No try it, Mr. Baddums. To fry it you'd have to crumb it up.

VON ZELL.—That's what I'm doing.

ALLEN.—I'm sure we all concur, Mr. Baddums. But seriously, let us take up our fish question.

JOHN.—Okay, what is it?

ALLEN.—You are asked to identify the following fish by the sounds they make under water. Mr. Fumes wants us to get three out of three. Here's the first sound.

SOUND.—*Bubbling sound . . . straw blown in glass of water.*

ALLEN.—Mr. Baddams.

VON ZELL.—That's the *Piscatorus blueplatibus*, or male halibut, calling its mate.

ALLEN.—Correct. And now, the second sound.

SOUND.—*Bubbling sound repeats.*

VON ZELL.—That's the mate answering.

ALLEN.—And what is she saying. Mr. Baddums?

VON ZELL.—Cut out the bubble talk, big boy.

CHARLES.—Duh. I got stage fright.

ALLEN.—Nobody asked you, congressman. Now, Mr. Baddums, the third and last sound in your fish trilogy.

SOUND.—*Sucking sound . . . straw siphoning bottom soda glass.*

ALLEN.—All right, Mr. Baddums.

VON ZELL.—I never heard a fish make that sound. Is it a swordfish honing?

ALLEN.—No.

VON ZELL.—A shad rowing?

VON ZELL.—No. Give up, Mr. Baddums?

VON ZELL.—Yes. What is it?

ALLEN.—It's a fellow in Liggett's drugstore finishing a chocolate soda.

VON ZELL.—Wait a minute. You said a fish.

ALLEN.—The man's name is Trout.

VON ZELL.—I been robbed.

ALLEN.—Roqueford Fumes happens to be my brother-in-law, if that clarifies matters, Mr. Baddums.

VON ZELL.—It certainly does.

ALLEN.—Very well. Mr. Baddums missed out on that one. And so $10 and a complete set of Farmer's Almanacs go to Mr. Roquefort Fumes of Bedspread, Iowa.

SOUND.—*Cash register rings.*

ALLEN.—And now . . . (*Aside*) Ah-ah. Take your hand out of that cash register, congressman.

CHARLES.—Oh. Sorrow. I thought I was still in Washington.

ALLEN.—Ha! Ha! Well the congressman's spontaneous unrehearsed fun seems to have brought us to the halfway mark. And our experts have cost Mother Murphy's Meatballs the trifling sum of $10. And now a word from our announcer, Milton Dross.

VON ZELL.—(*Classy*) Have you tried a Mother Murphy's Meatball lately? Remember, with men about the abattoir; with butchers, gluttons, bicarbonate salesmen; with men who know meatballs best, it's Murphy's two to seven. Later returns will be read as they come in.

ALLEN.—Thank you. Mr. Dross. Your little talk took exactly 25 seconds.

VON ZELL.—(*Aside*) Quiet. I'm not finished yet. (*Aloud*) Go to your neighborhood grocer and order Mother Murphy's Meatballs today!

ALLEN.—Mr. Dross has consumed 35 seconds.

VON ZELL.—Look for the big dead letters on the box!

ALLEN.—Forty-five seconds.

VON ZELL.—And remember. Mother Murphy's Meatballs come in three delicious flavors. With a few onions! With plenty of onions! And, phew, pass the Lifesavers.

ALLEN.—Sixty seconds, and go away, Mr. Milton Dross. And now, back to Information Tease. Denby String of Nil, Nebraska, wants you to complete the following musical phrase at the piano. Listen, gentlemen.

MUSIC.—(*Piano*) *Plays hunting call, omitting last note.*

ALLEN.—Can you finish this hunting call, Congressman Fluke?

CHARLES.—Duh—duh.

ALLEN.—You are, without a doubt, the worst guest expert we've ever had on Information Tease.

CHARLES.—Duh. I got stage fright. I'm stricken dumb.

ALLEN.—You'd better say something pretty soon or Mother Murphy will be out here ready to explode. Who can complete this hunting call? Mr. Tiernan?

VON ZELL.—Mr. Tiernan is asleep.

ALLEN.—Did he leave a call?

VON ZELL.—No.

ALLEN.—Let us have the musical question again. Not too loud, we'll wake Mr. Tiernan.

MUSIC.—(*Piano*) *Repeats hunting call, omitting last note.*

JOHN.—I can complete that phrase. Wait till I get to the piano.

ALLEN.—Mr. Bevant is going to the piano. Let us bow our heads in reverence, folks. Ready. Mr. Bevant?

JOHN.—Ready? Here it is.

MUSIC.—(*Piano*) *Plays call, slows down at last note, pauses, then hits flat note.*

ALLEN.—Uh-uh! Not quite, Mr. Bevant.

JOHN.—Oh! That's right. Here it is.

MUSIC.—(*Piano*) *Repeats, pauses, then hits sharp note.*

ALLEN.—You're getting warm, Mr. Bevant.

JOHN.—I've got it!

MUSIC.—(*Piano*) *Repeats, plays correct note, finishes with flourish of arpeggios and thunderous chords.*

ALLEN.—That is correct!

SOUND.—*Applause and cheers.*

ALLEN.—Congratulations, Mr. Bevant. We salute your unerring musical genius. The next question, congressman, is right up your alley, along with our constituents. Farnum Bag of East Haddock, Vermont, asks you to name the last three vice-presidents of the United States.

CHARLES.—Huh? Lemme see. (*Mumbles gibberish as though he may start talking*)

ALLEN.—Quiet, experts. I think the congressman is finally coming through.

CHARLES.—Wait a minute. (*Mumbles rapidly*)

ALLEN.—Don't weaken, congressman. We're with you.

CHARLES.—(*Slows down*) Ubble fibble dubble. (*Low*) I got stage fright. I'm stricken dumb.

ALLEN.—This is embarrassing, congressman. Can any of our experts?

SOUND.—*Door closes off-mike.*

VON ZELL.—Psst, Tifton! Mother Murphy's coming.

ALLEN.—Good heavens!

MIN.—(*Fading in*) I've stood enough of this, Mr. Battiman. It's going to stop right now.

ALLEN.—Dear Mother Murphy, this is a surprise.

MIN.—"Dear Mother," my bustle. This is getting monotonous.

ALLEN.—What, Mother?

MIN.—Every week, your guests on Information Tease get stage fright. They don't say a word.

ALLEN.—But—but . . .

MIN.—I'm through paying money to guest stars who don't even open their mouths.

ALLEN.—Can I help it . . .

MIN.—Stop interrupting, young man. If you don't get this guest ninny here to talk, you're all fired.

ALLEN.—Not that, Mother Murphy.

MIN.—Yes, that, Mr. Battiman.

ALLEN.—Congressman!

CHARLES.—Yeah?

ALLEN.—You've got to come through. You've got to talk.

CHARLES.—I'm doin' my best. But I got stage fright. I'm stricken dumb.

ALLEN.—Gad! What a dilemma.

VON ZELL.—Why don't you give him some easy question, Tifton?

ALLEN.—Yes. That might start him talking. I'll do it F.O.B. Congressman, who wrote Shakespeare's sonnets?

CHARLES.—Shakespeare's sonnets. Lemme see. Shakespeare's sonnets.

ALLEN.—I'll give you a hint. Was it Shake—Shake . . .

CHARLES.—Shake, brother. Remember me in the next election.

MIN.—He's hopeless! The program's almost over, Mr. Battiman. You've got 42 seconds to make him talk, or you're all fired.

ALLEN.—There must be some question here a congressman can answer.

JOHN.—He's a Republican, Tifton. Ask him something about politics.

ALLEN.—I've got it. Here's a card that ought to do the trick. Here, congressman, take this card.

CHARLES.—Okay.

ALLEN.—Can you answer that question?

CHARLES.—Duh. I got . . . (*Voice changes to boisterous politician*) Why, ladies and gentlemen, I will be delighted to answer this question.

VON ZELL.—Hurray! He's off!

CHARLES.—It is a privilege and an honor to deal with this subject. I can state without fear of contraction. I can . . .

ALLEN.—All right, congressman. Time's up. You can finish your answer next week. There you are, Mother Murphy. You wanted our guest to talk.

MIN.—You've saved Information Tease, Mr. Battiman. How did you ever do it?

ALLEN.—It only required the right question to get the congressman started, Mother.

MIN.—But what was the question?

ALLEN.—Here it is. Read it.

MIN.—"Who was the hero of the Battle of Manila"?

ALLEN.—Yes. If you want to get a Republican started today, all you have to do is mention Dewey! Go back to sleep, America.

MUSIC.—(*Orchestra*) *Bumper number.*

ALLEN.—May we remind you that next Wednesday night we bring you an outstanding personality?

JOHN.—Folks, meet a big shot.

SOUND.—*Shot.*

MUSIC.—(*Piano*) *Chord.*

ALLEN.—Your song of the week!

CHARLES.—"Oh, You Beautiful Dill, You Great Big Beautiful Dill."

ALLEN.—Psst, that's "Oh, You Beautiful Doll," not "dill."

CHARLES.—I'm in the pickle business, gerk!

MUSIC.—(*Piano*) *Chord.*

ALLEN.—And our next guest will be . . .

VON ZELL.—Don Magarrell. Maitre d'Airline for United Air Lines. Tune in Wednesday and hear the man who serves the highest meals in the world. Yet breakfast, lunch, dinner are free as the air!

VON ZELL.—Tomorrow night at 8 o'clock EST over most of these stations tune in to "Mr. District Attorney," the famous radio show that exposes rackets and confidence games that steal millions every year from the American public. Remember, 8 o'clock tomorrow, Thursday night.

ALLEN.—Good night!

MUSIC.—*Theme.*

Burns and Allen

GEORGE BURNS was born in New York; Miss Allen, his wife, was born in San Francisco. Both went on the stage while children.

Miss Allen's father was a song-and-dance man, and she made her first public appearance at the age of three and a half, when she danced at entertainments in San Francisco.

As a thirteen-year-old she spent the summer vacation doing a single act in vaudeville around San Francisco. With her three older sisters she next formed the vaudeville team of the Allen Sisters. Eventually this led them to Larry Reilly's company, where Miss Allen became a featured player of Irish colleen parts.

One by one, her older sisters left the Reilly show to return to San Francisco to take over the management of a dancing school. It became a tradition among them that, as the older one would give up the management of the school, the next in line would take over the job. Miss Allen did not cherish this task, so she refused the honor when her turn came. She remained with the Reilly show.

Today, all her sisters are married and live in San Francisco, where the two oldest have dancing schools. After several seasons with the Reilly company, during which time she became the headline attraction, Miss Allen left the show because she was refused billing. But jobs were hard to obtain, so she decided to give up the stage and entered a secretarial school to train for the post of a stenographer.

With a friend, she went to Union Hill, N. J., where her friend was trying out an act. Backstage she met George Burns, then doing a song-and-dance act with Billy Lorraine. Burns had started on the stage when he was twelve as the oldest of four boy singers who called themselves the "PeeWee Quartet." During the years that followed he was in hundreds of vaudeville acts with many partners.

"It got so folks would meet me on the street and ask, 'Who you with this week?'" Burns explains today.

After meeting Miss Allen, Burns dissolved his partnership with Lorraine and teamed with Miss Allen.

Miss Allen had been with the Reilly show so long that during the first season of their act she couldn't drop her Irish brogue, so she continued to use it. Later, she adopted her present successful characterization of the "dizzy" girl.

After four years as a team, Burns and Allen were offered a six-year contract with RKO theaters. They signed it and got married. They continued to play throughout the country, with annual trips to Europe. During those six years they received a number of Broadway offers but could not get a release from their agreement. On one of their European engagements they made their radio debut, appearing for fifteen weeks for the British Broadcasting Company.

During the last part of 1930 Burns and Allen made their film debut in short subjects for Paramount. When their RKO contract was completed January 8, Burns and Allen signed their film-stage agreement with Paramount on January 9, 1931.

While at the Palace, Eddie Cantor, who was on the same bill, asked Miss Allen to do five minutes with him on his Chase and Sanborn radio hour. She did and was so well liked that the Columbia Broadcasting System signed Burns and Allen as radio stars.

Burns and Allen

BRADLEY.—(*Cold*) Hellotion, my friends. The Hinds Honey and Almond Cream program.

MUSIC.—(*Orchestra and cast*). "*Vote for Gracie.*" (*fades*)

BRADLEY.—Starring George Burns and Hinds Honey, Gracie Allen, with Frank Parker, Ray Noble and his orchestra, and Truman Bradley speaking.

MUSIC.—(*Gracie and cast*). "*Vote for Gracie.*" (*Applause*)

GEORGE.—Thank you very much.

GRACIE.—Hello!

GEORGE.—Well, Gracie, we're back in Hollywood after your convention in Omaha, and what a time we had.

GRACIE.—Yes, wasn't it a wonderful reception?

BRADLEY.—Do you realize, Gracie, there were about a hundred thousand people on the streets and in the station to greet you?

GEORGE.—What about the one man who said "hello" to me?

GRACIE.—Yeah, weren't you thrilled?

FRANK.—And I loved those torchlight parades and thousands of girls throwing kisses at me.

BRADLEY.—And what a kick I got, Gracie, when I saw you riding down the main street with police escort, and Mayor Butler of Omaha sitting on your right hand and Governor Cochran sitting on your left hand.

GRACIE.—You see it was cold, and I forgot to bring my gloves.

GEORGE.—Well, that covers that. Did you ever see so many people, Bubbles?

BUBBLES.—No. It's the first time I ever saw a crowd bigger than I am.

GEORGE.—Gracie, that was a beautiful dress you wore, leading the grand march.

GRACIE.—I had that made especially for my campaign.

GEORGE.—That was a pretty low-cut back.

GRACIE.—I'm not like the other candidates; I believe in coming right out in the open.

GEORGE.—Well, at least you're showing plenty of backbone.

BRADLEY.—I never saw so many people in one place in my life. The congestion was awful, and, boy, what a time I had parking!

GRACIE.—I never have trouble parking. I usually have trouble after I park, if you know what I mean.

GEORGE.—I think I know what you mean.

GRACIE.—You see, when I'm out driving with a boy, we just pick a spot, pull up the brake, and clutch.

GEORGE.—Frank, by the way, what happened to you the night of Gracie's convention?

FRANK.—I was out all evening with a very cute girl, and did we have fun!

GEORGE.—Oh, I see. You don't bother with conventions.

FRANK.—No, that's why we had so much fun.

GRACIE.—My biggest thrill was to be made Honorary Mayor of Boys' Town. But I was surprised; I couldn't find Mickey Rooney there.

GEORGE.—Maybe Boys' Town didn't take up his option.

GRACIE.—Aw, don't be silly. He's too big to wear options.

RAY.—Just looking at those boys reminded me of my childhood.

GEORGE.—You mean the awkward age?

RAY.—Yes, when you look kind of funny and the girls won't go with you. It starts at thirteen.

GRACIE.—Ray, when is it over?

RAY.—I don't know, but I hope soon.

George.—Mine is coming to an end next year.

Ray.—I say, Gracie, I'm sorry I had to fly to San Francisco after the broadcast and missed your acceptance speech.

Bradley.—It was beyond description. Breath-taking! Fifteen thousand people, ten bands, people cheering, delegates from all over the country!

Gracie.—And when Mr. Raymond D. McGrath made the nominating speech, I'll never forget it. His words are still ringing in my ears. And when he said . . .

Man 1.—(*Fading in*) I shall not speak of the qualifications of our candidate for this high office. Everyone knows the qualifications which she possesses and knowing them, are for her anyway.

And so, because of these things which I have said and because of many things which I have not said and because of the Omaha Chamber of Commerce and because this is the time designated for me to do so, and because I have to get back to my peanut wagon, I hereby nominate for President of the United States, Gracie Allen.

Sound.—*Applause . . . cheers.*

Man 2.—And now the roll call of the states:
State of Alabama. (*Shout*)
State of California. (*Shout*)
State of New York. (*Shout*)
State of Nebraska. (*Shout*)
State of confusion. (*Big cheers*)

Sound.—*Applause . . . band . . . cheers.*

Man 3.—(*Over applause*) And now that the cheers are dying down, we are now about to hear the acceptance speech of our candidate, the Honorable Gracie Allen.

Gracie.—Ladies and gentlemen, members of the Surprise Party, citizens of Omaha, and friends:

I want to thank you for nominating me your candidate for President.

As I look around here in this coliseum and see thousands of trusting, believing faces shining up at me with love and respect, tears come into my eyes.

And do you know why? My girdle is killing me.

If I'm elected next November, and it's bound to come . . .

It usually does, comes right after October.

I'll be the first lady President that this country has ever had.

This campaign of mine hasn't been easy. My opponents have given me plenty of worry.

But I said to myself: "Grace"—I always call myself Grace when I'm talking to myself—I said: "Grace, be like a teakettle. When you are up to your neck in hot water, continue to sing."

You see when you're singing like a teakettle, you can also let off steam at the same time.

If you have listened to my opponents, you will have to admit that they have been very outspoken, and I'm the one who outspoke 'em.

Their attacks have only made me all the prettier. The mud that they threw turned out to be beauty clay.

I've been in the library in Congress time and time again, and I want to tell you that it's a shame . . .

There isn't a good story in the place.

The newspapers have asked me what I think of the **little** man.

I think they're cute.

The reason we need a woman in the presidential chair is to pave the way for other political jobs for women such as lady senators and lady congressmen.

Anybody knows that a woman is much better than a man when it comes to introducing bills into the house.

Just look at all the famous women in history!

The mother of Julius Caesar was a woman; Napoleon's wife was a woman. Why, half the married people in the United States are women.

Naturally there are candidates running in opposition to me.

I've been in the city of Omaha only three days, and I kissed Mayor Butler twice.

Can my opponents match that?

Some people say to me: "Don't count your chickens before they're hatched, Gracie. You haven't been elected yet."

Of course, there is a remote possibility of that. But should such a thing happen, I'll say what Mr. Dionne said to the nurse when she told him that he was the father of quintuplets: "*I demand a recount.*"

In conclusion, ladies and gentlemen, I want to thank you for nominating me.

Be true to yourself by being true to the "Surprise Party."

Stick with us until we get to Washington.

Remember the banana. When it leaves the bunch, it gets skinned. (*Applause*)

RAY.—Well, Gracie, I'm certainly sorry I wasn't in Omaha to hear that speech.

GEORGE.—The night of the convention a very funny thing happened to me. I tried to get in, and they didn't know who I was, and they threw me out of the back door.

GRACIE.—Yes, but I told them who he was.

GEORGE.—Yeah, and they invited me in again.

GRACIE.—And threw him out of the front door. (*Applause*)

BRADLEY.—How would you like to get a dollar's worth of hand lotion for only 49 cents? Well, that's exactly what you get in the Hinds Honey and Almond Cream special. Only 49 cents for the *big* dollar size Hinds. What a price! And what a lotion! Hinds Honey and Almond Cream brings extra-creamy, extra-soothing comfort to your dry, rough hands, and it's cooling to sunburned skin. This big money-saving Hinds special is selling *fast.* So hurry. Save half price now on Hinds big dollar size. Why, even at its regular price, this dollar Hinds Honey and Almond Cream is famous as the family *economy* bottle. It contains over twice as much lotion as the regular 50-cent bottle. And with this 49-cent Hinds autograph special, you also get a Gracie Allen autograph. It's on the bottle and detachable. Get Hinds 49-cent special tonight and use Hinds regularly for softer, prettier hands. Remember, the big dollar bottle of Hinds Honey and Almond Cream is on sale for 49 cents for a limited time only. And now Frank Parker.

MUSIC.—(*Orchestra and Parker*).—"*Yours is My Heart Alone.*"

GEORGE.—Gracie, until I saw your convention, I didn't think a silly campaign like this could get you so far. But now that we're nominated . . .

FRANK.—We? Don't be so plural, George.

GEORGE.—Yeah, this is no time for modesty. I feel that our party needs a business leader. A person with foresight, ingenuity, brains, intelligence.

GRACIE.—We'll have to get somebody else, George. I can't be everything.

GEORGE.—I know. So as your new campaign manager I've got some ideas in my *head* that will lead us to victory.

FRANK.—Sort of a hollow victory.

GEORGE.—Oh, yeah? Anyway, we're going to San Francisco next week.

SOUND.—*Knock on door.*

GEORGE.—Come in.

SOUND.—*Door slams.*

MAN.—Good evening. I'm Ed Pettis.

GRACIE.—What are you taking for it?

GEORGE.—Please. I'm George Burns.

MAN.—Oh. Er—er you're wanted on the phone outside.

GEORGE.—It might be important. I'll be right back.

SOUND.—*Door slams.*

MAN.—He's not wanted on the telephone. Miss Allen, I just wanted to bring you a message from the Surprise Party headquarters. I've come to tell you about one mistake in your campaign.

GRACIE.—Shouldn't George hear about this?

MAN.—No, he's a mistake. *And we've got to get rid of him.*

GRACIE.—Have you any idea what George means to me? Have you any idea what we've been to each other? Get rid of George? *How can I get rid of George?* Has anybody got any ideas?

MAN.—Now you're going to San Francisco next week, and you're going to do a campaign speech and a broadcast. And we of San Francisco are very progressive. We got rid of ferry boats; we got rid of miniature golf; we got rid of horse cars. *So you can certainly get rid of George.* Good-by.

SOUND.—*Door slam.*

GRACIE.—Well, that's that. (*To self*) The question is how to get rid of him.

FRANK.—Now let's see. How about throwing him off a high building?

GRACIE.—No, he gets dizzy.

BRADLEY.—How about drowning him?

GRACIE.—No, he catches cold too easily.

RAY.—I've got a peachy one. How about giving him some cyanide pills?

GRACIE.—Uh-uh, they're too fattening.

BUBBLES.—How about shooting him?

GRACIE.—No, *I couldn't possibly do that.* I haven't got a license

RAY.—Gracie, I've got an idea. Let's make him think he's sick and worry him to death.

GRACIE.—Oh, that's cute.

SOUND.—*Door slam.*

GEORGE.—Mister, I've been in every phone booth. Where's that man that was in here?

FRANK.—The man? What man?

GEORGE.—The man who sent me outside.

BRADLEY.—There was no man here.

GEORGE.—Then why did I go out?

GRACIE.—You didn't go out.

GEORGE.—Now wait a minute. If I wasn't here and I didn't go outside, where have I been?

GRACIE.—George, do you feel all right?

GEORGE.—Never felt better in my life.

GRACIE.—Frank, get him a glass of water.

GEORGE.—I don't want any water.

GRACIE.—Then why did you ask for it?

GEORGE.—I didn't ask for it.

GRACIE.—Then give it back to me.

GEORGE.—I haven't got it.

RAY.—George, are you trying to make us think you're crazy?

GEORGE.—I was never saner in my life.

GRACIE.—(*Aside*) That's what we're worrying about.

GEORGE.—Look, we haven't any time to lose. Next week we're going to San Francisco . . .

RAY.—When is George's birthday, Gracie?

GRACIE.—Next month.

RAY.—Too bad. He would have been thirty-nine.

GEORGE.—What do you mean, would have been thirty-nine? I will be thirty-nine.

FRANK.—Wanta bet?

GEORGE.—Quiet, Frank.

FRANK.—I'm not Frank. I'm Truman Bradley.

GEORGE.—If you're Truman Bradley, *Who is this?* I said, *Who is this?*

GRACIE.—George, where you're pointing, there's nobody there.

GEORGE.—Folks, I've had a hectic week, and I don't feel so well . . .

GRACIE.—Aw, George, you're just worrying for nothing. You're not half as sick as you look.

GEORGE.—Well, thanks.

GRACIE.—You've probably got a little touch of frozola of the bozola.

GEORGE.—Frozola of the bozola? What is that?

GRACIE.—Oh, it's really nothing. Very few people ever die of it.

GEORGE.—Good.

GRACIE.—Only the ones who have it.

GEORGE.—How long do you think I've got to live?

GRACIE.—I'll give you a little hint. Don't buy an all-day sucker.

GEORGE.—All right, so I'm sick. But anyway, when we go to San Francisco . . . What are the symptoms of frozola of the bozola?

GRACIE.—Why get upset? If you've got it, the autopsy will show it.

GEORGE.—What if I haven't got it?

GRACIE.—Then you died of something else.

GEORGE.—Well, now I feel better.

FRANK.—I'll tell you how to get rid of it. The first day you cut out meat; the second day you cut out starches; the third day you cut out liquids.

GEORGE.—What do I cut out the fourth day?

FRANK.—Paper dolls.

GEORGE.—Frozola of the bozola? I've never heard of that.

BRADLEY.—I don't think we should talk that way about George. He's such a nice fellow.

GRACIE.—Yes, wasn't he?

FRANK.—There never was a better pal.

GEORGE.—Yeah, he was a nice kid.

BRADLEY.—(*Tearfully*) He was kind, considerate, free with his money.

GEORGE.—Yeah, I'm gonna miss him.

GRACIE.—I'll never forget his face. Isn't it awful?

GEORGE.—It's like a bad dream.

BRADLEY.—(*Tearfully*) Can you imagine how I'll feel when I get up and say, "Don't forget to use Hinds Honey and Almond

Cream, it's good for rough, red faces." (*Crying*) My heart will be broken when I say, "You can get it at any toilet goods counter."

GEORGE.—Truman, what are you talking about?

BRADLEY.—The dollar bottle.

GEORGE.—Then why are you crying?

BRADLEY.—They're selling it for 49 cents. (*Applause*)

MUSIC.—"*Oakland to Burbank.*"

BRADLEY.—Due to conditions over which we have no control, George is still living. However, with the help of a sleeping powder and a small mallet, we now have him strapped in bed here in the Studio Emergency Hospital with the cast acting as the medical staff. *And here we are.*

GEORGE.—*Heavy breathing.*

FRANK.—Look, he's breathing heavy.

GRACIE.—I hope he can last a few minutes longer.

BUBBLES.—Why?

GRACIE.—He's got three more balloons to blow up for our party tonight.

GEORGE.—*Heavy breathing.*

SOUND.—*Balloon breaks.*

GRACIE.—We've got four more to blow up.

GEORGE.—*Groans.*

RAY.—Look, he's coming to. His eyelids are starting to flutter.

BUBBLES.—What a time to flirt.

GEORGE.—*Groans . . . sings "Ain't Misbehavin'."*

GRACIE.—Quick before he gets to the chorus, give him a sleeping tablet.

BRADLEY.—Which one?

GRACIE.—The one with the handle.

SOUND.—*Clunk.*

GEORGE.—Oh! (*Heavy breathing*)

BRADLEY.—Now remember, before he comes to, we've got to keep him here so he can't go to San Francisco.

GRACIE.—Now don't forget, Bubbles and I are nurses. Truman, you and Ray are doctors, and Frank, you're the patient in the next bed.

FRANK.—Okay, but let me give George the next sleeping tablet.

GRACIE.—Yeah, George will get a bang out of it.

GEORGE.—(*Groaning . . . singing "Ain't Misbehavin'"*) Where am I?

GRACIE.—Now, just lie quiet, Mr. Burns. You're suffering from a very horrible malady.

GEORGE.—What malady?

GRACIE.—Ain't misbehavin'.

GEORGE.—What happened? What am I doing here?

GRACIE.—You were operated on for frozola of the bozola.

GEORGE.—Did I have it?

GRACIE.—Back to back.

GEORGE.—Back to back? Gracie . . . Gracie . . .

GRACIE.—Yes, yes. Just lie quiet. Gracie will be here in a minute.

GEORGE.—Now wait, you're Gracie.

GRACIE.—No, I'm Nurse Crowley. You're delirious Mr. Burns. Just take it easy.

GEORGE.—Why am I tied down?

RAY.—This room happens to be upside down, and we don't want you to fall out of bed.

GEORGE.—Now listen to me, Ray Noble.

RAY.—I'm not Ray Noble. I'm Dr. Frankfurter, a skin specialist.

GEORGE.—This has gone from bad to wurst. Frank, what are you doing in the next bed? What's the matter with you?

FRANK.—Do you mean me, buddy?

GEORGE.—Yeah.

FRANK.—My name isn't Frank. I'm J. V. Dittenfest, Junior.

GEORGE.—J. V. Dittenfest, Junior?

FRANK.—Yeah, I was named after my son.

GEORGE.—You haven't got a son.

FRANK.—Could I help it if he died before I was born?

GEORGE.—What is this? Say, Truman?

BRADLEY.—I'm not Truman. I'm Dr. Alvin Johnson.

GEORGE.—I'll see if he's Truman Bradley. *What's good for rough, red hands?*

BRADLEY.—I don't know. I'm an ear specialist.

GEORGE.—You are, huh? *What can you get at toilet goods counters?*

BRADLEY.—The salesgirl's phone number.

GEORGE.—Bubbles, come here.

BUBBLES.—You mean me?

GEORGE.—Yes.

BUBBLES.—I'm sorry. I can't talk.

GEORGE.—Why not?

BUBBLES.—I'm an oxygen tent.

GEORGE.—I hope this is a dream.

GRACIE.—Now open your mouth, Mr. Burns.

GEORGE.—Ah.

GRACIE.—Wider.

GEORGE.—Ah—ah.

GRACIE.—Now swallow the spoon.

GEORGE.—Swallow the spoon?

GRACIE.—Yes, I gave you some medicine before, and I forgot to stir it.

GEORGE.—Hurry up, I want a sleeping tablet.

RAY.—Gladly, old boy, this one's on me.

SOUND.—*Clunk . . . whistle . . . bell.*

GRACIE.—Give the gentleman a cigar.

RAY.—Thank you!

GRACIE.—Truman, we'd better get a bottle of beer for George.

BRADLEY.—Is he thirsty?

GRACIE.—No, he's anemic. I want to give him a transfusion.

BRADLEY.—What if it kills him?

GRACIE.—We still get a nickel back on the bottle.

BUBBLES.—(*Laughs*) Poor George. Doesn't he look awful?

GRACIE.—(*Laughs*) Yes, doesn't he?

BUBBLES.—I wish he'd get well or something. I've got a date to see a double feature.

GRACIE.—What is the double feature?

BUBBLES.—Don Wilson.

RAY.—Look, George is waking up. Maybe we ought to give him something that will really put him to sleep.

GRACIE.—We're not allowed to give him any, dope. I mean we're not allowed to give him any dope.

GEORGE.—*Sings "Ain't Misbehavin'."*

SOUND.—*Clunk*

GEORGE.—Oh.

RAY.—What a terrible clunk.

GRACIE.—Yes, he certainly is.

BRADLEY.—Look, George is hardly moving. Get up. I say, George, get up.

FRANK.—Truman, let's tap his knee and test his reflexes.

BRADLEY.—All right.

SOUND.—*Tap . . . tap.*

BRADLEY.—I tapped his knee, but nothing happened.

GRACIE.—Yeah, what about the jerk?

FRANK.—He's still unconscious.

RAY.—I say, this is getting serious. Frank, you'd better go out and get a real doctor.

FRANK.—Okay.

SOUND.—*Door slams.*

BRADLEY.—Poor George. To think he won't be able to go to San Francisco.

RAY.—Yes, look at that bump on his head. It looks like Treasure Island.

GRACIE.—Yes, and his nose looks like Knob Hill.

BUBBLES.—And look at him with his mouth open. It looks like the Golden Gate.

GRACIE.—Yes, I can see the bridge.

SOUND.—*Door slams.*

FRANK.—This way, doctor.

DOCTOR.—Um-hum. How long has he been dead?

GRACIE.—Doctor, that's Ray Noble. This is the patient.

DOCTOR.—My, my, my. No pulse, no color, no blood pressure, no respiration, no reflexes.

GRACIE.—He ain't got nuttin', has he, doctor?

DOCTOR.—This is a very serious case, and he's got to be removed immediately.

GRACIE.—Oh, good.

DOCTOR.—There's only one place where we can save him. That's the Grandview Sanitarium, and I'd better take him there immediately.

GRACIE.—Swell! Where is it?

DOCTOR.—San Francisco.

GRACIE.—Oh. (*Applause*)

BRADLEY.—When you read a romantic love story, doesn't it make you dream of such happiness for yourself, of strong arms holding you close and warm, thrilling kisses? Of course! And you can help make those dreams come true! Keep yourself just as attractive and appealing and feminine as you know how! For one thing, make good use of Hinds Honey and Almond Cream. This fine, fragrant lotion helps keep your hands looking smooth, smelling fragrant, and *feeling thrilling to a man's touch!* And don't forget, now is the time for all women to buy Hinds. Why? Because it's on special *sale!* You get the big dollar size, for only 49 cents, less than half price! Just walk up to a toilet goods counter, put down 49 cents, and you get the dollar size Hinds Honey and Almond Cream, the biggest hand lotion special of 1940! It contains over twice as much lotion as the regular 50-cent bottle. And this is the same fine Hinds Honey and Almond Cream you've always known, extra-creamy, extra-softening! Ask for Hinds 49-cent special tonight. It's an autograph special, too, with a detachable Gracie Allen autograph on the bottle. Remember, this offer is good for a limited time only. The price is less than *half*, only 49 cents for the big dollar size of Hinds Honey and Almond Cream!

MUSIC.—(*Orchestra and* GRACIE).—"*I Can't Love You Any More.*"

BRADLEY.—Now you can enjoy *both:* Hinds *lotion* in *bottles*, hand *creams* in *jars*. Those smart red-and-white jars contain the fluffiest, creamiest hand cream Hinds could make! It comes in two sizes; 10 cents and 39 cents a jar. And don't forget the big Hinds lotion special, the dollar size for only 49 cents.

GEORGE.—Well, Gracie, say good night.

GRACIE.—George, just think. Next week Ray, Frank, Truman, Bubbles, and myself will all be up in San Francisco.

GEORGE.—Gracie, aren't you forgetting me?

GRACIE.—No.

SOUND.—*Clunk.*

GEORGE.—Oh. Good night, all! Ladies and gentlemen, we've got a big surprise for you tonight, and it gives me great pleasure to introduce the mayor of Los Angeles, the Honorable Fletcher Bowron. (*Applause*)

MAYOR.—Thank you, George, and hello, Gracie.

GRACIE.—Hello. Say, mayor, could you get my brother out? You see it wasn't really his fault . . .

GEORGE.—Quiet! Quiet!

MAYOR.—Ladies and gentlemen, and fellow members of the Surprise Party, I am very happy to be here tonight. And in my official capacity I hereby delegate Gracie Allen as Los Angeles' special ambassador to the San Francisco Fair for '40 next Wednesday.

GEORGE.—You know, mayor, Gracie was born in San Francisco.

MAYOR.—I know, and I want to thank San Francisco for sending Gracie to Los Angeles. And we've been waiting for years for a chance to send her back.

GEORGE.—I think you've got something there, mayor.

GRACIE.—Mayor Bowron, it was nice of you to come. This mayor of ours, say, he's pretty!

GEORGE.—Yeah.

GRACIE.—When I'm elected, I'm going to make Mayor Bowron a Secretary of the Interior so we can have some X-ray pictures taken together.

GEORGE.—Good night, all, and thank you, Mayor Bowron.

BRADLEY.—(*Over music*) And next Wednesday, over these same stations, George and Gracie and all of us will be back again, don't forget. And don't forget, for honeymoon hands it's Hinds Honey and Almond Cream.

Bob Hope

THIS show has made one of the most spectacular forward leaps in radio's history. It is pushing all the headliners and pushing them hard, and it threatens to shoulder its way to the top by the sheer force of its speed, the rapid-fire delivery of its central comedian, and the nitwit accessories that go with him: Brenda and Cobina, and Jerry Colonna, who is known as Yehudi.

The Bob Hope show gets a punishing rehearsal two days before each broadcast. Ten or eleven writers are at work on the shows all the time, and about ninety minutes' worth of material is actually played before an audience. Recordings are made of this hour-and-a-half ordeal and are played back and analyzed by Hope and his crew. Everything that missed fire is pulled out; so is much that did not get the reaction expected. The very best, in what would normally add up to three separate shows, is cut down to fill the time of one, and this device of a test show (not new but never so mercilessly prosecuted) is in a great way responsible for the superiority of the type of show the Bob Hope program is.

It is possible that some of the nonsense that goes on in this Tuesday evening half hour will work itself into the American language. One hears some of the phrases already, popping up on the street in the same way that "So's your old man" did twenty years ago. "You and your education"! "Oh, don't like poor people, huh"? "That's what I keep telling them down at the office." This latter one is probably too long to catch on, but "Greetings, Gate" has already become an American salutation.

Here is Bob Hope's show for March 12, 1940.

Bob Hope

GOODWIN.—The Pepsodent Show! . . . Starring Bob Hope!

MUSIC.—"*Thanks for the Memory*" . . . *First two bars.*

CHORUS.—Hello there, East and West,
The North, the South, the rest.
It's time for fun for everyone.
Bob Hope! Make with the jest!

HOPE.—Ah! Thank you so much.

How do you do, ladies and gentlemen. This is Bob Hope advising you to use Pepsodent while your teeth are still underpups, and they won't grow up to be "Golden Boys"! I'm a little tired tonight. I'm building a new house in North Hollywood, and I want to tell you that's hard work. I think I'll have to hire a carpenter to help me. It's one of those California all-weather houses . . . you know . . . six rooms, a big sun porch . . . and a direct wire to the coast guard! I decided to build a permanent home now that I'm doing pretty well in pictures. Of course, it's the only house on the block with wheels on it! . . . But I'm really putting up a nice house. The other day when the lumber came in . . . the termites were standing around smacking their lips and applauding! You'll like the inside of the house. It's really got a beautiful bathroom . . . when you want cold water, all you have to do is dig . . . when you want hot water . . . you just go deeper! The other day I turned on the faucet, and a Major Bowes' corroded unit came out! It's got three guest rooms . . . the green room, the blue room, and the jade room. It's really all the same room . . . we just change the lights for the first two and burn incense for the other! And I've got a new idea in the bedroom . . . the walls just pull out from the bed.

I have a Murphy bed and a Morris chair in my room, and the room is so small. The other morning Murphy woke up with an accent! One thing I don't like about the house is that it has a California Chamber of Commerce heating system.

Everytime you turn it on it yells, "Traitor." The house should have been finished a long time ago . . . But my architect drools, and every time he looks at the blueprints he inks in a couple of more rooms! The architect fixed it so that every time you go to the second floor you bump your head . . . He calls it the "Stairway to the Stars"! But still it's going to be the show place of the town. What other house in the neighborhood will have a neon fence? I got one of those new government loans on my house, and the government certainly protects its investments. The other day when it rained out here, Morgenthau called me up long distance to shut the windows! . . . And here's Skinnay Ennis and the Six Hits and a Miss, singing "Where or When."

MUSIC.—(*Skinnay Ennis, Six Hits and A Miss, and Orchestra*). "*Where or When.*"

HOPE.—That was Skinnay Ennis and the Six Hits and a Miss singing "Where or When" from "Babes in Arms." And here's why.

BRUNDAGE.—In this matter of choosing a dentifrice it isn't the *form* of dentifrice that's important; it's what's *in* it that counts; it's what's *in* it that does the work! Whether you choose tooth paste, powder, or new liquid for teeth, the only thing that matters is *results*. Doesn't that make sense? That's why Pepsodent should be your choice, no matter which form suits you best. Because Pepsodent, and Pepsodent *alone*, offers tooth paste, tooth powder, and liquid dentifrice, all of which give your teeth the sparkling benefits of irium. Irium is Pepsodent's patented, trade-marked cleansing ingredient that is showing millions the quick, *safe* way to a more dazzling smile. It's irium that spurs Pepsodent tooth paste, Pepsodent tooth powder, and Pepsodent liquid dentifrice into quicker, keener cleansing action, helps to brush away dingy surface stains, and persuades your teeth to gleam with full natural brilliance and does it gently and safely—for Pepsodent with irium is *proved safe* for tooth enamel. So choose the form of dentifrice *you* like best . . . paste, powder, or new liquid. Just make sure of one thing: If it's smoother, cleaner, brighter looking teeth you want, make sure your dentifrice is Pepsodent containing irium!

MUSIC.—*Tag.*

HOPE.—Yes, sir, good old Pepsodent liquid dentifrice . . . a drip in time saved mine.

GOODWIN.—Hello, Bob.

HOPE.—Hello, Bill. Say, you look great tonight. Look at those bright red cheeks and those flashing white teeth! Gee, what a picture . . . *sunrise over a picket fence!*

GOODWIN.—Oh, yeah! Well, look at your face, Bob . . . *moonglow over an avocado!*

HOPE.—Wait a minute, Bill. I'm in the pink of condition. Look at that stomach . . . flat as a pancake and hard as a rock.

GOODWIN.—Yeah. But, Bob, what happens if the lace breaks?

HOPE.—I take care of myself, Bill. About 6 months ago I sent an application to one of those correspondence school body builders . . . but the application must have gone to a cooking school by mistake.

GOODWIN.—What makes you think so?

HOPE.—After the fifth lesson I developed *lemon meringue biceps!*

GOODWIN.—Why, I've got a gymnasium in my attic. You know, I like to work on the parallel bars.

HOPE.—Yeah, that's fun. That was my brother's favorite sport. He'd work on the bars, and his pal would watch for the warden.

GOODWIN.—Why don't you do some bowling? There's a sport for you, Bob. Nowadays they've got the bowling alleys and poolrooms fixed up so you can't tell them from a beauty parlor.

HOPE.—I know, Bill. The other day I went into a place and told them I wanted an hour of pool and they gave me a bubble bath. Did you know, Skinnay Ennis and his thin brother work in the bowling alley across the street?

GOODWIN.—Do they? I never see them around.

HOPE.—They only work there mornings. Skinnay and his thin brother wait till the pins are set up; then they run between them and dust them off!

ENNIS.—Hiya, fellers.

GOODWIN.—Hiya, Skin.

HOPE.—Well, well, the little man that wasn't! How you doing, Skin?

ENNIS.—Man, I feel like a million upbeats! I got myself a new raccoon coat.

GOODWIN.—A raccoon coat? Why, Skinny, a big fur coat like that will tire you all out.

HOPE.—Skinnay solved that, Bill. On the bottom it's got *wheels!*

GOODWIN.—Gee, Skin, you look good! Are you exercising these days?

ENNIS.—Yeah, man, I'm feeling better all the time. Why, now every morning I get up . . .

HOPE.—Yes, and then what?

ENNIS.—Then what? Shucks, man, ain't that pretty good for a start?

HOPE.—But is it doing you any good?

ENNIS.—Sure it is. Look at my physique. Look at my build. I weigh 116 pounds and not an ounce of fat on me!

HOPE.—You should try my routine, Skin. I like badminton myself. Yesterday we played all afternoon.

GOODWIN.—Those feathers come off the birds pretty easily, don't they, Bob?

HOPE.—I'll say. At the end of the day there were so many feathers lying around, a turkey came in, took one look, and said, "My gosh, hand me that calendar!"

GOODWIN.—You know, Judy Garland's the real badminton player. That was a swell week end we all had out at her house, wasn't it?

HOPE.—It certainly was. I had a fine time.

ENNIS.—I was mighty glad Judy invited me, too. To show my appreciation, I treated Judy's folks to a big dinner at the Victor Hugo.

GOODWIN.—And to show *my* appreciation, I treated them to tickets at the theatre.

HOPE.—(*Pause*) Well, Judy's a great girl, isn't she?

GOODWIN.—She has a lovely home. And say, isn't that great Dane of hers a beautiful animal? He sure liked you.

HOPE.—Yeah. And that reminds me, do you think I should write Judy's mother a thank-you note . . . or just let the dog keep my hand?

GOODWIN.—I thought that week end up there did you a lot of good, Bob.

HOPE.—Yes, it did. Before I went out there, I could hardly raise the window in my bedroom.

GOODWIN.—And now?

HOPE.—Well, there's no use being silly about fresh air.

JUDY.—Hello, Mr. Hope!

HOPE.—Hello, Judy. I've been looking for you. I want to thank you for that wonderful week end we had at your house. I hope we didn't put your mother out too much.

JUDY.—Oh, no. Mother thought it was so nice that you could come on such short notice . . . you gave her!

GOODWIN.—Gee, Judy, thanks for inviting me over, too.

JUDY.—You're welcome, Mr. Goodwin. It was nice of you to help my mother cook the dinner.

HOPE.—Goodwin helped your mother cook the dinner? Oh, *that's* what it was!

GOODWIN.—That's what *what* was?

HOPE.—Oh, nothing. But that was the first chicken I ever ate with irium gravy! . . . But, Judy, I enjoyed everything so much I'm going to send your mother a nice autographed picture of myself.

JUDY.—Honest, Mr. Hope?

HOPE.—Why, sure.

JUDY.—*Free?*

HOPE.—Why, of course. I gave your father an autograph for nothing, didn't I?

JUDY.—Yes, and that reminds me. Daddy wants his pencil back.

HOPE.—I guess your mother thought we were pretty hungry the way we tore into that food we had for supper.

JUDY.—Oh, no. She was born and raised on a farm, she's used to those noises . . . But she did say that was the first time she ever saw anyone get sparks out of a knife and fork!

HOPE.—Gosh, everything was marvelous. You know, it was all new to me, having breakfast in bed.

JUDY.—By the way, Mr. Hope, my servant told me to tell you . . . when you eat in bed you should *sit up*.

HOPE.—I *thought* something was wrong. After I ate those soft-boiled eggs, *I looked like "Golden Boy."*

JUDY.—Our home isn't very big. Did you mind sleeping over the garage?

HOPE.—Oh, not at all. I had a beautiful *carbon monoxide* dream.

JUDY.—I guess Skinnay Ennis spent a restless night, too. You know, Mr. Hope, Skinnay walks in his sleep.

HOPE.—Does he?

JUDY.—Yes. I could hear him all night long banging against the walls of his iron lung.

HOPE.—Well, I slept all right, except I heard a peculiar noise during the night, sort of metallic clinking.

JUDY.—Oh, that! That was only daddy downstairs counting the silverware.

HOPE.—By the way it was the finest mattress I ever slept on the floor next to.

JUDY.—I meant to ask you before, Mr. Hope. Why did you stay in your room all Sunday afternoon?

HOPE.—Well, after all, Judy, it takes *me* a little time to *understand* the funny papers.

JUDY.—Was it exciting?

HOPE.—Exciting! I'll say it was . . . Dick Tracy almost caught *himself!*

JUDY.—Mr. Hope, you didn't get mad when those kids from across the street lighted a fire under you when you were sitting on the barbecue pit, did you?

HOPE.—No, I was just surprised. I thought someone had stolen my secret formula for the Hope Hotfoot.

JUDY.—You were nice about everything. My mother wants to thank you for mowing the lawn, and my brother wants to thank you, too.

HOPE.—Your brother wants to thank me for mowing the lawn?

JUDY.—Not exactly. He was lying on it at the time . . . and he has *always wanted one of those college boy haircuts!*

HOPE.—Well, I'm glad I did *something* right. I didn't look so good when we were out on the tennis courts. I thought I was a good tennis player, but I was really outclassed.

JUDY.—Well, don't you feel bad about it, Mr. Hope. Miss Robson is awfully fast on her feet.

HOPE.—Oh, I felt better after the beating she gave George Arliss.

JUDY.—I liked your tennis outfit. But weren't those shorts you wore kind of long?

HOPE.—Judy, those weren't shorts. They were my white flannel pants from high school graduation.

JUDY.—Well, they were up above your knees. Mr. Hope, don't you think it would be better if you just wore your socks without the garters?

HOPE.—I'll try that. Next time I'll just hook them over my kneecaps.

JUDY.—That was some sign you hung out in the street before the match.

HOPE.—I designed it myself, Judy—just a simple white banner with 2-foot red letters. Did you like the wording?

JUDY.—Oh, yes . . . "Tennis game now on . . . starring Bob Hope."

HOPE.—I thought I did very well in the first two games.

JUDY.—You did. I even liked you when they put the net up! Say, why did Mr. Ennis keep holding his tennis racket up to his face?

HOPE.—Judy, Skinnay had that racket built special. It's got smelling salts in the handle. I thought I was really good in my match with Mickey Rooney.

JUDY.—That was exciting.

HOPE.—I smashed the ball as hard as I could. Mickey smashed it right back. Boy, can he hit! He drove it so hard, when it stopped bouncing, the ball said, "Listen, fellers, can't we settle this thing some other way"?

JUDY.—We did have a good time, didn't we? But I'm so sorry the swimming pool didn't have any water in it.

HOPE.—Yes. It was nice of Mickey Rooney *not* to tell me!

JUDY.—Did you get hurt?

HOPE.—Of course not. It was all in fun. I can pick up a new shoulder blade anyplace.

JUDY.—Maybe if I sing my favorite song, you'll feel better.

HOPE.—Your favorite song? Who wrote it?

JUDY.—It's from "Babes in Arms." Mickey wrote it in the picture.

HOPE.—*Ouch!* Sing, Judy.

MUSIC.—(*Orchestra and Judy*). "*Good Morning.*" (*Applause*)

HOPE.—That was Judy Garland singing "Good Morning" from "Babes in Arms," and here's that man again.

BRUNDAGE.—All this week the druggists of the United States are celebrating National Pharmacy Week. The purpose of this annual event is to acquaint you with the many services rendered by your near-by drugstore. In your druggists' windows you will find many attractive values and many items which you need in your everyday life.

Among these items you will always find new Pepsodent liquid dentifrice, Pepsodent tooth paste, Pepsodent tooth powder, and Pepsodent antiseptic—the team mates of modern mouth hygiene. Perhaps your supply of these products is running low. If it is, purchase them tomorrow from your near-by druggist in appreciation of the friendly service he renders you 7 days a week, 52 weeks a year.

Remember—all this week is National Pharmacy Week!

MUSIC.—"*Stop, You're Breaking My Heart*" . . . *play on.*

GOODWIN.—And now Bob Hope brings you his version of the new song hit "Stop Kickin' My Heart Around"

MUSIC.—*Up and down.*

HOPE.—Gosh, I'm so excited, Bill. Imagine *us* having a date to go out tonight . . . and with *girls*, too!

GOODWIN.—Yeah, Bob. Gee, if we'd only known about Mother Mirandy's Golden Hair Wash 5 years ago!

HOPE.—(*Nervous laugh*) I'm actually going out with a girl! Where'll we take 'em, Bill? All the poolrooms are closed.

GOODWIN.—Don't worry about that, Bob. These girls are class. We'll take 'em for a ride on the Glendale bus.

HOPE.—(*Nervous laugh*) Am I dressed all right?

GOODWIN.—You shouldn't have worn those socks, Bob.

HOPE.—What's the matter with these socks?

GOODWIN.—One of them has a hole in the knee. And those open-toe shoes . . . why did you buy that kind?

HOPE.—I didn't buy them that way. It's just that my big toe is always in there punching! Say, how long are we gonna have to wait for those girls? What time is it, anyway?

GOODWIN.—It's a little after Tuesday.

HOPE.—Well, let's wait till a quarter to Thursday; and if they don't show up, we'll go stag!

GOODWIN.—I can't understand this, Bob.

HOPE.—Yeah, this is the third time this week I've been turned down. Gosh, what can be the matter? I read all the ads!

GOODWIN.—Well, Bob, there's something I ought to tell you, but you're an "unconscious offender."

HOPE.—I'm an unconscious offender?

GOODWIN.—Yes, Bob, your winter underwear always shows below your pants.

HOPE.—Well, can I help it if they come strapless now?

GOODWIN.—Gee, I *wonder* what's holding these girls up?

HOPE.—Yeah, and after they get here, I'll bet we'll still be wondering.

GOODWIN.—Say, Bob, supposing the girls don't show up at all? Shall we call those other two girls we know?

HOPE.—I don't know. What time do they get through at the laundry?

GOODWIN.—Well, I don't really know, now that Maisie is on mangles!

HOPE.—Is Maisie on *mangles* now? Gee, isn't it nice to know she's getting ahead!

GOODWIN.—Yeah. Say, you know I'm getting tired of always being stood up.

HOPE.—Yeah, it's just like these women. I give them the best years of my life, spend all my money, and what have I got out of it . . . *wallflower crouch!*

GOODWIN.—Bob, look who's coming! I think it's Skinnay Ennis!

HOPE.—You *think* it's Skinnay Ennis? Aren't you sure?

GOODWIN.—Listen, Bob, with Skinnay, even *he* isn't sure!

ENNIS.—(*Coming in*) Hiya, fellas! Well, well, so the two Romeos got stood up!

GOODWIN.—*It's a lie!*

HOPE.—Yeah, it's a lie! But how did you know?

ENNIS.—Man, I ought to know. I'm an expert on women.

HOPE.—Well, what about getting us a couple of girls for tonight?

ENNIS.—Say, I know a couple of swell coeds over at the college. They'll be just right for Bill and you. One's tall, and the other's stupid!

HOPE.—But are you sure you can get a date for us with them?

ENNIS.—Sure. Gimme a nickel, and I'll call up the slugs!

HOPE.—Is a nickel enough? Maybe you'll have to talk overtime.

ENNIS.—Listen, when I ask these Model T's if they want a date, they'll say "Yes" so fast I'll get 3 cents change! . . . Here, give me that phone.

SOUND.—*Receiver click . . . nickel dropping in slot.*

ENNIS.—Operator! Gimme Anaemic 2072! . . . Hello, girls . . . (*fading*) this is Skinnay Ennis . . .

MUSIC.—*In lightly and fade.*

BLANCHE.—All right, Skinnay. Thanks a lot for getting us the dates! Good-by!

SOUND.—*Receiver click.*

ELVIA.—Say, Brenda!

BLANCHE.—Yes, Cobina?

ELVIA.—These fellows Ennis is sending around, do you think they'll be like him?

BLANCHE.—Gosh, I hope not. I like my fellers to breathe naturally.

ELVIA.—Gee, they're from Hollywood, too. Guess they'll want a kiss. Maybe they may try to tempt us!

BLANCHE.—Tempt us? I'll say! The last feller I met from Hollywood didn't walk in with candy. He wriggled in on his stomach with an apple in his teeth.

ELVIA.—Gee, maybe he'll look at me, walk over and take my hand, look in my eyes, and then he'll . . .

BLANCHE.—Say, Cobina, stop holding yourself a preview!

ELVIA.—I bet they'll be here any minute now.

BLANCHE.—Gee, I'm all excited. I'm shaking all over just like I got *parsley!*

ELVIA.—Brenda, do you think Goodie will go for me?

BLANCHE.—Yes, but don't act too eager. We been out with lots of fellers before. *Tell 'em!*

ELVIA.—Of course we have. Gee, what a kiss that last guy I was out with gave me!

BLANCHE.—Did he kiss you so hard?

ELVIA.—Hard? (*Alum mouth*) *I talked like this for two days!*

BLANCHE.—Gee, I hope *these* boys are nice fellers. If your boy friend gets fresh, let me know and I'll smash him right in the kisser!

ELVIA.—Yeah, I'll let you know . . . *and smash you right back!*

BLANCHE.—Say, we better finish dressing right away, Cobina. What are you gonna wear? Your organdy creep de shiney or your *liver pill schlemiel?*

ELVIA.—Oh, I dunno. I wanna look good, but I wanna be ready to defend myself at the same time. Say, Brenda, have you seen my bottle of bay rum?

BLANCHE.—Don't you remember? We used it last night in the Martinis! . . . Well, whaddya know, Cobina! I can't find my false eyelashes!

ELVIA.—I got them. I'm brushing off my coat!

BLANCHE.—I wonder if they're too long? Should I cut them down to 3 inches?

ELVIA.—I don't know; but every time you wink your eye, you flag down the Super Chief! Gee, Brenda, I have such trouble with my stockings. Tell me, are my seams crooked?

BLANCHE.—On *your* legs, how else could they be?

ELVIA.—Say, shall I help you with your coiffure?

BLANCHE.—Yeah. Do you think I got enough glue on my head now?

ELVIA.—Sure.

BLANCHE.—Okay. Stick my hair on. And be careful. Last time you put it on sideways, and I had to leer at people all evening!

ELVIA.—Say, Brenda, how will I act when Goodie comes in?

BLANCHE.—Act like you did with your last boy friend . . . *if you can still remember!* Gee, I wonder what my goon looks like?

ELVIA.—Oh, I seen Robert a lot. He looks like a sculptor made him outa clay and forgot to let go of his nose!

BLANCHE.—Say, when it comes to talking about noses, we better not, believe me, kid!

ELVIA.—Gee, I'm so nervous. The boys should be here any minute!

SOUND.—*Loud metallic snap off-mike.*

BLANCHE.—They're on the front porch now.

ELVIA.—How do you know?

BLANCHE.—The bear trap just went off!

SOUND.—*Door opens . . . running footsteps.*

HOPE AND GOODWIN.—*Hello, girls!*

HOPE.—(*Pause*) You *are* girls, aren't you?

BLANCHE.—I'll say. My name's Brenda La Frenzy, but you can call me Muggsy for short!

GOODWIN.—Okay, mugg. When do we start muggin'? (*Laughs*)

BLANCHE.—Huh! Get a load of that character, willya! Quiet, you, or I'll sic a beetle on you!

HOPE.—Well, my name is Bob Hope.

BLANCHE.—Chawmed, I'm sure.

HOPE.—Huh? What?

BLANCHE.—I said, chawmed, dope! Cobina, hand me my lorgnette!

ELVIA.—It's all gone, Brenda. We had it for dinner with the cave-ier.

GOODWIN.—Say, what is this?

BLANCHE.—You know, we're definitely of the horsey set.

HOPE.—Really? Which one of you is Seabiscuit?

ELVIA.—Mr. Hope, *my* name is Cobina, and I think you're wonderful! Here, let me pat your face with my hand!

SOUND.—*Scratching noise.*

HOPE.—What was that?

ELVIA.—Nothing . . . *I forgot to use my hand lotion tonight!*

GOODWIN.—Well, what'll we do now? Shall we eat the sandwiches here or take a long hike in the country?

ELVIA.—Oh, that sounds like jolly fun. I'd love to see the old picnic grounds. I haven't seen them since I was a little girl.

HOPE.—It's too late for that, Cobina. They built *Los Angeles there!*

BLANCHE.—Say, wait a minute. Never mind that picnic stuff. Come on, J. Pierpont, let's go to a movie!

ELVIA.—Yeah, we ain't never seen a talkie!

HOPE.—No, let's stay right here. I like it.

BLANCHE.—Listen, we gotta go out somewhere. The dean of women won't let you boys stay here after 9 o'clock. Cobina, let's put on our sailor hats.

HOPE.—Sailor hats? What are you—part of the navy?

BLANCHE.—No, but we can dream, can't we?

ELVIA.—(*Off . . . loud*) It's cold out, Brenda . . . *You better wear your mackinaw!*

SOUND.—*Knock on door.*

BLANCHE.—Gee, that must be Professor Colonna—the dean of women!

SOUND.—*Very loud knock on door . . . then slight rip of splintering wood.*

ELVIA.—Yeah, that's the dean all right; I recognize his *knuckles.* Don't come in, Dean—we're getting dressed to go out!

COLONNA.—(*Off-mike*) *Why? . . . Is the joint on fire?*

ELVIA.—No. We've got a *date!*

COLONNA.—(*Off-mike*) What did you do? *Call for volunteers?*

BLANCHE.—Of course not! Wait till you see the boys who are visiting us! Come on in!

SOUND.—*Door opens.*

COLONNA.—Greetings, my little coeds! . . . *Eek! Who are these two deadheads?*

HOPE.—I'm very pleased to meet you, Dean Colonna. My name is Bob Hope. I'm on the Pepsodent program.

COLONNA.—Oh, well, *it could happen to anybody!*

ELVIA.—Boys, I'd like you to know that Dean Colonna is very popular here at school. Aren't you, Brush Mush?

COLONNA.—Ah, yes! All the girls here look up to me. All the teachers look up to me. In fact, everybody looks up to me!

GOODWIN.—But why, Dean?

COLONNA.—*I love to walk on stilts!*

HOPE.—Professor, are you acquainted with any of the other deans?

COLONNA.—Ah, yes. I know all the deans in the country. In fact, I once met Man Mountain Dean!

HOPE.—You really met Man Mountain Dean? What did he say?

COLONNA.—The conversation went like this: quote, "Shake hands, Colonna!" (*Sound, terrific crunch*) Unquote! Well, I must go now. But if there are any men in this room when the clock strikes 9, you girls will be expelled! So remember—"*Cinderella, stay out of his arms!*" . . . Good-by!

SOUND.—*Crash of glass . . . descending slide whistle . . . thud.*

HOPE.—Professor! *You went out of the window instead of the door!*

COLONNA.—(*Off-mike*) *All right, so I ain't neat!*

BLANCHE.—What'll we do now?

ELVIA.—I'll tell you what let's do. Let's dance! Brenda, will you play for us?

HOPE.—Is Brenda musical?

ELVIA.—I'll say she is! *Listen!*

MUSIC.—(*Drummer*) *Three tom-tom beats.*

BLANCHE.—*Yeah man!*

MUSIC.—(*Drummer*) *Three tom-tom beats.*

BLANCHE.—*Yeah man!*

MUSIC.—(*Drummer*) *Three tom-tom beats.*

BLANCHE.—*Yeah man! I wanna hat with cherries! . . . Believe me, kid!*

ELVIA.—Come on, Bobbsy, let's dance! Hold me tighter.

HOPE.—All right. But is this a new grip, or are you smuggling in an octopus?

BLANCHE.—Gee, Billsy, look at them dance!

ELVIA.—You know, you boys ought to get out of here now. It's almost time for the curfew! Listen!

SOUND.—*One lousy gong.*

HOPE.—So that bell is curfew?

BLANCHE.—Yeah. Sometimes when we got a good date, they give us *four* bells!

SOUND.—*Knock on door.*

ELVIA.—It's the dean of women! Hurry, boys! Throw on a couple of sarongs and floor mops and the dean will think you're a couple of coeds!

HOPE AND GOODWIN.—Okay!

SOUND.—*Scurry of feet.*

GOODWIN.—I'm ready. Did you find a floor mop to put on your head, Bob?

HOPE.—No. I'm wearing a Fuller sink brush. How do I look?

GOODWIN.—You'd look better in the sink! . . . Come on!

SOUND.—*Knock on door.*

COLONNA.—(*Off-mike*) Who's in there? As if I didn't know.

HOPE.—(*Falsetto*) Go away, Dean, we're not here any more. I mean there aren't any boys in here!

COLONNA.—(*Off-mike*) I'll see about that!

SOUND.—*Door opens.*

HOPE, GOODWIN, ELVIA, AND BLANCHE.—(*All giggle like girls*) Hello, Dean!

COLONNA.—Greetings, Gate! Are these the "Four Daughters"—or is it something I ate?

ELVIA.—No, Dean Colonna, these are our grandmothers!

GOODWIN.—(*Falsetto*) Yes, I'm Cobina's grandmother!

COLONNA.—Oh, grandma, what big teeth you have!

HOPE.—(*Falsetto*) The better to sell Pepsodent with, my dear! . . . And I'm Brenda's grandmother—*believe me, kid!*

GOODWIN.—(*Whispers*) Hey, Bob, pssst! Look at your dress. It fell off!

COLONNA.—Aha! A grandmother in Hart, Schaffner and Marx unmentionables!

HOPE.—Quick, Brenda! Turn out the lights!

SOUND.—*Click.*

BRENDA.—Run for it, boys!

HOPE.—Come on, Brenda! Give me your hand so you won't trip in the dark!

SOUND.—*Running footsteps.*

HOPE.—At last! We're alone! . . . Kiss me, Brenda!

SOUND.—*Loud kiss.*

HOPE.—Hey, what are you doing with that fuzz on your lip? Are you Brenda?

COLONNA.—No, I'm Dean Colonna—*believe me, kid!*

MUSIC.—*Play off.*

GOODWIN.—For thrills . . . chills . . . action . . . romance . . . tune in Pepsodent's smashing dramatic hit Mr. District Attorney—every Sunday night on another network.

Judy Garland appeared on tonight's program through the courtesy of Metro-Goldwyn-Mayer.

Don't forget Pepsodent with Irium brings you Bob Hope next Tuesday night at this same time.

This is the National Broadcasting Company.

The Aldrich Family

by CLIFFORD GOLDSMITH

IN THE person of Henry Aldrich, Clifford Goldsmith has introduced to radio one of the best comedy characters on the air today. The mad skirmishes between his extremes of buoyancy and depression are all very ludicrous and pathetic and believable. He is the same Henry who had so much trouble with authority in "What a Life" and, in fact, came directly to radio from Broadway, together with all his bad habits, his impecuniousness, his schemes, his suspicions, his parents. And, what is more important, he came with Ezra Stone, who created the role in the original stage production. He is a combination of Penrod Schofield, Baby Snooks, Willie Baxter, Tom Sawyer, and quite a little bit of himself. With this show Clifford Goldsmith revealed himself as one of the most resourceful writers in radio.

Here is a Halloween story, heard on October 31, 1939.

The Aldrich Family

Music.—*Jell-O pudding fanfare.*

Mrs. Aldrich.—(*Calling*) *Hen-ry! Henry Aldrich.*"

Henry.—"*Coming, mother!*"

Music.—"*This Is It*" . . . *Fade out behind.*

Von Zell.—The Aldrich Family! Starring Ezra Stone and written by Clifford Goldsmith, brought to you by Jell-O puddings, those delicious new desserts all America's talking about!

Music.—*Stone opening . . . fade for.*

Von Zell.—Do you remember when *you* were in your teens? Well, when you listen to Henry Aldrich and his pals, we think you'll sorta be able to detect a little of yourself. For Henry Aldrich is a typical American boy, from a typical American family. Just listen, and see if I'm not right.

Music.—*Out.*

Von Zell.—As our scene opens we find the Aldriches seated at the dinner table.

Mary.—Have I told you what I'm going to wear, mother?

Mrs. Aldrich.—No, Mary.

Mary.—I'm going to sew maple leaves all over my dress.

Mr. Aldrich.—*Where* are you going to wear a dress like that?

Mary.—To the Halloween party tomorrow night, father. Wherever you look, all you'll see of me is maple leaves.

Henry.—Maple leaves?

Mary.—Yes.

Henry.—You're going as a tree?

MARY.—As a tree that's just turned.

MRS. ALDRICH.—Henry, eat your lemon pie.

HENRY.—I don't care for any pie, mother. Father, was there a letter of any kind for me this morning?

MR. ALDRICH.—Nothing that I saw, Henry.

HENRY.—Are you sure you looked carefully?

MR. ALDRICH.—There was a letter, if I remember, for your sister.

MARY.—That was my invitation to the party.

HENRY.—Oh.

MRS. ALDRICH.—And what are you going to wear, Henry?

HENRY.—I, mother? I'm not even going.

MRS. ALDRICH.—Aren't you invited, Henry?

HENRY.—Mother, the reason I'm not going is I don't care to. That's the only reason in the world I'm not going.

MRS. ALDRICH.—(*Impressed*) Well, Henry.

HENRY.—Of course.

MRS. ALDRICH.—Aren't you even going to *taste* your pie, Henry?

HENRY.—I'm not hungry.

MR. ALDRICH.—Let me look at you, Henry.

HENRY.—Father, mother, may I be excused from the table?

MRS. ALDRICH.—If you don't want anything more.

HENRY.—(*Fading*) There's something I want to see in here.

MRS. ALDRICH.—(*Low*) Sam, *what* is the matter with Henry?

MR. ALDRICH.—After all, Alice, just because a boy isn't going to eat a piece of your lemon meringue pie doesn't mean that he is coming down with anything.

MRS. ALDRICH.—Well, I know it isn't the pie. That's the best crust I ever made.

HENRY.—(*Off*) Mary, where did you put that invitation you got?

MARY.—On the living room table, I guess.

MRS. ALDRICH.—(*Low*) Why do you suppose he wants to look at that?

MARY.—(*Calling*) Why do you want to look at it, Henry?

HENRY.—(*Off*) No reason. I was just wondering what kind Kathleen sent out this year.

MRS. ALDRICH.—Mary, *has* Henry received any invitation?

MARY.—Why, I supposed he had.

MR. ALDRICH.—Alice, may I have another piece of that pie, please?

MRS. ALDRICH.—Sam, can't you think of anything but your appetite when something may be wrong with your son?

MR. ALDRICH.—What would you like to have me do?

MRS. ALDRICH.—You can at least call him in and talk to him, dear.

MR. ALDRICH.—Yes, of course. (*Calling*) Henry.

HENRY.—(*Off*) Yes, father.

MR. ALDRICH.—Won't you come here, please?

HENRY.—(*On*) Yes, father.

MR. ALDRICH.—Henry, your mother would like to speak with you.

MRS. ALDRICH.—Sam Aldrich!

HENRY.—You'd like to speak to me, mother?

MRS. ALDRICH.—(*Trying to be very casual*) Tell me, Henry, you've *had* an invitation to go to that party tomorrow night?

HENRY.—An invitation?

MRS. ALDRICH.—Yes.

MR. ALDRICH.—Can't you answer your mother, Henry?

HENRY.—But, father, even if Kathleen begged me, I wouldn't want to go.

MARY.—Why not?

HENRY.—Because, in the first place, I went to her party last year. You certainly don't think I want to go 2 years in succession, do you?

MARY.—Well, *I* want to go again this year.

HENRY.—But, Mary, you're an entirely different type from me. You're much more easily amused.

MARY.—Why, Henry Aldrich!

HENRY.—But, you are, Mary. The whole thing is so foolish. All they do is dress up in costumes.

MARY.—But they dance, Henry.

HENRY.—Sure. That's another thing. They dance.

MRS. ALDRICH.—All right, dear, all right. But we aren't deaf!

HENRY.—(*In the same pitch*) I'm not shouting, mother. I just want you to understand how I feel. (*Continued*) And besides, Barbara Pearson isn't even going to be at the party.

MARY.—But Betty Walker is.

HENRY.—Betty Walker is?

MARY.—Of course.

HENRY.—Is that right? Well (*fading*), even so, I still wouldn't be interested.

MRS. ALDRICH.—Where are you going, Henry?

HENRY.—(*Off*) Just into the living room.

MRS. ALDRICH.—(*Low*) I'm going in there and talk to him.

MR. ALDRICH.—(*Off slightly, . . . and determined*) May I have a piece of pie, please?

MRS. ALDRICH.—You'll have to eat Henry's.

MR. ALDRICH.—(*Off*) Thank you.

MRS. ALDRICH.—Henry.

HENRY.—What are you coming in here for, mother?

MRS. ALDRICH.—Henry, sit down a minute.

HENRY.—Well?

MRS. ALDRICH.—What *are* you going to do tomorrow night?

HENRY.—Nothing.

MRS. ALDRICH.—Not a thing? Mary is going to be out, and your father and I will be out.

HENRY.—But if Kathleen doesn't want me, I hope you don't think I'd go, do you?

MRS. ALDRICH.—It isn't because she doesn't want you, dear. You must remember, Mary and Kathleen are older than you.

HENRY.—What difference should that make?

MRS. ALDRICH.—Well, there may be times when they would prefer being with boys of their own age. Don't you think there might?

SOUND.—*Door opens off.*

DIZZY.—(*Off*) Hi, Henry! Is it all right to come in without knocking?

HENRY.—Where did you come from, Dizzy?

DIZZY.—(*On*) I just dropped in to see about something. Evening, Mr. Aldrich. Where, where is Mary?

MARY.—(*Approaching*) Here I am.

DIZZY.—Hi! I'll bet you can't guess what I've got in this big box, here.

MARY.—What is it?

DIZZY.—It's my costume for the party. Would you like to have me show you folks a private preview?

MARY.—I don't think you better show it, Dizzy.

HENRY.—I'm not going to the party.

DIZZY.—You're not going, Henry? You're not going!?

MARY.—He wasn't invited, Dizzy.

MRS. ALDRICH.—Mary!

HENRY.—That's not the reason I'm not going.

DIZZY.—But I'm positive you were invited!

HENRY.—You are?

DIZZY.—Sure. At least, I *thought* she told me she was going to invite you.

HENRY.—Father!

MR. ALDRICH.—Yes, Henry.

HENRY.—Are you sure there wasn't any mail for me this morning?

MR. ALDRICH.—Yes, Henry, I am quite positive.

HENRY.—Well what do you know about that?

DIZZY.—It'll probably come in tomorrow's mail.

MARY.—Henry, I thought you didn't care anything about going.

HENRY.—I don't, Mary. Only don't you think if Kathleen's decent enough to think of me, I shouldn't offend her?

DIZZY.—Gee, the whole town's going to be there.

HENRY.—Who?

DIZZY.—The same gang we had last year.

HENRY.—Yeah? The whole crowd? Is that right?

DIZZY.—Sure.

HENRY.—Father, I know this is unexpected, but could I have enough money to rent a costume?

MR. ALDRICH.—About how much would it come to?

DIZZY.—Well, I'll tell you what I got for $2.

MARY.—Dizzy!

DIZZY.—I don't mind telling you.

MR. ALDRICH.—For $2?

DIZZY.—You can get costumes at any price. Say, Henry, I just had an idea. Why don't I take my costume back, and you and I rent one together?

HENRY.—Just one for the two of us?

DIZZY.—Sure.

HENRY.—What kind?

DIZZY.—They've got a horse there they'll rent for $6.

HENRY.—A horse?

DIZZY.—Sure, we'll go as a horse!

HENRY.—Do you think any girl would want to dance with a horse, Dizzy?

MRS. ALDRICH.—Well, whether they would or not, we're not spending any $6 on a costume.

DIZZY.—I'll pay three-fifty, Mrs. Aldrich, if Henry'll let me be the front end.

MRS. ALDRICH.—It seems to me we ought to be able to fix up a very nice costume right here at home.

DIZZY.—In the way of a horse, Mrs. Aldrich.

MRS. ALDRICH.—Perhaps not a horse, exactly.

MARY.—Why don't you go as a ghost, Henry?

HENRY.—I wore a ghost costume once, Mary, and practically suffocated.

MARY.—That shouldn't be so bad.

HENRY.—Did you ever dance with a sheet over your head?

MARY.—I've danced with some boys that might just as well have had.

DIZZY.—You're not referring to me, are you, Mary?

MRS. ALDRICH.—Sam, I know of the very thing.

MR. ALDRICH.—What is it?

MRS. ALDRICH.—It's upstairs in the attic!

HENRY.—In our attic?

MRS. ALDRICH.—Sam, do you remember that costume you wore when we went to that dance just after we were married?

MR. ALDRICH.—I do.

HENRY.—What is it?

MRS. ALDRICH.—George Washington!

HENRY.—George Washington! George Washington! Mother, do you think I want to go to a Halloween party as George Washington?

MRS. ALDRICH.—I certainly don't see why you couldn't.

MARY.—I know where the costume is, mother. (*Fading*) I'll run up and get it.

HENRY.—You needn't get it for me, Mary.

MRS. ALDRICH.—But wait, dear. You haven't seen it.

DIZZY.—Between ourselves, Mrs. Aldrich, I think Henry would look better as a horse.

MR. ALDRICH.—That costume was good enough for me to wear once.

MRS. ALDRICH.—And you took first prize in it.

DIZZY.—Was it a Halloween party, Mr. Aldrich?

MR. ALDRICH.—No, I wouldn't say it was a Halloween party.

HENRY.—In all my life I have never seen George Washington at a Halloween party.

MRS. ALDRICH.—That's the point. No one has ever thought of it before.

HENRY.—Dizzy, would you like to swap with me, and you go as George Washington and take first prize?

MARY.—(*Approaching*) Here it is, Henry. Look, Henry, it's darling!

HENRY.—Blue satin trousers!

MR. ALDRICH.—Of course.

HENRY.—And they're short trousers! What do I wear below them?

MRS. ALDRICH.—You wear your black shoes and a pair of my stockings.

HENRY.—Your stockings, mother!

MRS. ALDRICH.—Who will know the difference?

HENRY.—Well, at least I will! You don't think I could ever hold my head up in your stockings, do you?

DIZZY.—Look at the coat, Henry.

HENRY.—Sure! It's even got lace on it!

MRS. ALDRICH.—Just put it on, so we can see how you look.

HENRY.—Mother!

MRS. ALDRICH.—Please put it on, dear.

HENRY.—Okay.

MARY.—And here's the wig.

HENRY.—Mary!

MRS. ALDRICH.—Henry!

HENRY.—I'll put it on, but my heart won't be in it.

MRS. ALDRICH.—My goodness, dear. Stand back. Push the wig up off your eyes.

HENRY.—Like this?

MARY.—Not all the way back, Henry.

MRS. ALDRICH.—Dear, you look just exactly the way your father did that night he wore that to the ball.

MR. ALDRICH.—(*Startled*) I looked like that?

DIZZY.—To me he looks quite a little like a horse.

HENRY.—Mother! Couldn't I please rent a costume?

MRS. ALDRICH.—Do you have enough allowance left?

HENRY.—If you'd give me a little extra.

MR. ALDRICH.—I thought we were going to keep within your allowance, Henry.

HENRY.—Say! I know what I can do!

DIZZY.—What?

HENRY.—Never mind! Wait till you see me. Father, could I borrow your hammer and saw tomorrow?

MR. ALDRICH.—What for, Henry?

HENRY.—I'm going to make my costume.

MUSIC.—*Bridge.*

SOUND.—*Hammer pounding on metal.*

MRS. ALDRICH.—(*Off*) Henry! Henry Aldrich!

DIZZY.—(*On*) Henry!

SOUND.—*The pounding stops.*

HENRY.—What'll you have, Dizzy?

DIZZY.—Your mother's calling you.

HENRY.—(*Calling*) You calling me, mother?

MRS. ALDRICH.—Where are you?

HENRY.—Down in the basement.

MRS. ALDRICH.—Doing what?

HENRY.—Making my costume.

MRS. ALDRICH.—What are you making it out of? Sheet iron?

HENRY.—Wait'll you see it! Has the morning mail come yet!

MRS. ALDRICH.—Not yet, dear.

HENRY.—Well, the minute it does, let me know.

MRS. ALDRICH.—(*Fading*) All right.

HENRY.—Dizzy, are you sure Kathleen is sending me an invitation?

DIZZY.—She's sending one to practically everyone else.

HENRY.—Isn't that strange?

SOUND.—*The pounding starts.*

DIZZY.—Henry! Henry! Hey, Henry!

SOUND.—*The pounding stops.*

HENRY.—You speaking to me?

DIZZY.—*Why* won't you tell me what you're making?

HENRY.—Sure, then you'll go and tell everybody else, and all the girls will know who I am.

DIZZY.—You aren't going to go as a locomotive, are you?

HENRY.—A locomotive! (*The pounding begins and stops*) Could you hold this wash boiler up just a minute?

DIZZY.—You're going to put it on, Henry?

HENRY.—Sure. Now wait'll I get my arms through these holes I knocked in it. (*Cloth tears*) Gee did I tear my shirt a little?

DIZZY.—Only about 6 inches.

HENRY.—I've got my arms through.

DIZZY.—Isn't that hole for your neck a little tight?

HENRY.—It feels quite comfortable. Now look, Dizzy, you see those pieces of stovepipe there?

DIZZY.—Don't tell me you're going to put those on, too.

HENRY.—When I raise my right leg, you slip one on.

DIZZY.—(*Grunting as we hear the metal scratching*) When you once get this all on tonight, Henry, how are you going to be moved to the party?

HENRY.—This won't be hard to walk in.

DIZZY.—Noooo!

HENRY.—Now you see those tin cans over there?

DIZZY.—Say, Henry, do you realize this is a dance we're going to?

HENRY.—Put one can on each foot. And don't talk.

DIZZY.—Remember, though, if you tip over, you're as good as lost.

HENRY.—Got them on?

DIZZY.—Yes. Now let's see you walk.

SOUND.—*Mild clanking.*

HENRY.—See that, Dizzy. There's practically nothing to it.

DIZZY.—The girls'll have a nice time dancing with you. They just might as well waltz with a meat grinder.

HENRY.—Dizzy, you see that tin funnel right here on the floor?

DIZZY.—Yeah.

HENRY.—Could you please pick it up for me?

DIZZY.—What are you going to do with that?

HENRY.—That's my hat. I'm the Tin Woodman from "The Wizard of Oz."

SOUND.—*Door bell rings off.*

HENRY.—Mother! Mother!

DIZZY.—Are you dying, Henry?

MRS. ALDRICH.—(*Off*) Yes, Henry.

HENRY.—Is that the mailman?

MRS. ALDRICH.—I think it is, dear.

HENRY.—Well, wait. *I'll* be right up.

SOUND.—*Metal clanking as he starts to walk.*

DIZZY.—Henry, you're going to kill yourself.

HENRY.—I'm going to get my invitation. Come on.

SOUND.—*Clanking.*

DIZZY.—You don't think I'm going to walk behind you and risk my life, do you?

SOUND.—*Clanking continues.*

MRS. ALDRICH.—(*Closer*) What in the world is going on there?

HENRY.—Nothing, mother. I'm just coming upstairs.

DIZZY.—It's Frankenstein, Mrs. Aldrich.

SOUND.—*Terrific crash.*

HENRY.—(*Yelling*) Dizzy! Catch me!

MRS. ALDRICH.—(*Screams*) Henry!

SOUND.—*Clanking stops.*

MRS. ALDRICH.—Henry Aldrich, what on earth did you fall into?

HENRY.—I was in it before I fell. It's your wash boiler.

DIZZY.—Stop talking, Henry; and when I lift your head up, hold your legs stiff.

HENRY.—(*Grunting*) Okay.

SOUND.—*Clanking.*

DIZZY.—(*Grunting*) I got you part way up.

HENRY.—Come on now. A little higher.

DIZZY.—If you fall down at the dance, Henry, you needn't count on me. There!

HENRY.—Okay.

SOUND.—*Clanking up the stairs.*

MRS. ALDRICH.—Henry, you can't go to any dance in that outfit.

HENRY.—Mother, it's just a case of getting used to it.

DIZZY.—Of who getting used to it?

HENRY.—Has the mail come?

MRS. ALDRICH.—I suppose it is at the front door.

HENRY.—Well, gee whiz, let me go and get it.

DIZZY.—I'd like to see you tear an envelope open in that outfit.

SOUND.—*Metal scratching on wood.*

MRS. ALDRICH.—Just a minute, Henry, I'll open the door for you. We would still like to use that door.

SOUND.—*Door opens.*

HENRY.—Thank you, mother.

SOUND.—*Clanking continues.*

MRS. ALDRICH.—*Must* you walk on the hardwood floors?

HENRY.—I won't scratch them.

SOUND.—*Metal scratching on wood.*

MARY.—(*Approaching*) Here's the mail, mother.

HENRY.—Could you give me mine, Mary?

MARY.—Well, for goodness sakes, Henry!

DIZZY.—I won't let him hurt you.

HENRY.—Won't you hand me my invitation, Mary?

MARY.—Look at all there is. Here are two letters for mother, one for father.

HENRY.—Never mind those, Mary. I'd like mine.

MARY.—Well, just a minute, Henry. Here's one for me.

DIZZY.—Kathleen's invitations are in yellow envelopes.

MARY.—Here are two more for father. (*Curious*) One of them is from Buffalo, New York.

HENRY.—Mary! Is Buffalo, New York, important at a time like this?

MARY.—There isn't any for you.

HENRY.—I know; but how could a thing like that happen? (*Clanking*)

MRS. ALDRICH.—Henry, dear, would you mind not sitting down in that good chair with that wash boiler on? (*Clanking*)

HENRY.—But, gee whiz, all this work for nothing. I thought, Dizzy, you said she was going to invite me.

DIZZY.—Well, don't blame me if she didn't, Henry.

HENRY.—I've got to stay home tonight?

MARY.—Henry, I'm going over to Kathleen's later on, and I'll ask her whether you are invited?

HENRY.—Oh, no, you won't, Mary. If she doesn't want to send me an invitation, she needn't.

MRS. ALDRICH.—Mary! If Kathleen does mention the party tonight, I think it would be perfectly all right to at least give her a chance to ask whether Henry is coming.

MARY.—Of course it would.

DIZZY.—You're marring the wallpaper, Henry.

HENRY.—Well, can you stand me up, please?

MARY.—Shall I speak to Kathleen, Henry?

HENRY.—Don't ask her outright, Mary. Just say it's too bad Henry hasn't any place to go tonight. Sort of subtle, see?

MUSIC.—*Play off.*

VON ZELL.—Henry Aldrich will be back with us in just a moment. Well, as the feller says, there's a time for everything! And, folks, the season that lies just ahead of us is sure the time for parties! From Halloween in October, all the way through April Fools' Day! And all of 'em mean good things to eat, too! Swell dishes like Jell-O Butterscotch Pudding! You know, just about everybody is making Jell-O Butterscotch Pudding a "part of the party" these days, the real guest of honor! And no wonder! This grand, golden dessert has a truly festive flavor that fits in with all kinds of fun and feasting! It has all the gay appearance of a party dish, too, especially when served with snowy whipped cream, dark delicious dates, or maybe a sprinkling of shredded coconut! But the big thing is its marvelous mellow taste! That wonderful, buttery, brown-sugar flavor that everybody loves! So keep Jell-O Butterscotch Pudding handy for all party occasions, along with those two other tempting desserts: smooth, delicate Jell-O Vanilla and rich, glossy Jell-O Chocolate Puddings! Then you'll know why these new Jell-O puddings are the dessert all America's talking about!

MUSIC.—*Sneaks in during last few sentences . . . then up to a finish.*

MRS. ALDRICH.—(*Calling*) Mary!

MARY.—(*Off*) Yes, mother!

MRS. ALDRICH.—Will you ask Henry to come down here to the living room, please?

MARY.—Yes, mother. I'll call him.

MR. ALDRICH.—It seems rather late, though, to be breaking news like this to him, Alice.

MRS. ALDRICH.—Sam, do you think we really should go to that bridge party this evening?

MR. ALDRICH.—But we accepted the invitation weeks ago.

MRS. ALDRICH.—But, Sam, we ought to stay home with Henry. It's Halloween.

SOUND.—*Slow clanking off.*

HENRY.—(*Approaching*) Where are you, father?

MR. ALDRICH.—Right here, Henry.

HENRY.—(*On*) Just a minute while I make this turn.

MRS. ALDRICH.—Henry, your father wants to speak with you.

HENRY.—With me, father? With me?

MRS. ALDRICH.—I think I'll go upstairs.

MR. ALDRICH.—Henry, your mother has asked me to give you a rather unpleasant message.

HENRY.—Well?

MR. ALDRICH.—Mary was over at Kathleen's a few minutes ago.

HENRY.—Well?

MR. ALDRICH.—I'm afraid, son, you're not invited.

HENRY.—Kathleen said I wasn't?

MR. ALDRICH.—All I know is Mary assumed from Kathleen's conversation you were not.

HENRY.—But, gee whiz, I must be. I'm practically the only one in the whole crowd that isn't.

MR. ALDRICH.—(*Kindly*) Don't you suppose there will be other Halloweens?

HENRY.—I certainly hope there won't be any more like this.

MR. ALDRICH.—Henry, there are going to be a great many times in your life when things won't go exactly the way you'd like to have them. And when they do, there's only one way to take them.

HENRY.—But, dad, this is so trivial. Kathleen just forgot to ask me.

MR. ALDRICH.—Whether she forgot or not, the gentlemanly thing to do is stay away from any party to which you are not invited.

MARY.—(*Approaching*) Father, where's mother?

MR. ALDRICH.—Upstairs, I think, Mary.

MARY.—(*On*) Henry, do you think I look like a maple tree?

HENRY.—(*Holding back the tears*) Sure. (*Clanking*)

MARY.—Where are you going?

HENRY.—(*Fading*) Up to my room. Where do you think? And take this off. (*Clanking*)

MR. ALDRICH.—Why are you putting on your coat this early, Mary?

MARY.—I'm taking some cakes over to Kathleen's, father. And when Tommy Bush comes back, tell him his costume is right here in the hall.

MR. ALDRICH.—He's going to put it on here?

MARY.—It's so much nearer to Kathleen's if he does.

SOUND.—*Door opens.*

MRS. ALDRICH.—(*Off*) Don't stay out too late, Mary.

MARY.—I won't. Good-by.

SOUND.—*Door closes.*

MRS. ALDRICH.—Get your things on, Sam.

MR. ALDRICH.—(*Calling*) Henry! Henry!

HENRY.—(*Off*) Yes, father.

MR. ALDRICH.—Come down here a minute.

HENRY.—(*Approaching*) You changed your mind? I can go anyhow?

MRS. ALDRICH.—No, dear. Will you try to understand if your father and I go out to an engagement that we promised to go to a long time ago?

HENRY.—I'll be here all alone?

MRS. ALDRICH.—You mean to say a boy as old as you minds being alone?

HENRY.—No, I don't mind, mother. But I'm going to be *all* alone?

MRS. ALDRICH.—If we didn't have to go, we wouldn't think of leaving you.

MR. ALDRICH.—If anyone comes to the front door, Henry, I'd be very careful whom I let in.

HENRY.—You think anything might happen?

MR. ALDRICH.—No, not a thing. But on Halloween I'd simply be careful. Put the chain on the door.

HENRY.—Sure.

MRS. ALDRICH.—Good night, dear.

HENRY.—Good night.

MR. ALDRICH.—Good night, son.

SOUND.—*Door opens.*

MRS. ALDRICH.—Don't sit up too late.

HENRY.—I won't.

MRS. ALDRICH.—(*Off*) Good night.

SOUND.—*Door closes . . . Telephone rings . . . it rings again . . . slow clanking*

HENRY.—I'm coming to the phone. (*Clanking . . . receiver lifts*) Hello? Who? Mary isn't in right now. Mrs. Aldrich isn't in either. No, ma'am. There's nobody here but me. Is that you Aunt Harriet? Gee, I'm certainly glad to hear your voice. No I don't mind being alone. What is there to be afraid of? (*Door bell rings*) I wonder what that could be? Our front doorbell rang. (*Doorbell rings . . . voice low*) Hold the line, while I look out the window and see who it is. (*Pause . . . clanking . . . doorbell rings . . . pause . . . clanking . . . voice low*) Aunt Harriet, are you still there? I think it's a man in a brown coat. Yeah, he's got a hat on. (*Doorbell rings*) I'm not afraid. Gee whiz, what is there to be afraid about? You wouldn't like to get in your car and come over, would you?

SOUND.—*Doorbell rings . . . pounding on door.*

DIZZY.—(*Off*) Hey, Henry! Can't you let a guy in here?

HENRY.—(*Coming to life*) Aunt Harriet, I've got to let Dizzy in! Good-by! (*Receiver hangs up . . . clanking . . . pounding on door*) Is that you I see through the window, Dizzy?

DIZZY.—(*Off*) Who do you think it is?

SOUND.—*Door opens.*

HENRY.—Hi!

DIZZY.—Hi. Come on, Henry. Let's start for the party.

HENRY.—I'm not going.

DIZZY.—You're not going?

HENRY.—Kathleen didn't invite me.

DIZZY.—All right, what if she didn't? Come along anyhow.

HENRY.—No.

DIZZY.—Who'll know the difference?

HENRY.—Mary will be there.

DIZZY.—What's that package there on the floor?

HENRY.—How should I know what it is?

DIZZY.—It's from the Century Costume Company. That's where I got my outfit.

HENRY.—It's probably something Mary was going to use.

DIZZY.—I wonder what it is? Do you mind if I open it just a little?

HENRY.—I don't care whether you open it.

SOUND.—*A string breaks . . . paper rattles.*

DIZZY.—Henry! Look!

HENRY.—What about it?

DIZZY.—Look at it! It's the horse they wanted to rent me!

HENRY.—(*Interested*) Yeah?

DIZZY.—Henry, why don't we use this?

HENRY.—It isn't ours.

DIZZY.—Is Mary going to wear it?

HENRY.—Of course she isn't.

DIZZY.—Is your father going to?

HENRY.—(*Pleading*) Listen, Dizzy, my father said it wouldn't be right for me to go any place I'm not invited.

DIZZY.—Who's going to know you're even there? I'll be in the front legs, and you'll be in the back. Kathleen and Mary won't even see you.

HENRY.—You don't think so?

DIZZY.—How could they? Here, put on the pants for the hind legs.

HENRY.—Okay.

DIZZY.—I'll be getting into the front legs. Here, throw this blanket over your head. (*At this point the conversation of both boys becomes slightly muffled*) I'll put my head up inside the horse.

HENRY.—Okay.

DIZZY.—Now put your hands on my shoulders. Can you see?

HENRY.—Did you ever try to see in pitch dark? Let's go.

DIZZY.—How are we going to open the front door?

HENRY.—That's for you to figure out. Can you find it?

DIZZY.—I think so. No. Wait a minute, Henry, these are the hall stairs we're starting up.

HENRY.—This isn't going to lead to any good, Dizzy.

SOUND.—*Door opens.*

DIZZY.—I've got the front door now. You close it as we go out.

HENRY.—Sure. I hope I closed it.

DIZZY.—Be careful of the front steps, Henry. (*We hear them going down the steps*) Are you down yet?

HENRY.—How would I know?

DIZZY.—Come on, now, let's run.

HENRY.—You're crazy!

DIZZY.—Come on! Get up, there! (*There's a thud*) Ouch! Henry! I think I broke my neck.

HENRY.—What's the matter?

DIZZY.—I think we hit a tree!

MUSIC.—*Bridge . . . segue to dance music from a piano . . . voices . . . Halloween horns and general confusion . . . the voices of Dizzy and Henry are still muffled when they speak.*

HENRY.—Dizzy! Dizzy!

DIZZY.—Where are you, Henry?

HENRY.—I'm right where I've been for the last 2 hours. Inside this horse.

DIZZY.—You ever have a better time, Henry? We've danced with every girl here.

HENRY.—What fun do you think I've had?

DIZZY.—Four times we've danced with your sister.

HENRY.—She probably thinks we're somebody else.

DIZZY.—Keep quiet, Henry. (*Falsetto*) How do you do, Miss. Would you like this dance? Oh, pardon me!

HENRY.—What's the matter?

DIZZY.—That's a chair.

MARY.—Hello, Tommy.

TOMMY.—(*Sulking*) Hello, Mary. What I want to know, Mary, is who's inside that horse.

MARY.—Why?

TOMMY.—There are several reasons. And if it's the one I think it is . . .

HENRY.—(*Low*) Come on, Dizzy. Let's get away from here.

DIZZY.—Maybe we better.

HENRY.—Let's go over and try to get some punch.

MUSIC.—*Begins again.*

DIZZY.—I can't drink any more.

HENRY.—Maybe you can't, but I haven't had any yet. Come on.

DIZZY.—How are you going to drink it under there?

HENRY.—Can't you pass it under your legs?

DIZZY.—Okay. Come on. (*A terrific crash of glass . . . people scream*) Let's go.

HENRY.—What was that?

DIZZY.—That was the punch.

HENRY.—Tell me, Dizzy, have you seen Betty Walker?

DIZZY.—Sure. We just finished dancing with her, you dope.

HENRY.—With my girl? Are the decorations nice?

DIZZY.—They're swell.

HENRY.—I think I would have been a lot better off if I'd stayed home.

DIZZY.—(*Falsetto*) How do you do, Mary Aldrich. Would you like to dance once more?

MARY.—Won't you tell me who you are?

DIZZY.—I'm the Prince Charming that was turned into a dragon. Come on, Mary.

HENRY.—Dizzy, this is no time to tango.

DIZZY.—I like to tango.

MARY.—What was that?

DIZZY.—Nothing. I was just talking to myself.

TOMMY.—Wait a minute there! Who's inside that horse?

SOUND.—*Thud.*

HENRY.—Who hit me?

TOMMY.—I did.

MARY.—Tommy Bush!

SOUND.—*Thud.*

DIZZY.—Cut it out. Do you want to choke me to death?

TOMMY.—Let me pull that thing off your head!

MARY.—Henry Aldrich! Where did you come from?

HENRY.—I?

TOMMY.—I *thought* this was where my costume went.

MARY.—Henry, do you realize father has telephoned here twice for you?

HENRY.—He wants me?

TOMMY.—And you can pay for this costume!

DIZZY.—Where are you going, Henry? I think I'd better be leaving.

HENRY.—I'm going home.

MUSIC.—*Bridge.*

MR. ALDRICH.—Henry, I don't believe I've ever been quite so disappointed.

HENRY.—But, father. I don't think Kathleen even knew I was there.

MR. ALDRICH.—That isn't the point, Henry. I left you here on your honor. Not only did you take a costume that didn't belong to you, but when your mother and I came home, we found the front door wide open.

HENRY.—*Wide* open?

MR. ALDRICH.—Well, Henry, what are we going to do about it?

HENRY.—What would you suggest, father?

MR. ALDRICH.—I think it would be much better for you to do the suggesting.

HENRY.—I have to tell you what my own punishment is to be?

MR. ALDRICH.—You do. And I want you to tell me quickly.

HENRY.—Well, would you—would you be willing not to give me any allowance for the next 4 weeks?

MR. ALDRICH.—I think that is an excellent suggestion.

HENRY.—All right. No allowance for the next 4 weeks.

MR. ALDRICH.—And what else would you suggest?

HENRY.—What else?

MR. ALDRICH.—That is what I said.

HENRY.—Well, suppose I go to bed an hour early every night next week?

MR. ALDRICH.—That is agreeable with you?

HENRY.—Yes, sir. I realize I've got to learn sometime, and I might as well get it over.

MR. ALDRICH.—Would you like to suggest anything more?

HENRY.—Anything more? Well, I'm pretty sure that's enough to make me *think* the next time.

MR. ALDRICH.—And you have nothing else to suggest?

HENRY.—Supposing I help mother with the dishes all next week, too?

MR. ALDRICH.—You've never had a punishment as severe as this, have you, Henry?

HENRY.—I'll say I haven't.

MR. ALDRICH.—You're quite sure you feel it is only fair.

HENRY.—Yes, sir.

MRS. ALDRICH.—(*Approaching*) Sam.

MR. ALDRICH.—Yes, Alice.

MRS. ALDRICH.—Are you and Henry through?

MR. ALDRICH.—We are. Supposing you march up to bed, son.

HENRY.—Good night, mother.

MRS. ALDRICH.—Good night, dear.

HENRY.—And I want you to know, father, I feel pretty much ashamed to think I went to the party.

MRS. ALDRICH.—I'm glad to hear you say that, dear.

MR. ALDRICH.—No allowance next month, to bed an hour early every night next week, and you're to help your mother with the dishes every day.

HENRY.—Yes, sir. And if you can think of anything else you'd like to have me do, I'd be glad to do that, too.

MR. ALDRICH.—That will be all.

HENRY.—(*Off*) Good night, father.

MRS. ALDRICH.—(*Low*) Sam, no boy ever lived that didn't disobey his parents now and then.

MR. ALDRICH.—And by the same token, no boy ever lived that didn't have to be punished now and then.

HENRY.—(*Off*) Father.

MR. ALDRICH.—Yes, Henry.

HENRY.—I almost forgot to tell you. Aunt Harriet phoned just after you left.

MRS. ALDRICH.—What did she want, dear?

HENRY.—She said she wrote you a letter a couple days ago and wondered why you hadn't answered it.

MRS. ALDRICH.—Thank you, Henry.

MR. ALDRICH.—I remember getting it yesterday morning. I put it here on the living room table.

MRS. ALDRICH.—It isn't there now, dear.

SOUND.—*Drawer opens.*

MR. ALDRICH.—Here it is in this table drawer with the rest of my mail.

MRS. ALDRICH.—What does she say?

MR. ALDRICH.—Well, well. I wonder . . .

MRS. ALDRICH.—Is it some bad news?

MR. ALDRICH.—I'm not even looking at her letter. I'm looking at this one addressed to Henry.

MRS. ALDRICH.—To Henry? Sam Aldrich, that's Henry's invitation!

MR. ALDRICH.—How did it get in with my mail?

MRS. ALDRICH.—You got the mail yesterday morning yourself, Sam. I remember distinctly your getting it.

MR. ALDRICH.—Yes, yes. Henry, Henry!

HENRY.—(*Off*) Yes, father?

MR. ALDRICH.—Could you come down here a minute, please?

HENRY.—I've only got half of my pajamas on, father.

MRS. ALDRICH.—Please come down here at once! Sam Aldrich, I could cry.

HENRY.—(*Approaching*) Did you think of something else you want me to do, father?

MR. ALDRICH.—Henry, I just found something of yours in this top drawer.

HENRY.—You did?

MR. ALDRICH.—Supposing during next month, we double your allowance.

HENRY.—You double it?

MR. ALDRICH.—And if you would like to, you may stay up 15 minutes later than usual each evening next week.

HENRY.—Are you kidding me?

MR. ALDRICH.—And, Alice, during the same period, I'll help with the dishes.

HENRY.—Mother, is father out of his head?

MUSIC.—*Aldrich play off . . . segue to fast tune . . . fade for*

VON ZELL.—"On a recent trip to San Diego," says Mrs. Alice Franconi of Boston, Massachusetts, "my husband wrote me about a wonderful dessert he had discovered in a little Spanish restaurant there. He said the waiter told him it was 'Hel-yo' Pudding! So I searched every book I could find on Spanish cooking. But nothing doing, until suddenly I realized that 'Hel-yo' was merely the Spanish pronunciation of Jell-O!"

Well, this letter of Mrs. Franconi's was so interesting, ladies and gentlemen, that *we* wanted to meet her and wanted *you* to meet her, too; so we invited her to New York as a guest of Jell-O puddings, with all expenses paid. And she's standing right here beside me now. Mrs Franconi, what did your husband say when you told him about your discovery?

MRS. FRANCONI.—When he got home, I had a big bowlful of Jell-O vanilla pudding all ready for him, with dates and coconut in it, just the way he'd had it in San Diego. And we both agreed that the laugh was on him for traveling a couple of thousand miles to find a marvelous dessert that was never any farther away than our corner grocery! But, as my husband said, it was worth the trip!

VON ZELL.—Well, your husband's not alone in that, Mrs. Franconi! Thousands of *other* husbands, yes, and boys and girls, too, are going for Jell-O vanilla pudding every *day* in a big *way* because its mellow, thrilling vanilla flavor is just as good as it can be!

Folks, you'll all want to try this rich, creamy dessert, as well as Jell-O's delicious butterscotch pudding and Jell-O chocolate pudding, decorated with whitecaps of foamy whipped cream! So *tomorrow* do as all America's doing. Order all three of these popular new desserts: Jell-O chocolate, vanilla, and butterscotch pudding!

MUSIC.—*Up to finish.*

HENRY.—Mother.

MRS. ALDRICH.—Yes, Henry.

HENRY.—Would you like to have me go over to the store and get some soap?

MRS. ALDRICH.—Do we need any?

HENRY.—That isn't the point. I'm going to take up music.

MRS. ALDRICH.—I beg your pardon?

HENRY.—There's an advertisement here that says if you save 3,000 soap wrappers, you get a silver cornet free.

VON ZELL.—(*Chuckling*) Be sure to listen next week at this same time for more adventures of Henry Aldrich. The Aldrich Family, starring Ezra Stone, is written by Clifford Goldsmith. Original music composed and conducted by Jack Miller! Harry Von Zell speaking and wishing you good night, for those delicious new desserts all America's talking about Jell-O puddings!

MUSIC.—*Jell-O pudding fanfare.*

VON ZELL.—Erza Stone is now appearing at the Biltmore Theatre in the George Abbott Farce "See My Lawyer."

BEST VARIETY SHOW

The Pursuit of Happiness

by ERIK BARNOUW, JOHN TUCKER BATTLE, CARL CARMER, NORMAN CORWIN

THIS superb series had its origin in an idea conceived by Edward Klauber, executive vice-president for CBS. What he wanted was not easy to state and harder to satisfy: a show that was, first of all, thoroughly entertaining, but a show that was also rich in things American and one that would, at the same time, recall to the active, conscious mind of the listener an increasing respect for his own heritage by bringing him forgotten pages from the lives of his ancestors; reanimated pictures of events grown stale by repetition or bad handling; music that had a meaning and a history; authentic scenes of Americans, living and dead, in the midst of their great moments. And it did not matter whether these moments were fiery or placid.

The Pursuit of Happiness was a flag-waving show, and it had the good sense not only to admit this at the beginning but to insist upon it throughout the run of the series. Flag waver number one was Burgess Meredith, whose voice and youth and declamatory enthusiasms made him exactly right for a show of this kind. Flag waver number two was lumbering, neighborly Carl Carmer. Meredith waved the Stars and Stripes, while Carmer moved around in the woods, waving various flags depending on where he was: the Bunker Hill flag, the flag of the Federated Colonies, the Rattlesnake ("Don't Tread on Me") Revolutionary flag. Meredith kept the show going as master of ceremonies from one of Columbia's playhouses and introduced talent; Carmer (for many of the shows) moved around America and introduced the scenes and people he met.

With the aid of George Faulkner, one of radio's better writers, W. B. Lewis, CBS vice-president in charge of broadcasts, got the programs started and after a few weeks turned the responsibilities of its production over to his assistant, a brainy and tireless radio man named Davidson Taylor. Norman Corwin was the director for all the shows.

A great deal of material was explored in order to get the right dramatic spots for each show, and something of the immense energies that went into CBS' determination to find and deliver the best talent of the country can be appreciated from the list of performers who appeared in one or more of the shows. It was a magnificently ambitious undertaking, and it struck American audiences hard and joyously. Its suspension, after many months, removed from the air not only the nation's most American show but its best variety show as well.

Here are some of its guests:

Ray Middleton, Virginia Verrill, Eddie Green, Raymond Massey, Mary Jane Walsh, Joe Cook, Carl Carmer, Frederic March, Gertrude Niesen, Robert Benchley, Carl van Doren, Paul Robeson, Jimmie Durante, Walter Huston, Mary Eastman, Danny Kaye, Abbott and Costello, Charles Laughton, Elsa Lanchester, Jane Froman, Sterling Holloway, Maxine Sullivan, Louis Armstrong, Franchot Tone, Beatrice Kaye, Howard and Shelton, Joan Edwards, Philip Loeb, Gertrude Lawrence, Charles Ruggles, Jane Cowl, the Calypso Singers, the Marshalls, Clifton Fadiman, Ethel Barrymore, Charlie Butterworth, Philip Merivale, Ruth Gordon, Ethel Merman, Bert Lahr, Lon Chaney, Jr., Roman Bohnen, Doc Rockwell, Walter Hampden, Pinocchio, Richard Bennett, Whitford Kane, Maxwell Anderson, Kurt Wiell Ballad, Henry Hull, Betty Field, Mildred Bailey, Lionel Stander, Miriam Hopkins, Betty Hutton, Sam Levine, Frank Luther, Frances Farmer, Hiram Sherman, Barry Wood, Leadbelly, Kay Lorraine, Victor Moore, William Gaxton, Donald Cook, Nancy Carroll, Len Doyle, Buddy Clark, Roy Atwell, Rex Ingram, Orson Welles, Gale Sondergaard, Woody Guthrie, Edward Arnold, Ray Collins, Sheila Barrett, the Golden Gate Quartet, Walter Cassel, the Modernaires.

The show I have selected to reprint was heard on Sunday afternoon, January 7, 1940.

The Pursuit of Happiness

MUSIC.—*Theme.*

MEREDITH.—The Columbia Broadcasting System presents The Pursuit of Happiness, with Ruth Gordon, Philip Merivale, Eddie Green, Carl Carmer, Mary Jane Walsh, Mrs. Edward MacDowell, and, as your master of ceremonies, Burgess Meredith.

MUSIC.—"*Of Thee I Sing.*"

MEREDITH.—Life, liberty, and the pursuit of happiness—of these we sing.

Recently a young man, aged nine, who edits a little home magazine which he distributes to neighbors, wrote an editorial about this program of which we're very proud. He wrote . . .

BOY.—It makes you realize how when a country isn't *scared* all the time, the people make up fine songs and swell jokes and write good plays.

MEREDITH.—You said it, son. And these things, fine songs, swell jokes, good plays, they spring up in a land where a man can let himself go.

And so, with this in mind, here's a song in which two Broadway song writers let themselves go. (*Music in*) Their idea is almost a threat to our institutions, but we feel it deserves a hearing. Two New York boys, getting a little weary with their dizzy surroundings, suggest that we "Give It Back to the Indians!" The song is by Rodgers and Hart, and it's sung by Mary Jane Walsh, who does the number in the current Broadway hit "Too Many Girls."

MUSIC.—(*Orchestra and Walsh*) "*Give It Back to the Indians.*"

verse:

Old Peter Minuit had nothing to lose when he bought the isle of Manhattan.

For 24 dollars and a bottle of booze they threw in the Bronx and Staten.

Pete thought that he had the best of the bargain; but the poor red man just grinned,
And he grunted "ugh" meaning okay in his jargon for he knew Poor Pete was skinned.
We've tried to run the city, but the city ran away
And now Peter Minuit—we can't continue it—

Broadway's turning into Coney—Champagne Charlie's drinkin' gin.
Old New York is new and phoney—give it back to the Indians.
Even Harlem's getting darker—no more jokes to make us grin.
M.G.M.'s got Dotty Parker—Give it back to the Indians.
Take all your Reds on the boxes made for soap,
Whites on Fifth Avenue—Blues down in Wall Street losing hope.
Big Bargain today—Chief, take it away.
Come, you busted city slickers—better take it on the chin.
Father Knick has lost his knickers—give it back to the Indians.

The Music Hall has presentations—but you simply can't get in.
Try to jump those excavations—Give it back to the Indians.
Shakespeare doesn't get a showing when those strip-tease girls begin.
Yet "Tobacco Road" keeps going—Give it back to the Indians.
Bound on the North by the Bronx—a pretty view—
East by Long Island smoke,
West by New Jersey pots of glue,
South Brooklyn's asleep—Chief, no want to keep.
Swing bands give you heebie-jeebies; Dewey's put an end to sin
Men wear clothes like Lucius Beebe's—Give it back to the Indians.

MEREDITH.—Thank you, Mary Jane. Miss Walsh to me. And while we're busy letting ourselves go, who could be a better man to invite to the proceedings than Eddie Green?

GREEN.—Thank you.

MEREDITH.—You remember Eddie. When he lets his imagination loose on the history of our country, the results are amazing. For instance, Eddie, what do you think of the idea of giving Manhattan back to the Indians?

EDDIE.—I think the rights of minorities ought to be considered.

MEREDITH.—The rights of minorities? In what way?

EDDIE.—Well, Mr. Meredith, you got to consider those poor Indians. How do you know they want it back?

MEREDITH.—You've got something. Tell me, while you're at it, would you and the rest of you historians give us some more inside dope on the early days of our country?

EDDIE.—Okay, we'll tell you a story about the American revolution.

MEREDITH.—Revolution, eh? Who's going to play George Washington?

EDDIE.—Me.

MEREDITH.—*You* are? Whose idea was that?

EDDIE.—Mine.

MEREDITH.—Well, you're on your own.

EDDIE.—Okay, Mr. Meredith. It was this way. Back in the days when America was just gettin' started, it used to belong to a king of England, name of George the Third. (*Music in*) An' one day he was settin' in his palace, an' he had a bad case of the blues.

MUSIC.—*In.*

KING.—Ugh. What the use of bein' the king of England if I got to get wet every time it rains. This here palace leaks like a sieve. Chancellor of the Exchequer, I commands you to git this roof fixed right now.

CHANCELLOR.—I is sorry, yo' majesty, but the roof fixin' man say he got to have cash money in advance, an' us ain't got a penny. The royal treasury is empty.

KING.—Then tax somebody. Tax them Americans of ours; that's all they is good for anyhow.

CHANCELLOR.—We is already taxin' 'em for everything but the air they breathe.

KING.—Then tax 'em for that. General Cornwallis, go tax the Americans.

CORNWALLIS.—I just got back from taxin' the Americans, an' all I got was this black eye. It's that man George Washington again.

KING.—George Washington hit you in the eye?

CORNWALLIS.—Uh huh. An' in the nose too.

KING.—That's treason.

CORNWALLIS.—That's what I told him, an' he just laughed.

KING.—Now I *is* mad. General Cornwallis, you and General Howe git your armies and cannons, and somebody git me my umbrella. Us is goin' to America an' collect some taxes.

MUSIC.—*Bridge . . . opening bars of "Rule Britannia."*

KING.—Messenger, go tell George Washington that I is here in America, an' I double dog dares him to come and see me.

MESSENGER.—Yassuh, King. (*Fades*) I'll tell him.

KING.—Now, Cornwallis, you an' General Howe git on each side of the throne here, an' have your cannons ready just in case.

VOICE.—(*Fading in*) King, there's an American outside say he want to see you.

KING.—Who is he?

VOICE.—I don't know, but he got a eagle settin' on his shoulder, an' he wavin' a flag colored like a barber pole, red an' white stripes with stars up in the corner.

CORNWALLIS.—Oh, oh. That's him. That's George Washington, all right.

KING.—Uh, well, uh, show him in.

GEORGE.—(*Fading in*) I is already in. Is you the king that double dog dared me to come see you? Well, here I is. You want to make somethin' out of it? If you does, just knock this eagle off my shoulder.

KING.—Now wait a minute, Mistuh Washington. Don't go flyin' off the handle. Set down an' have a cup of tea, an' let's talk this thing over.

GEORGE.—I don't want no tea, and I is too busy to set down.

KING.—Busy doin' what?

GEORGE.—Buildin' a country. Us done built Boston an' Philadelphia an' New York. An' we just startin' on Chicago. What you want to see me about?

KING.—Well, tell you the truth, George, I needs a little more taxes. You got to pay up.

GEORGE.—I ain't gonna do it. Taxation without representation is tyranny.

KING.—Egad, man, you knows you can't run no country without no taxes.

GEORGE.—Ain't it the truth. But us Americans reserves the right to be robbed by Americans that Americans shall not perish from the earth.

KING.—But I got to have tax money to buy bullets an' gunpowder an' red uniforms for my army. Us got a war on over there in Yurrup.

GEORGE.—You boys *always* got a war on over in Yurrup. That's why us Americans moved away from Yurrup, so us could settle down an' tend to our own business.

KING.—Phooey. What kind of business is more important than the war business?

GEORGE.—Well, King, I'll tell you. Us *Americans* likes to plow the ground and raise good stuff to eat. Us likes to build houses and live in 'em. Us likes to work hard, endurin' the heat of the day; an' in the cool of the evening when the dancin' an' singin' begins, us Americans do dearly love to take our pleasures.

KING.—But ain't you got no respect for us royalty?

GEORGE.—Well, I don't want to hurt yo' feelin's, yo' majesty, but to tell the truth we ain't.

KING.—That settles it. I'm gonna sic my army on you and shoot some sense in you.

GEORGE.—Okay, big shot, you deal the cards, an' us will play 'em like they fall.

KING.—How about meetin' me halfway, an' save the bullets an' gunpowder.

GEORGE.—No sale, King. Us Americans likes our liberty whole hawg or none.

KING.—Man, you Americans is crazy as June bugs. What you gwine do when my well-trained, unbeatable, colossal, invincible, and super army swoops down on you?

GEORGE.—Shoot 'em in the wishbone.

KING.—You ain't got no army.

GEORGE.—Maybe not. But us is got some awful tough farmers.

KING.—Phooey. Them ragamuffin army of yours ain't even got no shoes on. They couldn't run a hundred yards over that rough ground.

GEORGE.—Us don't aim to run.

KING.—This here is revolution, that's what it is. You Americans is committin' revolution.

GEORGE.—You catches on quick for a king, y' know.

KING.—I hereby declares war.

GEORGE.—Us hereby accepts.

KING.—British Army, blow the horns.

SOUND.—*Fanfare of all the brass*

GEORGE.—American Army, blow the horn.

SOUND.—*Definitive phrase of "Yankee Doodle" on kazoo.*

KING.—British Army, shoot them Americans.

SOUND.—*Heavy fusillade of cannon and muskets.*

GEORGE.—American Army, shoot them redcoats.

SOUND.—*One cannon comedy whistle tracer and paper bag explosion . . . five or six musket shots followed by ad lib crys of "Ouch," "Ahwah," "Oh, me," etc., from British.*

KING.—(*Sotto voce*) They ain't got many guns, but they sho kin shoot straight. (*Calls*) George Washington, does you surrender?

GEORGE.—(*Calls*) Naw! King George the Third, does *you* surrender?

VOICE.—Let's surrender, yo' majesty. Them Americans fights too rough.

KING.—(*Calls*) Okay. Since yo' all wants it, I surrenders.

GEORGE.—(*Fading in mike*) All right, King, just sign the Declaration of Independence. That's right. Now, let's shake hands an' let bygones be bygones. Okay, George 3?

KING.—Okay, George W. No hard feelin's.

GEORGE.—No hard feelin's. Patrick Henry, ring the Liberty Bell, an' ring it loud.

HENRY.—The bell is cracked, George.

GEORGE.—Okay. Den strike up the band!

MUSIC.—*Band plays "America" . . . four voices on-mike sing "God Save the King" while four louder voices sing "America" . . . Second verse swells into chorus of "America."*

MEREDITH.—The role of father of our country, in this original radio sketch by John Tucker Battle,* was played by Eddie Green, and that of King George, our country's father-in-law, by Jimmy Baskett.

Now, we've spoken, on this program, of that particular freedom of spirit without which there can be no vital art, music, or literature. Some people have the romantic view that art thrives in garrets, on fear and privation. But that's not so. It thrives on confidence, security, and peace.

The Pursuit of Happiness brings you today a woman who is so convinced of this that she has devoted most of her long and generous life to the practice of this ideal, to seeing that creative talents get the peace of mind they need. She is Mrs. Edward MacDowell, widow of the greatest of American composers. And she has been brought to our studio by Carl Carmer, roving reporter for The Pursuit of Happiness. Mr. Carmer will introduce her to you.

CARMER.—Our news story today, Buzz, begins in Europe 60 years ago when an American girl-musician met the brilliant

* John Tucker Battle, in his hilarious series Heroes Was People, revealed himself over seven years ago as one of the finest comedy writers in radio. He had previously, and has many times since, proved himself one of its most useful actors.

young American composer, Edward MacDowell. They had been married a dozen years in 1896 when they bought a deserted farmhouse in Peterboro, New Hampshire, and went there to live. Then from a log cabin, which his wife had given him, flowed MacDowell's greatest music.

Before he died in 1908, MacDowell told his wife how much the cabin had meant to him. He said he wished that all creative workers in America could enjoy similar conditions. His wife's answer was to incorporate the now famous MacDowell Colony and deed to it the 600 wooded acres of their Peterboro farm, all devoted to giving some 50 or more American painters, writers, composers, sculptors each summer seclusion, quiet, and freedom from wearisome responsibility.

Mrs. MacDowell is eighty-two now, but she's still managing the colony. And I've brought her here to ask her whether the scheme really works.

MRS. MACDOWELL.—I can tell you that 12 Pulitzer prizes have been won by work done at the colony. Does that answer your question?

CARMER.—It ought to, Mrs. MacDowell. And you have had many famous people as colonists?

MRS. MACDOWELL.—Sometimes their work at Peterboro *makes* them famous. A little known poet came to us at the very beginning. When he died a few years ago, Edwin Arlington Robinson took his place among America's immortals. Then there were a couple of unknown schoolteachers, Thornton Wilder and Hervey Allen; a former insurance agent, DuBose Heyward; and an obscure poet named Carl Carmer, who came to write "Stars Fell on Alabama."

CARMER.—Just one more question Mrs. MacDowell. In September, 1938, a great hurricane swept away 300 acres of the colony woods, destroyed the roads, broke in the roofs of the studios, left the colony a scene of utter desolation. You were just eighty-one then, as I remember. What did you do about it?

MRS. MACDOWELL.—I bought a stump puller. I borrowed some money and rented a sawmill. I gave concerts to make money to pay back what I'd borrowed. The colony will be cleared and ready to open again next June.

CARMER.—And speaking of concerts, Mrs. MacDowell, you're going to play for us, aren't you? One of your husband's compositions?

MRS. MACDOWELL.—I'll be happy to, if you can listen to the playing of an old lady. Would you like to hear "To a Water Lily"?

CARMER.—Played by an old lady who licked a hurricane at the age of eighty-one? We'd love it!

MUSIC.—(*Mrs. MacDowell*). "*To a Water Lily.*"

MEREDITH.—Thank you, Mrs. Edward MacDowell.

From this story of art in our day The Pursuit of Happiness turns back through the centuries to the very beginnings of American literature, the letters and diaries of our first settlers. Among the most moving of those are the letters of love exchanged between John Winthrop, governor of the Massachusetts colony, and Margaret Winthrop, his wife.

As Margaret, you will hear a brilliant and versatile actress, whom Broadway has applauded in "Ethan Frome," "Three-Cornered Moon," Wycherley's "Country Wife," and many other successes, Ruth Gordon. As John Winthrop you will hear Philip Merivale, famed for his portrayal of George Washington in "Valley Forge" and now starring in the play "Ladies and Gentlemen."

The words spoken in the following dramatization are all, every one of them, from the actual Winthrop letters and journals. The documents have been arranged for radio by Lydia Perera. We present (*music in*) the story of the Winthrops, with Ruth Gordon and Philip Merivale.

MUSIC.—"*Margaret*" *motif up and hold under.*

MEREDITH.—It is the year 1627, in Groton Manor, county of Suffolk, England. At a desk in the study sits a woman, Margaret Winthrop, writing . . .

MARGARET.—My sweet husband,

I received your most kind and comfortable letters and the things you sent, for which I heartily thank you. I blush to hear myself commended, knowing my own wants. But it is your love that conceives the best and makes all things seem better than they are.

I confess I cannot do enough for thee; but thou art pleased to accept the will for the deed and rest contented.

I have many reasons to make me love thee whereof I will name two: first, because thou lovest God, and secondly, because that thou lovest me. But I must leave this discourse and go about my household affairs. I am a bad housewife to be so long from them, but I must needs borrow a little time to talk with thee, my sweetheart.

My good mother commends her love to you all and thanks you for her tobacco. She would pray you to be careful of yourself that you take no cold.

Thus with my due respect to thyself, thanks for my linens, my love to my sons, I commit thee to God and rest,

Your faithful and obedient wife,
Margaret Winthrop

MUSIC.—"*John*" *motif up and under.*

MEREDITH.—And from London, where his business affairs have brought him, John Winthrop answers . . .

JOHN WINTHROP.—(*Hand cue*) My sweet wife,

I should mend and grow a better husband, having the help of so sweet a wife, but I grow still worse. I was wont heretofore, when I was long absent, to make some supply with volumes of letters; but I can scarce afford thee a few lines (it being now 11 of the clock this Tuesday night).

Thy kind heart must gather a great deal of matter from a few scribbled words.

I will send thee some pepper in my son's box. Thou shalt receive in it also a book of the news this week. I will remember M., her gown and petticoat and the children's girdles. Our friends here are indifferent well and desire to be commended to thee. So with my blessings to our children and my most entire affection to thyself, I kiss my most sweet wife and rest

Thy faithful husband,
Still present with thee in his most unkind absence,
John Winthrop

Oh, Postscription! Thou must be my Valentine for none hath challenged thee.

MUSIC.—"*Transition*" *motif . . . segue to* "*John*" *motif. . . .*

MEREDITH.—In 1629 we hear much talk of New England, the Massachusetts Bay Colony. John Winthrop is more than involved, but in his letters to his wife he makes small reference to it. He is already weighing in his mind the greatest decision of his life: that of sailing across the seas to America, the land of the Indians.

In a most offhand way he writes . . .

JOHN WINTHROP.—My dear wife,

I send thee herewith some papers concerning New England. I would have my son Forth read the book to thee; for the loose papers let him write them out better and then read them.

MEREDITH.—Events march quickly. As October, 1629, draws to a close, the shadowy idea has already become a concrete and imminent fact. In spite of the warnings of the more timid, John Winthrop and many others have decided to sail to New England.

MUSIC.—*In.*

JOHN WINTHROP

Mine own, my best beloved:

I must now begin to prepare thee for our long parting which grows very near. I know not how to deal with thee by arguments; for if thou wert as wise and patient as ever woman was, yet it must needs be a great trial to thee, and the greater because I am so dear to thee.

I purpose (if God will) to be with thee upon Thursday come senight, and then I must take my farewell of thee for a summer's day and winter's day.* The Lord, our good God, will, I hope, send us a happy meeting again in his good time. Amen.

MARGARET

The Lord, our good God, will, I hope, send us a happy meeting again in his good time. Amen. Remember to put me up some

* Blend: John and Margaret speak simultaneously, but the former fades off-mike while the latter advances. At the end of a sentence, Margaret has taken over the speech, the effect being that of reading John's letter aloud.

Cardon's and Cardon's seed. Let the cow be killed against I come home, and let my son Henry provide such peas as will porridge or else none.
Thy frail yet faithful husband,
John Winthrop

MUSIC.—"*Margaret" motif . . . segue to "John" motif.*

JOHN WINTHROP.—My faithful and dear wife,

It goeth very near to my heart to leave thee; but I know to whom I have committed thee, even to him who loves thee much better than any husband can, who hath taken account of the hairs of thy head and put all thy tears in his bottle.

I hope the course we have agreed upon will be some ease to us both. Mondays and Fridays, at five of the clock at night, we shall meet in spirit till we meet in person.

Neither can the sea drown nor enemies destroy nor any adversity deprive thee of thy husband and children. Therefore I will only take thee now and my sweet children in mine arms and kiss and embrace you all and so leave you with my God. Farewell, farewell.

MUSIC.—*Under following.*

MEREDITH.—March the twenty-ninth, 1630. Easter morning.

JOHN WINTHROP.—About 10 of the clock we weighed anchor and set sail.

MEREDITH.—On April seventh, eight ships loomed upon the horizon. Were they pirates?

MUSIC.—*Agitation until announcer comes in.*

JOHN WINTHROP.—Whereupon we prepared to fight with them, and out of every ship were thrown such bed matters as were subject to fire. We drew forth our men and armed them with muskets and other weapons and instruments for fireworks. All things being thus fitted, we went to prayer upon the upper deck.

MEREDITH.—But the eight ships were friendly and saluted the *Arbella*. For a few days all was peaceful.

JOHN WINTHROP.—We stood on our course merrily.

MEREDITH.—Then came 10 days of gale and rain. Many were sick. The ship was damaged. What comment did John Winthrop make in his journal?

JOHN WINTHROP.—Here I think it is good to note that all this time since we came from the Wight, we had cold weather. I wish therefore, that all such as shall pass this way in the spring have care to provide warm clothing.

MEREDITH.—Winds and high seas continued.

MARGARET.—Mondays and Fridays, at 5 of the clock at night, we shall meet in spirit till we meet in person.

MEREDITH.—The entire month of May came and went. The *Arabella* still held to her course. On June the first . . .

JOHN WINTHROP.—This evening we saw the new moon more than half an hour after sunset, being much smaller than it is at any time in England.

MEREDITH.—On Tuesday, June the eighth, after 70 days at sea they sighted land. What were John Winthrop's feelings? After long and bitter weeks on the ocean how did he describe his first glimpses of America? He merely said . . .

JOHN WINTHROP.—There came a smell off the shore like the smell of a garden.

MEREDITH.—On Monday, June the fourteenth, they anchored in a protected harbor and set foot on the shore.

MUSIC.—*Into tragic, autumnal feeling.*

MEREDITH.—Less than a month later his son Henry Winthrop was drowned in a creek near Salem.

JOHN WINTHROP

My dear wife,

I only write now that thou mayest know that yet I live and am mindful of thee in all my affairs. We have met with many sad and discomfortable things, and the Lord's hand hath been heavy upon my self in some who are very near to me: My son Henry, my son Henry, ah, poor child! Yet we may not look at great things here.* It is enough that we shall have heaven though we should pass through hell to it.

MARGARET

It is enough that we shall have heaven though we should pass through hell to it.

Be not discouraged by anything thou shalt hear from hence, for I see no cause to repent of our coming hither; and if I were to come again, I would not have altered my course, though I had forseen all these afflictions. I shall expect thee next summer and by that time hope to be provided for thy comfortable entertainment.

MEREDITH.—But in the meantime, life was far from comfortable for the governor and his colony of Puritans. A torrential rainstorm washed away two sides of Winthrop's new home; scores of colonists fell ill. Mr. Gager died. Captain Weldon died. Smith of Buxall and his wife died. Shiploads of food were delayed, and scores more died of famine. The springs ran dry. (*Fading*) Many died of scurvy. Disease began to spread . . .

JOHN WINTHROP.—My dear wife,

We are here in a Paradise. Though we have not beef and mutton, etc., yet, God be praised, we want them not. Our Indian corn answers for all.

MARGARET.—Mondays and Fridays, at five of the clock.

JOHN WINTHROP.—Remember to come with store of fresh provisions and a large strong chest or two, well locked, to keep these in. Be sure to have ready at sea a small stewing pan and a case to boil a pudding in and sack to bestow among the sailors.

MARGARET.—Mondays and Fridays, at five of the clock.

JOHN WINTHROP.—For physic you shall need no other but a pound of Dr. Wright's Electuariu Lenitivu and his direction to use it, a gallon of scurvy grease to drink a little five or

* Blend to Margaret's voice, as before.

six mornings together, with some saltpeter dissolved in it, and a little grated or sliced nutmeg.

I will here break off. I am sorry to part with thee so soon since we meet so seldom and my much business hath made me too often forget Mondays and Fridays. I will say nothing of my love to thee and of my longing desire towards thee; thou knowest my heart. Grace and peace be with you all.

Thine,

John Winthrop

MUSIC.—"*Margaret*" *motif.*

MEREDITH.—We do not know how Margaret replied to these letters from the colony. But we do know how she felt when she finally received word that she might sail. She wrote to her son John in London:

MARGARET.—Blessed be our good God for the good news which we have heard out of New England. I am glad that thy self and the rest of my company are willing to accompany me; we shall all join together, I hope, and be of one mind to suffer what God hath layed out for us and to rejoice together.

MEREDITH.—So in August, 1631, Margaret Winthrop sailed to America. On the fourth of November John Winthrop and his wife were reunited. There was great rejoicing on the part of the colonists; cannons were set off in celebration of the ship's arrival, and presents brought to the Governor's house as symbols of welcome.

What did John Winthrop say? He could not trust himself beyond the 12 simple words which he wrote in his journal.

JOHN WINTHROP.—November the eleventh, 1631. We kept a day of Thanksgiving at Boston.

MUSIC.—*Chord.*

MARGARET.—There is a time to plant and a time to pull up that which is planted, which I could desire might not be yet, but the Lord knoweth what is best and His will be done.

MUSIC.—*Conclusion.*

Applause.

MEREDITH.—Thank you, Ruth Gordon and Philip Merivale.

We'd like to return, for a moment, to that nine-year-old editor, who wrote in his home magazine on the subject of The Pursuit of Happiness. He went on to say:

BOY.—It makes you feel that America is full of energy and good ideas, and no matter how much of a jam we may be in, we'll come out Okay.

MEREDITH.—Ladies and gentlemen, what can we add to that? Join us next week for another half hour dedicated to life, liberty, and the pursuit of happiness. Till then, keep singing.

MUSIC.—"*Of Thee I Sing.*"

ANNOUNCER.—Theatres throughout the country will soon be showing an important new motion picture, starring Burgess Meredith, our own master of ceremonies. The Pursuit of Happiness will present next Sunday a preview of this picture. It is "Of Mice and Men," John Steinbeck's gripping tale of the Southwest. We will bring you Burgess Meredith as George and Lon Chaney, Junior, his co-star, in his screen role of Lennie. Roman Bohnen will play the part of Candy.

The program next Sunday will also present Bert Lahr and Ethel Merman in a comedy scene fresh from Broadway's new hit, "Du Barry Was a Lady."

The Pursuit of Happiness is directed by Norman Corwin and written by Erik Barnouw, with music under the direction of Mark Warnow.

This is the Columbia Broadcasting System.

Meet Mr. Weeks

PROGRAMS of this sort are, to my mind, sufficient refutation to the claims of the ladies who won't listen. Meet Mr. Weeks was the most charming and successful literature program of the past year. It was newsy and sincere, and it had a lot of laughs. It won and held a tremendous audience. There was never a hint of heaviness in the series, no hooting in the trees of tradition, no noisy take-offs. The show "stayed on the ground" and hummed along pleasantly with a lot of pleasant books and pleasant people. If the enjoyment of literature could be made as real for students as Mr. Weeks has made it for those who heard his programs, there would be less playing of hooky and a great deal more profitable and voluntary reading than there are under the present system of requiring sophomores to memorize Pope. Weeks said that books were fun, and he proved it every Tuesday night. I have selected his half hour about diaries and diarists. All the shows were worth hearing, and I hope that a permanent record of the whole six months of them will come out as a book. It would be a good book to own.

I will let Lewis Titterton, my good friend, introduce you to his good friend Mr. Weeks. Here is his note about the series:

The man who is today editor of the *Atlantic Monthly* inherits a very great tradition. Every predecessor—and there has been but a handful in the long life of the magazine—has been a man of exceptional distinction. It was my good fortune to serve with Mr. Weeks as one of the assistant editors of the *Atlantic Monthly* under Mr. Ellery Sedgwick in 1925, and, through the years of our friendship, I have seen for myself the development of a man recognized today as one of the finest editors in the country.

The fact that Edward Weeks had for several years been delivering public lectures was what led me to consult with him and then with my colleagues at NBC regarding the launching of a series of mature programs that would deal in an attractive way with literature. Mr. Weeks was good enough to prepare a sample talk of his own, indicating where a guest could be introduced, and he came down to New York and read it to me. It was fortunate that there was a meeting of our press and program departments in session, and I could think of no harder test than to take Mr. Weeks upstairs and ask him to go through the performance again. He did so, and the result was unanimous approval. So we launched the program and, after meditating on all the customary titles, such as The Editor's Easy Chair and The Literary Lion's Den, we felt we could do no better than choose the informal one of Meet Mr. Weeks. That people met him and came to look forward to his weekly programs was amply evidenced by the steady stream of letters which at once began to come in.

His guests were drawn from the ranks of the stage, the newspaper world, the university, the publishing house, and the author's study. With practically no exceptions they seemed to catch the meaning of the phrase "the human side of literature," which was used in the opening of each program, and the result was a relaxed and easy atmosphere such as we had hoped for but scarcely dared to count upon.

As for Mr. Weeks himself, he is about forty years old, slender, with delicately balanced nerves, of medium height—but, above all, he is an editor, with a passionate interest in what is written and in people who write.

Meet Mr. Weeks

ANNOUNCER.—This twelfth successive Tuesday evening we send out again the invitation to you to Meet Mr. Weeks. As many of you know, the general subject of this series is the "human side of literature"—and few things are as human as a diary. Today's subject, then, is "What's in a Diary," and today's guest is that distinguished member of the American stage, Miss Ruth Gordon. Now without delay, ladies and gentlemen, we invite you to Meet Mr. Weeks.

WEEKS.—Good evening! "Should you wish to make sure that your birthday will be celebrated three hundred years hence, your best course is undoubtedly to keep a diary. Only first be certain that you have the courage to lock your genius in a private book and the humor to gloat over a fame that will be yours only in the grave. For the good diarist writes either for himself alone or for a posterity so distant that it can safely hear every secret and justly weigh every motive. For such an audience there is need neither of affectation nor of restraint. Sincerity is what they ask, detail, and volume; skill with the pen comes in conveniently, but brilliance is not necessary." That is Virginia Woolf speaking, the best critic of her sex in England. And how right she is! "Sincerity, detail, and volume," these certainly are the three indispensable ingredients of any good diary.

I suspect that the impulse to write a diary hits a good many people on New Year's Day. Then, if ever, time stands still. We look ahead, and we promise ourselves to live with fresh determination. We are going to pay *all* our bills; we are going to be more considerate of our wives; we are going to spend more time with our children. In this optimistic mood it suddenly occurs to us that life is good fun—and what a fool we are not to keep a record of it!

Anyone has it in his power to keep a good domestic diary. The most complete domestic diary was written by an Englishman, John Evelyn. He began it on his twenty-first birthday, in the year 1641, and thereafter for 65 years he hardly missed a day. Evelyn was on terms of intimacy with the last two Stuart kings. He suffered under Cromwell, fought against the Dutch, lived through revolution and plague. He loved trees, gardens, and butterflies. Above all he was a great gentleman. You will find no secrets and no scandal in his pages. What endears him to us is his refreshing sincerity.

Evelyn describes his friend Mrs. Godolphin, who "loved to be at funerals" and who chose habitually "the dryest and leanest morsels of meat." A lover of architecture, he had no use for Knoll House, that huge manor in Kent. He called it "a large, old-fashioned structure." Walking by himself one day, he peered into the window of a poor, solitary thatched hut and there saw a young man carving a crucifix and carving so beautifully that Evelyn took him and his woodwork to the court and so discovered a great artist, Grinling Gibbons. And though Evelyn loved his daughter Mary, his grief at her death did not prevent him from counting the number of empty carriages drawn by six horses apiece that attended her funeral.

One of the most remarkable things about John Evelyn is that he kept his diary religiously till he was eighty-six years old. A diary is so easy to begin and so hard to keep going. I made my first try in 1917. Three months after my nineteenth birthday I sailed for France to serve as an ambulance driver with the Moroccan division. In my kit bag was a small, red leather diary. I got a good head start on that diary as we made our leisurely way across the Atlantic, and I found plenty to describe in the French training camp. After 34 days we joined our division at Verdun, and precisely at that point my diary came to an end. Things began to happen too fast for me to write them down. When I came off duty, I wanted to sleep. The rest was silence. If my experience is typical—as I think it is—we can mark down a fourth essential for a diarist: a method of shorthand so that he can cover the day quickly.

The most honest diary in the world was written in shorthand. I mean the Diary of Samuel Pepys (1660–1669). It covers hardly 10 years of his eager maturity. Yet with that shorthand, which he managed so skillfully, Pepys wrote a total of one million three hundred thousand words, never hesitating to describe his most secret thoughts and actions.

Did Pepys expect the world to read his diary after his death? Not, I think, at the first. But before long he was writing with a fierce concentration, and in his old age we find him labeling and numbering the volumes which he bequeathed to his old college in Cambridge.

Samuel Pepys was a successful man of affairs, working like fury to build up the King's navy, playing his lute, flirting, fussing over his household, quarreling and making up with his wife, firing the maids, whipping the page boy, relishing his food and drink, and adoring from afar Lady Castlemaine, the sight of whose petticoats on the clothesline at Whitehall thrilled him to the marrow.

Open the diary anywhere, and you find yourself looking at a man's heart. Pepys's relations with his wife should be required reading for all couples contemplating divorce. It would teach some of them forbearance. Listen:

"February 28th, 1665. Come home, I to the taking my wife's kitchen accounts at the latter end of the month, and there find seven shillings wanting, which did occasion a very high falling out between us. I indeed to angrily insisting upon so poor a thing, and did give her very provoking high words, calling her beggar, and reproaching her friends, which she took very stomachfully and reproached me justly with mine, and I confess, being myself, I cannot see what she could have done less. We parted after many high words very angry, and I to my office to my month's accounts, and find myself worth one thousand two hundred and seventy pounds—for which the Lord God be praised."

There speaks every man. But see how honestly Pepys tried to redeem his hasty temper.

And here is a passage which might have been written yesterday, so well does it describe the affectionate skirmish between man and wife:

"June 4th, 1667. To the office all the afternoon, where I dispatched much business to my great content, and then home in the evening, and there to sing and pipe with my wife, and that being done, she fell all of a sudden to discourse about her clothes and my humours in not suffering her to wear them as she pleases, and grew to high words between us, but I fell to read a book aloud in my chamber and let her talk, till she was tired and vexed that I would not hear her, and so become friends, and to bed together the first night after four or five that she hath lain from me by reason of a great cold she had got."

The fire of London was one of the great disasters of Pepys' day, and I should like to read his description of it to show with what vivid detail he wrote:

"September 2nd (Lord's Day) 1666. Jane called us up (he means the serving maid woke them) about three in the morning, to tell us of a great fire they saw in the City. So I rose and slipped on my night-gowne, and went to her window. I thought it far enough off; and so went to bed again and to sleep. By and by Jane comes and tells me that she hears that above three hundred houses have been burned by the fire we saw, and that it is now burning down all Fish-street, by London Bridge. So I down to the water-side, and there got a boat and through bridge, and there saw a lamentable fire. Everybody endeavouring to remove their goods, and flinging into the river or bringing them into lighters that lay off; poor people staying in their houses as long as till the very fire touched them, and then running into boats, or clambering from one pair of stairs by the water-side to another. The poor pigeons, I perceive, were loth to leave their houses, but hovered about the windows and balconys till they were, some of them burned their wings, and fell down. Having seen the fire rage every way, and nobody, to my sight, endeavouring to quench it, but to remove their goods, and leave all to the fire, and having seen it get as far as the Steele-yard, and the wind mighty high and driving it into the City; and everything, after so long a drought, proving combustible, even the very stones of churches.

"To Whitehall, and there up to the King's closett, and I did give them an account dismayed them all, and word was carried in to the King. So I was called for, and did tell the King and Duke of Yorke what I saw, and that unless his Majesty did command houses to be pulled down nothing could stop the fire. They seemed much troubled, and the King commanded me to go to my Lord Mayor from him, and command him to spare no houses. At last met my Lord Mayor in Canning-street, like a man spent, with a handkercher about his neck. To the King's message he cried, like a fainting woman, 'Lord, what can I do? I am spent; people will not obey me. I have been pulling down houses; but the fire overtakes us faster than we can do it.' Met with the King and Duke of Yorke in their barge, and with them to Queenhithe. So near the fire as we could for smoke; and all over the Thames, with one's face in the wind, you were almost burned with a shower of fire-drops. The churches, houses, and all on fire and flaming at once; and a horrid noise the flames made, and the cracking of houses at their ruine. So home with a sad heart."

It's a long jump from Pepys to those little leather diaries which parents give their children for Christmas. You will see why I mention these in just a minute. My guest this evening is Miss Ruth Gordon, an American actress who has captivated many an audience in New York and London. Last winter, Alexander Woollcott told me that Miss Gordon had written a most delightful diary. I published some of it in the *Atlantic*, and I am going to ask her to tell us how she wrote it in just a minute. But first let me present her to you. Miss Ruth Gordon. Miss Gordon, when did you first begin to keep a diary?

GORDON.—Back in January, 1914, when I was a senior in the Quincy High School in Massachusetts.

WEEKS.—And why did you keep it?

GORDON.—Mr. Weeks, a friend of mine gave me for Christmas a blue morocco-bound diary. In our household there was a spirit of thrift which compelled us to use any and every gift. Whether we *enjoyed* using it was beside the point. So you see I had to keep that diary. But I never really confided in it. I simply wrote down the bare actualities.

WEEKS.—Will you show me what you mean by "actualities"?

GORDON.—Well, for instance, Mr. Weeks, on January 1, 1914 (that was the day my diary began), I wrote this: "This afternoon, after going to the dentist, called on Mrs. Nickerson and had a nice time. Molly Brown was married tonight. We were invited but papa hasn't a dress suit so we couldn't go." Now, reading those simple words, Mr. Weeks, you couldn't understand what lay behind them.

WEEKS.—You mean the fact that you couldn't go to that wedding is a story in itself?

GORDON.—Why, it was a tragedy. You see, we lived in the shabby half of a double house in Wollaston, and there my mother and father and I and our cat hoped, dreamed, and somehow scrimped along—scrimped along on $37.50 a week which my father earned as foreman at a factory in Boston. The arrival of that wedding invitation caused great excitement, but the fact had to be faced that my father had no dress suit; and so after quite a little talk and figuring, my parents decided to send a cut-glass water pitcher as our present and with it our regrets. That water pitcher cost just under $4. You see, going or not going, either way, set us back financially.

On the evening of the wedding my father was in a taciturn mood all through supper. Perhaps he was remembering the days when he and mother had first come to Wollaston, a young couple, full of high hopes. He knew that mother was pining for that reception, and to conceal his own disappointment he was good and cross.

After supper I drifted out, ostensibly to play, but once outside I rushed headlong to the scene of the great event. There I stood humbly gawking until well after 9 o'clock. As I wandered dreamily into our front hall, my father's voice brought me back to my senses. "Where have you been?" he demanded. "Only up watching the wedding," I answered, innocent of class pride, for the last time in my life. "Why, you old goat!" my father shouted at me. "You old goat!" he kept on shouting, and, grabbing me by the ear, he thumped my head down on our golden-oak dining table, while my mother made faces over his shoulder that I wasn't to mind or get upset. "You got no earthly pride. You're yellow! You're as yellow as an old goat!"

Now, Mr. Weeks, how, at seventeen, could I ever have written down all that humiliation into my diary?

WEEKS.—In other words, it is only today, a good many years later, that you are able to fill in that diary without evasion?

GORDON.—Yes, that's quite true. It wasn't until I reread the old diary years later that I felt the impulse to tell the whole story concealed behind those short, cryptic phrases. So you see, I have really had to write a second diary.

For example, on January 22, 1914, I wrote this sentence: "Father has bronchitis and is at home." Packed away in those few words is the whole story of his fresh-air fad.

You see, father had been a sailor for a good many years, and he liked exercise. He joined a gymnasium class in the Y.M.C.A., and eventually we received an invitation to go to an evening exhibition in which father was to take part. I went with mother; and as we settled ourselves in the front row of the balcony my mother whispered, "For my sake try and act as though you liked it, and I'll do something nice sometime for you." But father turned out to be the chief source of entertainment, owing to the fact that he was years older than anyone else performing, and also because he looked so odd in his old-fashioned two-piece bathing suit. I sat wishing the balcony floor would open up and let me fall right through; for every time it would be my father's turn people around us would say, "Oh, good! Here comes the old feller," or "Oh, look at that old one go!" It was awful, but the worst was yet to come. As my father finished a somersault and rose awkwardly from the mattress to continue with a run around the track, a good 2 inches of bare skin showed in back between his jersey and his bathing pants. People around us were convulsed, but I sat there wondering that God did not show some mercy and strike our family dead. My mother told me not to act so silly and said that she guessed people knew what bare skin looked like and hoped I never had anything worse to be ashamed of. I hoped that my father would have some sense and hurry us home after it was over, so that we could retire into permanent privacy with our disgrace, but so insensitive was he that instead he invited us all to accompany him to the old Thorndike Hotel on Boylston Street for a dish of raspberry sherbet. It was the only time that my mother and father and I were all in a hotel together.

Oh, how could bronchitis have attacked my father after all we had been through for his health?

WEEKS.—It's curious, isn't it, Miss Gordon, what a big difference there is between that little blue diary you kept in 1914 and the illumination of it which you find it possible to give today?

GORDON.—I think perhaps a girl of seventeen, half child, half woman, is inevitably confused. She can't be expected to analyze her own emotions and feelings very clearly.

For example, I find in my diary a little note that reads: "This morning I went up to Kay's, and coming home we met Clarke Boynton! I was so thrilled!"

That's the only mention of Clarke Boynton, but I shall always be indebted to him for the first grown-up compliment I ever received. He said that I had a "cute shape." He did not say it to me personally but to my friend Gladys Bain. At least she said that he said it to her. My ears could hardly believe it at the time, and even now I scarcely know what to think. All my pictures of that period certainly belie the fact, and Clarke Boynton, who, by the way, had a cute shape himself, was very popular with the girls and could surely never have wasted so much as a fleeting glance on me. However, it opened up a new field of thought. I used to repeat the phrase over and over again, softly to myself; and, although steadfastly disbelieving it, I must say it gave me a good deal of simple pleasure. It helped to take up some of the slack of my spare time.

So Clarke colored my dreams, and yet I don't think that in real life I ever said more to him than a shy hello; but I know that whenever I met him on the streets of our town I became so self-conscious that my normal gait suddenly changed to that of some poor soul stricken with locomotor ataxia.

WEEKS.—Evelyn has given us the domestic diary, and Pepys the most honest the world has known. Miss Gordon and I have spoken of those youthful beginnings which sometimes develop into a true and lovable record. Last but not least there is the craftsman's diary, the diary of an artist in which from day to day he sets down the measurements of his work, the ideas he means to build with, the criticism of his contemporaries, and those little arrows of humor and observation which are part of the day's adventure.

Few modern authors have written as prodigiously as Arnold Bennett. He worked his way up through Fleet Street. He scored innumerable hits with his plays and his novels. He left us one fine and durable book in the "Old Wives' Tale," and in addition he left behind him a craftsman's diary of a million words which, believe me, makes shrewd and spicy reading. I prefer to let Arnold Bennett speak for himself, and so without any regard for dates I am going to quote a few of those chuckling sentences which make up his daily chronicle.

"June 26th. In an article today I wrote: 'Meat may go up in price—it has done—but books won't. Admission to picture galleries and concerts and so forth will remain quite low. The views from Richmond Hill or Hindhead, or along Pall Mall at sunset, the smell of the earth, the taste of fruit and of kisses—these things are unaffected by the machinations of trusts and the hysteria of Stock Exchanges." The *Westminster Gazette* quoted this and more, but it left out the words "and of kisses." Characteristic of the English newspaper!

"April 21st. London. Palace Theatre. Pavlova dancing the dying swan. Feather falls off her dress. Two silent Englishmen. One says, 'Moulting.' That is all they say.

"Thursday, November 2nd. Today I wrote five articles; two reviews; two articles on 'The Black Tulip' play, and my weekly 'household notes.'

"Thursday, October 31st. Dined with Sir James Barrie. Good short dinner. He told me that he didn't smoke till he was twenty-three and that he wrote 'My Lady Nicotine' before he had ever smoked. He said when he first came to London, he dined on tuppence a day (four ha'penny buns or scones) for a year, eating them in the street, and ate little else. He wrote about two articles a day and—if lucky—sold one in six.

"Monday, May 25th. Two hours' walk in the rain in the forest this after-tea, when ideas for my play, my novel, and a story, 'The Cat and Cupid,' simply bubbled up out of me.

"Sunday, November 14th. Marguerite's dog woke me up last night after I had had three hours' sleep. After that my nerves were too tightened for me to try even to sleep (as I had just finished my play). I lay awake and listened, rather frightened, to the various noises, all very faint, that I could hear. (I had quietened the dog with a slipper.) Marguerite, the clocks, another noise, regular, that I couldn't and don't understand, and then still others, faint ones beneath these. About five I began reading Taine on Balzac, and came across some magnificent pages of generalizations about the art of observation.

"Wednesday, August 14th. Some months ago, at intervals, I seemed to detect a very slight temporary deterioration of my eyesight. Then I noticed nothing. Today I was conscious of a certain uneasiness in the organs. Several times there was a mist before my eyes, as there is now—a mist which I can dispel by a strong effort of the will, but which returns. I wonder whether this is the end of my hitherto magnificent eyesight, or whether it is merely due to my having got up too early this morning.

"Wednesday, April 1st. Yesterday and today I drafted the whole of the play 'The Snake Charmer,' 1 act.

Eyesight troubling me again—due to careful (not small) writing of my novel.

I expect I am as happy now as I can be. I have learnt a lot, and am learning."

Writers of any persuasion will learn more than they ever knew about their trade from reading these inquisitive, witty, and always ambitious comments which make up the journals of Arnold Bennett. More than any modern writer I know he shows us how to live 24 hours a day.

The night after Christmas, I had the audacity to identify a list of 10 heroines drawn from my favorite books, each of whom I believed would be a stimulating and useful companion were we marooned together on a desert island. Since then a number of listeners have asked for the list of my 10 young ladies, and others have written in to remind me of heroines who were friends of theirs.

I have also received one expostulation from Cicero, Illinois, which I want to get off my conscience at once. Then we'll come back to the heroines. Says one listener:

"My Dear Mr. Weeks:

"If the editor of (let us say) *Love Tales* were to speak of François Villon as 'Frankoyz Vil-lon,' you might well exclaim, "Dear me, what a barbarian!"

"When I heard the editor of the *Atlantic Monthly* last night say "Don Jewan" for "Don Hwan" all I could think of was Arriba España!

Yours truly,
Fred B. Hurt"

Yes, Mr. Hurt, my pronunciation of "Don Juan" was deliberate. I believe Lord Byron intended the anglicized version to be used in connection with his poem.

Apart from that minority report, my mail has seductive suggestions. Here, for instance, is one from Yanceyville, North Carolina:

"Dear Mister Weeks:

"Suh, I heard your radio discussion of last night: 'Ten Gals and Me at Nassau.' I congratulate you not only for your courage, but your *catholicity* of taste. I rise to protest, however, that you did not include the Queen of Sheba in your entourage. There's a gal who *lived* in the desert, who could take a thousand mile trip on a camel, and upon arrival at a distant destination, pull an evening dress and jewels out of her bag, and dazzle old Solomon. I omit all references —being a high-minded gent—to what she did to St. Anthony.

Sincerely yours,
David L. Cohn"

From Morgantown, North Carolina, Mrs. Dorothy H. Avery makes this pertinent inquiry:

"Dear Mr. Weeks:

"I liked your collection of desert island companions in the main, but would suggest Imogen instead of Juliet (she wouldn't vapor so much); Cleopatra instead of Helen (bet she'd be more intellectually stimulating); and Rebecca of Sunnybrook Farm somewhere. Scarlett, Elizabeth Bennett and Mary Thorne have my whole-hearted vote.

"Why don't you ask the ladies in your audience for their choice among fictional men? Mr. Knightley would be a sensible person to have along, for one."

Maryland Club
Baltimore, Maryland

"My Dear Mr. Weeks:

"May I invite your attention to the possibility that you neglected a most important side of the question in your discussion of the most satisfactory female companions for a man on a desert island? I make the point that very much depends upon the specific man—that the woman most satisfactory to one man in this situation might be quite unsatisfactory to another man.

Sincerely,
Francis Fielding Reid"

My guest next week will be Mr. David McCord. He and I intend to read together from the letters and verses of those "Poets Who Made the World Laugh"; so, until next Tuesday, good night!

ANNOUNCER.—We have been honored today by the presence on our program of Miss Ruth Gordon, the distinguished American actress, and we thank her cordially for having joined us. Meet Mr. Weeks is a public service presentation of the Blue Network of the National Broadcasting Company, RCA Building, Radio City, New York.

The Human Adventure

One of the most strenuous and intelligent efforts to bring good educational material to radio is the effort behind the series known as The Human Adventure. These shows first reached the air in midsummer, 1939, and have been heard weekly ever since. Their objective is to present dramatic interpretations of the progress being made in university research throughout the world, progress in any of the thirty thousand research projects that are now being worked on by scholars and scientists in this country and in the centers of learning throughout the civilized world.

Shows of this sort are hard to assemble and hard to write. They are hard to assemble because so many of the finest men in the field of active research are either too modest to talk or too inarticulate to know how. And there are many, too, who are reluctant to say anything significant to broadcasters for fear that, in the course of its being dramatized, the end product will come out as something more sensational than lucid.

They are hard to write because the terms that will most accurately describe the findings of these research efforts are terms unfamiliar to most listeners, and they are hard to write because the background necessary to a true understanding of almost any important scientific problem is not a part of the equipment of most of those in the radio audience.

In the necessary process of simplification much has to be sacrificed in order to be widely understood. I doubt if the series, as a whole, has either pleased or satisfied the scientists. But, then, few things please scientists anyhow; they would not be good scientists if it were otherwise.

In a program series of this sort, radio's point of view must be as simple as this: If the information is substantially clear and completely accurate (even if slightly bobbed), the show has fulfilled its real duty. It has brought to listeners the result of a lot of hard and unrewarded work, in this case, work that is important, contemporary, and progressive. And, in its wake, the series has left something else of value, an active respect for learning and the learned.

A wide variety of subjects has been covered in the past year, subjects under the patient scrutiny of thousands of men and women who are giving their quiet lives to the business of finding answers where there have been no answers before. The series has moved into fields as remote from each other as are zoology and aeronautics. The Black Plagues of Europe, imagery of childhood, Einstein, Arthurian legends, termites, the dime novel, the role of the abnormal individual in politics, supersonics, uranium 235, Babylonian business practices, the transformation of female chicks into roosters, advances in cancer control, the ghetto in America, hobo jungles, dental decay, train whistles—these and many hundreds of other questions in active research have been dealt with or are on schedule for future programs. Actors move in and out of the pages of these diversified hours with syringes, folios, bottles of snake venom, ether cones, bird notes, and Irish poetry. Every once in a while they smash an atom or two or put somebody to sleep in a new way.

All the programs have the great advantage of freshness in that they have carried their stories to the point of most recent development. They have brought the listener up to date and have read for him, not the last chapter of the complete story but the last one to be written thus far. The series is prepared through cooperation between CBS and the University of Chicago. It is written by the staff of the radio department at the university, under the supervision of the department's director, Sherman Dryer. The broadcasts originate in New York City, and the entire series has been, and is being, directed by Brewster Morgan of the Columbia staff.

This, to my mind, is the year's best dramatized educational program. The series has been on the air for the past fifty weeks and has delivered a great variety of information in highly acceptable treatments. This particular script, the story of childbirth, is a positive indication of the courage of radio to deal with problems of primary public interest. The broadcast that I am reprinting was performed on June 29, 1940.

The Human Adventure

ANNOUNCER.—The Human Adventure!

MUSIC.

NARRATOR.—The University of Chicago, in collaboration with the Columbia Broadcasting System, presents The Human Adventure.

WOMAN.—The story of the birth of a baby!

NARRATOR.—The Human Adventure, for the first time on radio, tells the story of childbirth, takes you behind the scenes of a modern lying-in hospital, reveals the actual medical treatment of expectant mothers.

MUSIC.—*Up to tag.*

ANNOUNCER.—This series of broadcasts represents the work of universities. We bring you the exclusive accounts of research in all fields of knowledge. A university's job is to learn, and you and all mankind may benefit from its knowledge. The universities are your investment in a better life.

MUSIC.—*In.*

MAN.—Mary. Mary, I haven't time for breakfast this morning. I'm late.

WOMAN.—Well, sit down and have a cup of coffee. I poured it out.

MAN.—Thanks, honey. Where's my brief case?

WOMAN.—On the table in the living room.

MAN.—Oh, yeah. Gosh, why didn't I put those papers in last night.

WOMAN.—(*Pause*) Tom, there's . . .

MAN.—Well, I'll just carry them in my hand till I get in the train.

SOUND.—*Cup and saucer.*

MAN.—Still too hot.

WOMAN.—Tom, there's something we must talk about.

MAN.—Uh-huh.

SOUND.—*Papers rustling.*

WOMAN.—I've suspected it now for a couple of weeks.

MAN.—Uh-huh.

WOMAN.—Well, yesterday . . .

SOUND.—*Train whistle . . . cup and saucer.*

MAN.—There's my train. So long, honey.

WOMAN.—Tom, don't run away.

MAN.—I'll be home early. Meet me at the station at 5:55.

WOMAN.—Tom, I have something to tell you.

SOUND.—*Train whistle closer.*

MAN.—Well, for Pete's sake, what is it, darling? I'll miss that . . .

WOMAN.—I—I'm going to have a baby.

MAN.—Can't you . . . Huh?

SOUND.—*Footsteps.*

MAN.—No!

WOMAN.—Yes.

MAN.—Sure?

WOMAN.—Sure.

MAN.—Gosh!

SOUND.—*Train whistle.*

MUSIC.—*Up full.*

MUSIC.—*Introduction and hold.*

NARRATOR.—Today in America, June 29, 1940, from now, 8:30 P.M., EDST, while this program is on the air, until the clock in our studios strikes 9, about 140 babies will be born. The greatest human adventure in the experience of man will take place. And this year in America, more than two million new lives will breathe the air of their strange new world. And those that survive will grow to build new cities, till black earth, sing new songs.

MAN.—I guess my wife's all right, isn't she, nurse?

NURSE.—Perfect. Just a normal delivery.

MAN.—She seems awful tired.

NURSE.—Naturally. Everyone is tired after labor. Now she needs rest. You were very wise, Mr. Johnson, to bring your wife to the hospital so early. If every mother was as careful and came for her prenatal care regularly before the baby was born, we'd all have healthier babies and sounder mothers.

MAN.—How long will she be here, nurse?

NURSE.—About 10 days.

MAN.—Gosh!

NURSE.—No work for Mrs. Johnson until she is strong again.

MAN.—Sure thing.

NURSE.—And plenty of milk and vegetables as well as rest. These next few weeks are just as important as the last 9 months.

MAN.—Thanks to all of you here for all you've done.

NURSE.—Don't thank us. From the moment your wife registered in this lying-in hospital 8 months ago, that baby was ours as well as yours.

MUSIC.—*Up in curtain to finish.*

NARRATOR.—A pleasant scene, a typical scene, even a trite scene, where Mr. and Mrs. Johnson are lucky enough to share the advantages of one of our few modern lying-in hospitals in America. Careful prenatal care, expert obstetrical deliveries, close observation, and scientific isolation of mother and child after birth.

MUSIC.—*In and behind.*

NARRATOR.—The story of this accomplishment begins many years ago in a Viennese hospital, with a man called Ignaz

Philipp Semmelweiss, of the University of Vienna, Vienna, 1847. The No. 1 obstetric clinic of the general hospital. Of every nine women that give birth, one dies of childbed fever. And while women wail, a priest with a black robe and a tinkling bell walks through the ward of life and death mumbling the last sacrament.

SOUND.—*Bell to background.*

PRIEST.—Te igitur clementissime Pater, in nomine Patris et Filii et Spiritus Sancti.

WOMAN.—Doktor! Herr Doktor, please let me go home. Let me have my child at home. I will die here! I know it! Please Doktor Semmelweiss.

SEMMELWEISS.—Courage and rest, gnädige Frau.

WOMAN.—Rest? How can I rest when I know I shall die like the others? How can I rest, Herr Doktor, when I am all day reminded of death? That bell, the priest's bell!

SEMMELWEISS.—Dr. Schultz.

SCHULTZ.—Ja, Dr. Semmelweiss?

SEMMELWEISS.—Do me a favor. Ask that priest not to march through these wards again with his death bell. These poor women will go mad.

SCHULTZ.—Ja, Dr. Semmelweiss.

SEMMELWEISS.—And, Dr. Schultz, do these women a favor, wash your hands before you come into the wards.

SCHULTZ.—*My* hands? Why, they're clean!

SEMMELWEISS.—Dr. Schultz, where were you before you made your rounds in No. 1 clinic?

SCHULTZ.—Anatomy laboratory.

SEMMELWEISS.—So?

SCHULTZ.—We are performing an autopsy on a woman who died with fever.

SEMMELWEISS.—You came directly then to this clinic to examine the women in labor?

SCHULTZ.—I . . . Herr Doktor Semmelweiss, I object to your constant questions. You are not an attorney, nor am I a criminal.

SEMMELWEISS.—That remains to be seen. Did you wash your hands after you examined the unfortunate woman in the autopsy laboratory?

SCHULTZ.—My hands are clean. See for yourself.

SEMMELWEISS.—I see nothing. You must remember, Herr Doktor, that even a doctor's hands may carry disease.

MUSIC.—*Up and down for bridge.*

NARRATOR.—The next day found Dr. Semmelweiss with the chief of the obstetrical staff Dr. Klein.

KLEIN.—Semmelweiss, you are making a fetish of childbirth fever.

SEMMELWEISS.—Since when is death a fetish?

KLEIN.—But the causes of childbed fever are well known: bad diet and the natural fear and chilling of women in labor. Even Virchow will tell you it's bad air. "Atmospheric cosmic telluric influences."

SEMMELWEISS.—Fancy words! Ignorance! The disease is caused by dirt, decomposed animal matter, and filth on a doctor's hands. If your internes would take the trouble of washing their hands with chlorine water, fewer women would die in your hospital.

KLEIN.—(*Sarcastically*) And how do *you* know, Herr Doktor Semmelweiss?

SEMMELWEISS.—I will tell you how I know. We have two obstetric clinics: No. 1 and No. 2. In No. 1 the mortality rate is 11.3 per cent. In No. 2 the mortality rate is only 2.7 per cent. In No. 1 clinic the women are examined by fingers of internes contaminated in the autopsy lab after they have worked on fatal cases of childbed fever. In clinic No. 2 only midwives attend deliveries. Midwives never go near the morgue. Therefore, less contamination—fewer deaths.

KLEIN.—Very pretty hypothesis proving nothing.

SEMMELWEISS.—You almost talk like a scientist, Herr Doktor Klein.

KLEIN.—Semmelweiss, for a long time I have been thinking of discharging you for your stupidity and insults.

SEMMELWEISS.—That will eliminate Semmelweiss, not childbed fever. My appointment here ends a year from now. Let me prove to you in that year that my hypothesis is correct. Whatever our personal difficulties, you are a scientist, Klein. Let me experiment. Let *me wash the hands* of *your* staff in clinic No. 1.

MUSIC.—*Agitato.*

NARRATOR.—And Semmelweiss did wash their hands clean of death. The next morning all the doctors in clinic No. 1 were assembled before him.

SOUND.—*Ad libs of internes.*

MUSIC.—*Out.*

SEMMELWEISS.—Mein Herr Doktors, these are the orders. I want the delivery room spotless: clean sheets, sterile clothing, sterile sponges, antiseptic instruments. And clean your hands! Soap and water alone may not remove the poison. Soak your hands in a solution of chloride of lime! That will be all. (*Ad libs*)

MUSIC.—*Up and down behind.*

NARRATOR.—And that was all. The simplest clues sometimes help solve the most baffling mysteries. In only 3 weeks Dr. Semmelweiss reported . . .

SEMMELWEISS.—The mortality rate from childbed fever dropped from 11.3 per cent to only 3 per cent.

NARRATOR.—And in one year, he reported . . .

SEMMELWEISS.—Mortality rate dropped from 3 per cent to the all-time low of the Vienna Lying-in Hospital, only a little over 1 per cent.

NARRATOR.—And in that same year, Herr Dr. Klein reported . . .

MUSIC.—*Out abruptly.*

KLEIN.—Semmelweiss, you are discharged!

SEMMELWEISS.—I have been expecting that, Dr. Klein. But I've proven my point. We know how to wipe out childbed fever. We have saved the lives of thousands of women.

KLEIN.—You are impetuous. You quarrel and cannot take orders.

SEMMELWEISS.—Wrong again, Dr. Klein. I can take orders. Good-by.

MUSIC.—*In and behind.*

NARRATOR.—Disheartened, Semmelweiss left Vienna and for a time filled the chair of Professor of Obstetrics at the University of Budapest. There he continued his experiment, successful experiments against death. But before the day that a backward and bigoted world would accept his amazing but simple discovery, Semmelweiss, the realist who hated obvious sentiment, became a martyr. While working on childbed fever, he died of that same septic infection.

MUSIC.—*Up and out.*

NARRATOR.—Sir William J. Sinclair, of the University of Manchester wrote the epitaph.

MUSIC.—*Sad and Sneak.*

SINCLAIR.—We deplore the martyrdom of Semmelweiss, but we can find some comfort in the reflection that he did not struggle in vain and that he did not suffer in vain. The whole civilized world was soon to enjoy the fruits of his discovery. He had thrown the light of scientific progress into a region hitherto shrouded in the darkness of Egyptian night.

MUSIC.—*Up and down.*

NARRATOR.—Today, in America, in modern hospitals, cleanliness has all but banished childbed fever. The obstetrical procedure of the up-to-date physician throughout the country has made this dread disease a matter of ancient history.

MUSIC.—*Up.*

NARRATOR.—Today in America, in the city of Chicago, there stands one of the most modern lying-in hospitals in the world. Founded by the courage and perseverance of the famous Professor Joseph B. De Lee of the University of

Chicago, it carries on the work of Semmelweiss and countless other university scientists who have added to our knowledge of obstetrics, who have given their lives that death and pain may no longer plague mothers. Dr. De Lee emphasized the fact that the ordinary general hospital is not the safest place for women in labor. This was his hope when he said . . .

De Lee.—If babies must be delivered in a hospital, then it must be a hospital *built for that one purpose only*, far away and free from other sickness and death.

Music.—*Up.*

Narrator.—Today in America a woman applies for admittance to a lying-in-hospital. The first step, the examination by a doctor.

Doctor.—Good morning.

Woman.—Good morning, Doctor.

Doctor.—You're . . .

Woman.—Mary Johnson. I mean, Mrs. Tom Johnson.

Doctor.—(*Laughs*) Oh, yes. This your first baby?

Woman.—Yes, we want a baby very much, but I'm a little frightened.

Doctor.—There's nothing to be afraid of, Mrs. Johnson. To bring a baby into the world is a perfectly normal and beautiful thing, especially if the woman is well and happy.

Woman.—Oh, I feel fine.

Doctor.—Good. Now just a few simple questions, and then we will give you a thorough physical examination. How old are you, Mrs. Johnson?

Woman.—Twenty-six.

Doctor.—Ever been sick? Any operations?

Woman.—Had my tonsils out when I was a little girl. Otherwise I'm all there.

Doctor.—(*Laughs*) Have you been to your dentist recently?

Woman.—Last year.

DOCTOR.—Better see him again. Care of the teeth is very important. How long ago do you think your baby's life began?

WOMAN.—About 2 months ago.

SOUND.—*Door opens and shuts off.*

DOCTOR.—Oh, nurse.

NURSE.—Yes, Doctor?

DOCTOR.—This is Mary Johnson.

NURSE.—How do you do? I'm Miss Roth.

WOMAN.—Pleased to meet you.

DOCTOR.—Prepare Mrs. Johnson for complete examination. Height, weight, urine specimen, Wassermann. That's to determine venereal disease, Mrs. Johnson.

WOMAN.—Yes, I know. Tom and I had a Wassermann test done before we were married.

DOCTOR.—Good. We will also take measurements of your pelvic bones. That is very important. And after the examination we will prescribe proper diet and exercise so that the baby is properly nourished and develops normally.

WOMAN.—My, oh, my! Quite a fuss over a baby that hasn't even been born yet.

DOCTOR.—Yes, quite a fuss. But the baby, though not born, is already a living thing. Both of you need care. That baby is not only yours now but ours, as well. And we're going to watch that baby.

MUSIC.—*Up and down.*

NARRATOR.—And so the first examination was over. Mary Johnson, mother, was now the concern of the doctors and scientists of the lying-in hospital. Prenatal care, the first stage, was given Mary as often as necessary. She and her baby were under the watchful eye of a doctor, benefiting from all his knowledge of modern scientific research, research that would bring a mother and child safely through the greatest of all human adventures—birth. Further examinations followed at intervals of a few weeks or even weekly. Two months later . . .

DOCTOR.—How do you feel, Mary?

WOMAN.—Just fine, but awful hungry all the time.

DOCTOR.—(*Laughing*) That baby has an appetite. Do you ever have headaches?

WOMAN.—No. But my back aches some.

DOCTOR.—Dizziness?

WOMAN.—No. But I sometimes trip when I walk, and Tom gets awful scared.

DOCTOR.—Nothing to worry about. The baby is getting heavier and probably unbalances you. Nurse.

NURSE.—Yes, Doctor. Hello, Mary. My, don't you look well today.

WOMAN.—Thank you, Helen.

DOCTOR.—And, nurse, tell Mary about a proper support to help her carry her baby and ease her back. And then prepare her for another complete examination.

MUSIC.—*Up and down.*

NARRATOR.—The seventh month.

DOCTOR.—Position of the fetus correct. Watch your diet, Mary. Plenty of minerals, calcium, iron. That means milk, plenty of milk and eggs, meat, fruits and vegetables. You need energy. But watch your weight, Mary. Twenty pound increase is just right. Nurse, prepare Mrs. Johnson for complete examination.

MUSIC.—*Up and down.*

NARRATOR.—The eighth month.

DOCTOR.—Fetal heartbeat . . . 1 . . . 2 . . . 3 . . . 4 . . . 5 . . . 6.

SOUND.—*Heartbeat up and down to background.*

DOCTOR.—Beat steady and strong. That's fine. Your own pulse is good. Blood pressure, 110. Everything in shape.

MARY.—I'm glad.

DOCTOR.—Rest and exercise now, Mary. In the next few weeks the pains will come. Do not be frightened. It is a normal way of childbirth. We'll speak to your husband about bringing you to the hospital in plenty of time. And, nurse, give Mrs. Johnson a list of clothing the baby will need.

MUSIC.—*Up and down.*

NARRATOR.—The Lying-in Hospital, a baby is born!

SOUND.—*Scrubbing of hands.*

DOCTOR.—My mask, please, nurse. Keep on scrubbing, Jones.

ASSISTANT.—You know, Doctor, this scrubbing your hands for 10 minutes is the worst chore in the profession.

DOCTOR.—(*Amused*) Well, when you've delivered as many babies as I have, you'll get used to it. There! Time's up.

NURSE.—(*Fading in*) Here's your gown, Doctor.

DOCTOR.—Right. How's Mrs. Johnson?

NURSE.—She's had her shower bath. Birth passage sterilized.

DOCTOR.—Did she eat her lunch?

NURSE.—Every bit.

DOCTOR.—Good. Gloves, please.

NURSE.—Yes, Doctor.

DOCTOR.—(*Through mask*) How regular are her pains now?

NURSE.—Every 3 minutes, Doctor.

DOCTOR.—We'd better go in then.

SOUND.—*Walking.*

DOCTOR.—Hello, Mary. How are you?

WOMAN.—I'm sort of afraid.

DOCTOR.—You mustn't be. If you are afraid, your muscles contract and the baby will only come harder. Remember all the things I told you about your body, how it is built, and how a baby is born. Then you won't be afraid.

MUSIC.—*Up and down.*

SOUND.—*Background gentle noises of doctor's instruments . . . tinkling of glass bottles, etc., to run through the scene.*

DOCTOR.—Anesthesia ready, Dr. Brown?

BROWN.—Ready.

DOCTOR.—Apply only when I give you the word. Not before. She is a healthy girl. This will be a natural birth.

MUSIC.—*Birth theme up and down.*

DOCTOR.—Blood pressure?

BROWN.—120.

DOCTOR.—Fetal heartbeat?

BROWN.—Steady.

DOCTOR.—Beautiful, beautiful. Contractions normal.

MUSIC.—*Up and down.*

DOCTOR.—All right, Brown. When I give the word, when I see the baby's head, apply anesthesia.

BROWN.—All set.

MUSIC.—*Up and down.*

DOCTOR.—Anesthesia!

SOUND.—*Anesthesia.*

DOCTOR.—Beautiful, beautiful.

SOUND.—*Slap of doctor's hands on baby's rump . . . baby starts to cry . . . then a lusty yell.*

MUSIC.—*To tag.*

NARRATOR.—A baby is born, and a young man stands bewildered at the bedside of his wife.

MAN.—Happy, darling?

WIFE.—Yes! But I'm pretty tired.

MAN.—I'm kinda tired myself.

WIFE.—It's a girl, Tom.

MAN.—Oh, that's all right.

WIFE.—But she weighs over 8 pounds. Did you see her, Tom?

MAN.—Oh, yeah, I saw her.

WIFE.—Does she look like me, Tom?

MAN.—Well, no! I mean— well, you know I wasn't very close. It was behind that glass window.

WIFE.—You're not disappointed 'cause it's a girl, are you, Tom?

MAN.—Don't be silly. I'm happy—happy you're Okay. Its a wonderful baby, I guess those wrinkles kinda smooth out after a while.

WIFE.—(*Laughing*) Oh, Tom, your face!

MAN.—Gosh, what did I say now? Don't cry.

WIFE.—I'm not crying. I'm laughing.

MUSIC.—*Up and down.*

NARRATOR.—For the first time on radio you have heard the story of childbirth. Why was this story told? Professor Howard W. Haggard of Yale University answers for us.

HAGGARD.—The position of women in any civilization is an index of the advancement of that civilization. Accordingly, the advances and regressions of civilization are nowhere seen more clearly than in the story of childbirth.

NARRATOR.—All that has gone before paints a pleasant portrait of motherhood in the United States. Unfortunately, our task is not complete without the cold shower of fact. Equipped as our scientists are, with all the knowledge and experience of a century of careful research, here is the situation. Says Dr. Fred Adair, Professor of Obstetrics and Chief of Staff of the University of Chicago's Lying-in Hospital . . .

ADAIR.—More than 10,000 mothers died in childbirth in the United States in the year 1939. The percentage of maternal deaths in this country was one of the highest in the civilized world. One to two mothers die for every 275 to 300 births. Three-fourths of maternal deaths in this country are due to controllable causes. (*Pause*) Of the 275 babies born, 13 will die before they are a year old, and about one-half this same number are born dead.

NARRATOR.—This is a portrait of the American Madonna and child painted with cold figures in the year of our Lord 1940. And there is no excuse for this portrait. The best scientific thought and the best scientific care are at the command of the prospective mothers of America. It remains for society to reap the rewards of scientific achievement. And while half the civilized world is telling a story of destruction and death, today we in America paused to tell the story of birth—the greatest *human adventure!*

MUSIC.—*Up full to finish.*

ANNOUNCER.—(*Should be at least thirty-five years old*) Universities are places of research, storehouses of knowledge. They represent your investment in a better life.

Each year American universities spend 50 million dollars to support 30,000 research projects. Does that sound like a lot of money? Well, let's see—30,000 research projects divided into 50 million dollars equals only 4 dollars and 50 cents per day per project! For this small sum you and all mankind receive the benefits of centuries of knowledge applied to modern problems, to modern living.

You are the stockholders in the libraries, the laboratories, the quiet halls of learning that are America's universities. You are the beneficiaries in the Human Adventure.

Next week The Human Adventure tells the story of the Black Death, a scourge which swept over Europe with a silent force more deadly than 50,000 bombers. Listen next week to the story of the Black Death!

The Human Adventure is presented each week at this same time, in the interest of learning, over a coast-to-coast network by the University of Chicago in collaboration with the Columbia Broadcasting System.

BEST WESTERN

The Lone Ranger

by FRAN STRIKER

Every July, Detroit's Department of Recreation gives a school field day on Belle Isle. This year, 1933, it promised the children that the Lone Ranger would appear in person. He did, masked, on a white horse. The police were prepared to handle a crowd of 20,000—the most that Belle Isle could hold comfortably; 70,000 came. The children broke through the lines and knocked one another down, struggling to get near their hero. The situation became so dangerous that the police had to appeal to the Ranger himself to restore order. He never dared make another public appearance.

So reads a paragraph in an article by J. Bryan III, in the issue of October 14, 1939, of the *Saturday Evening Post.*

This famous program is heard three times a week over 140 stations. Half of these stations carry the "live" show, and half broadcast it by transcription. It is radio's most vital wood pulp and is heard not only throughout America and Canada, but in Hawaii and New Zealand. The program originates from the studio stage of Station WXYZ in Detroit.

The Lone Ranger is an American institution, hero of small boys and old women alike. The scripts are wonderfully horrible and horribly wonderful at the same time, and the cry "Hi-Yo, Silver" has about the same effect on hungry American multitudes as "Dinner is served"! Millions of people leave off what they are doing and do something else. The Lone Ranger is radio's busiest and most powerful crusader for the better life. He is a Lochinvar and Robin Hood, and he has just enough William S. Hart about him to be thoroughly muscular. He is a rage, a phase, a landmark, very definitely a radio entity who for the sake of posterity and the contemporary record deserves the next few pages. Herewith is script No. 1000, written by Fran Striker and performed over the Mutual Broadcasting System on June 30, 1939.

The Lone Ranger

ANNOUNCER.—Smith's Corners people went about their daily routine, little suspecting the tragedy that was coming at noon. It all began with the arrival of many hundred head of cattle, which approached the town in a commonplace way.

SOUND.—*Cattle hoofs.*

ANNOUNCER.—Caleb West noticed it on the outskirts of the town . . .

CALEB.—Wonder whar that stock is comin' from. Yew any idees, sheriff?

SHERIFF.—Nope. I didn't know of any ranch located north o' here.

CALEB.—Downright odd. I . . . Hey, sheriff, ain't that the Bar Jay brand on some of them?

SHERIFF.—By darn, Caleb, that's what it looks tuh be! Bar Jay, sure enough.

CALEB.—An' that's the Bar Jay dewlap! Thunder! Bar Jay ain't no cattle to bring *here now!* Old Blake was robbed a few . . .

SHERIFF.—*Caleb!* That there is the cattle that was stole from *Blake!* I'm goin' tuh have a *talk* with them hombres that's point ride . . .

SOUND.—*Fast shots, back . . . Cattle squeal.*

CALEB.—Look out, sheriff.

SHERIFF.—*Hey, what the . . .*

SOUND.—*Ad libbed fast shots . . . distant shouts . . . stampede starting.*

SHERIFF.—That'll stampede that cattle! Hey, you blame fools, stop that shootin' . . .

PETE.—(*Back*) Thar's the sheriff.

VOICE.—Let him have a couple.

CALEB.—That's Pete Brogan!

SHERIFF.—Stand where . . . (*gasp*)

CALEB.—Sheriff! Sheriff . . .

SOUND.—*Stampede up . . . sustain.*

ANNOUNCER.—Hard-riding two-gun men intentionally stampeded the herd of cattle, throwing fast shots toward where the sheriff and Caleb West stood in surprise. Both men sprawled on the ground while the frightened cattle thundered through the heart of Smith's Corners . . .

SOUND.—*Cattle stampede up . . . shouts ad libbed . . . "Stampede! . . . Git tuh cover! . . . It's a stampede! . . . Look out . . . Shoot anyone that shows! Cover the boys in the bank there."*

ANNOUNCER.—Guns roared whenever a townsman showed himself. The people working in the bank were suddenly surprised by men who dashed through the door . . .

LOOMIS.—Don't leave no one tuh know who we are! Clean 'em up!

SOUND.—*Guns blast . . . shouts of "Wait!" "Don't shoot."*

LOOMIS.—*That's the stuff! Now clean out the bank.*

SOUND.—*Ad libbing voices . . . "Make sure we don't overlook no cash . . . Pete ain't in favor o' slipshod work . . . Fill them sacks, and don't talk so much."*

ANNOUNCER.—(*Over the ad lib*) While grim-faced men looted the bank, others of the same powerful gang rushed old Ma Healy in the express office.

MA.—(*Yell*) What's this mean? Git outen here, yuh . . .

SOUND.—*Shot.*

MA.—*Gasp.*

VOICE.—Okay, *boys*, take that Wells Fargo cash an' the bullion from Goold Curry an' make it fast! Pete cain't keep that stampede goin' all day!

SOUND.—*Stampede fade in again.*

MUSIC.—*Cover . . . excitement . . . then change to . . . soft.*

ANNOUNCER.—Smith's Corners mourned that night. The ruthless attack of Pete Brogan's gang and their wanton gunplay left no less than a dozen people dead and many more wounded. The one doctor in town worked as fast as he could, but he couldn't begin to attend to all the injuries. An Indian, a stranger to everyone in town, appeared quite unexpectedly, and his skill in dressing gunshot wounds impressed even the stern sheriff.

SOUND.—*Water as wound is bathed.*

SHERIFF.—That'll do, Tonto. I c'n bandage that my own self.

TONTO.—Ugh!

SOUND.—*Rap on door.*

SHERIFF.—Who's callin' on you, Caleb?

CALEB.—(*Call out*) Who's thar?

MA.—(*Outside*) It's me, Ma Healy. Is the sheriff in there, Caleb?

CALEB.—Come on in, ma!

SOUND.—*Door opens.*

MA.—Sakes alive, it's a wonder you wouldn't stay around the scenes of . . . Why, sheriff . . . whar'd you git that wound?

SHERIFF.—Evenin', ma.

CALEB.—He took a bullet, when the "Brogan outfit" first hit town.

MA.—An' run intuh town tuh git thar right after things had happened?

SHERIFF.—Why not?

MA.—An' worked all this time with a slug in yer hide? Why, dad-rat you, yuh need someone tuh see that sech blame foolishness don't kill yuh!

SHERIFF.—I didn't have time tuh git patched up then. But how're you?

MA.—Fit as a fiddle!

TONTO.—That not true! You hit by bullet!

MA.—Aw, shucks, Injun, that didn't no more'n give me a headache but not near the headache this blamed Brogan outfit causes. What're yuh aimin' tuh do about 'em, sheriff?

SHERIFF.—That's what I'd like tuh know!

MA.—I seen a couple 'o the snakes. I c'd describe 'em! That's why I hunted you up.

SHERIFF.—Tain't no use, ma!

MA.—No use! I thought yuh wanted descriptions of all of 'em that you c'd git!

SHERIFF.—That uz last week. Things has changed.

MA.—How?

SHERIFF.—Brogan has fetched outlaws from half a dozen states intuh this part of the country! He's holed up in the badlands, an' it'd take more'n an army tuh git him!

MA.—What? More'n an army?

SHERIFF.—That's what I says!

CALEB.—He's got a regular fort up there, ma.

SHERIFF.—Surrounded by rocks that stand 20 foot high. Why, he c'n sit there inside them rocks an' spot a man comin' 10 miles off. A dozen men inside there could stand an army off!

MA.—Yuh know where they're at?

SHERIFF.—Yep. There ain't no mystery about it!

MA.—And yuh can't git 'em?

SHERIFF.—Ma, they ain't but one thing we c'n do! That's tuh sit tight an' hope an' pray that from now on Brogan will leave Smith's Corners alone!

MA.—An' let the skunk git away with all he done tuhday?

SHERIFF.—That's right!

MA.—But what about the army! Doggone it all, move the army here, an' let 'em use cannon tuh rout them rats from their hide-out.

SHERIFF.—Ma, I guess you don't know how far it is tuh where the army is located! What's more, the army is busy fightin' redskins. They got their hands full. It's up tuh the law tuh keep men like Brogan subdued.

MA.—An' the law cain't do nothin' . . . but sit with its fingers crossed. Why, blast yer hide, Sheriff . . .

CALEB.—Sheriff, hain't they some chance of *starvin'* 'em out?

SHERIFF.—Humph! They got springs there, ain't they?

CALEB.—Cain't live forever on *water*.

SHERIFF.—They got food enough stored there tuh last 'em a year! I tell yuh, Ma, Brogan has made a regular business out of bein' an outlaw. He's gone from thievery tuh murder, then tuh cattle stealin' and tuh more murder. Now he's organized in sech a way that he can attack every town inside 2 days' ride of his hide-out, an' they ain't no force of lawmen big enough tuh touch him!

CALEB.—He stole the cattle—just so he could stampede 'em an' chase folks outen the street when he attacked the town.

SHERIFF.—Where'd that Injun go?

MA.—I see him slip out when I come in.

SHERIFF.—*Shucks*! I wanted to ask him a few things.

CALEB.—He's likely gone tuh see if they's any more wounds that need takin' care of.

TONTO.—(*Outside*) Git um up, scout!

SOUND.—*Hoofs start and sustain.*

MUSIC.—*Tonto gallop.*

ANNOUNCER.—Hard riding brought Tonto, the faithful Indian companion of the Lone Ranger, to a prison camp many miles west of Smith's Corners at daybreak. Convicts were already at their work, building a bridge and improving a stage trail.

SOUND.—*Construction work, shoveling, chopping, etc. . . . hoofs clattering to halt.*

WARDEN.—*Howdy*, redskin!

TONTO.—*Whoa, scout! Whoa, feller.*

WARDEN.—What's on yer mind?

TONTO.—Me, Tonto. Where white friend?

WARDEN.—Who d'you mean?

TONTO.—Feller come yesterday. Him make plenty talk!

WARDEN.—Ridin' the white stallion?

TONTO.—That right.

WARDEN.—Wal, me an' him talked aplenty, like you say. Then he rid out north o' here.

TONTO.—Him go *north?*

WARDEN.—That's right, Injun. North!

TONTO.—Not go um east?

WARDEN.—Nope. Was he tuh go east?

TONTO.—Him say, meet-um Tonto! Him not come!

WARDEN.—Um, now that's right curious! He ast a heap o' questions about these men here.

TONTO.—Ugh!

WARDEN.—Wanted tuh know if they'd done anything real serious, an' I told him most o' them was servin' time fer desertin' the army.

TONTO.—Um!

WARDEN.—Then, while we was talkin', a couple gents come up, an' they spoke fer a time with this hombre that rid the white hoss. Then the three o' them started out northard.

TONTO.—Git um up, scout!

SOUND.—*Hoofs start . . . fade out.*

MUSIC.—*Tension interlude.*

ANNOUNCER.—Tonto felt a vague apprehension, when told about the two men with whom his friend had ridden away. He knew that the Lone Ranger went into the convict camp with his face disguised but unmasked. He also knew that the Lone Ranger would have met him in Smith's Corners, if someone hadn't prevented this. What the Indian did not know was that Pete Brogan and a couple of his men were at that very moment talking on the trail . . .

SOUND.—*Background of clumps in place.*

PETE.—Soyuh picked this hombre up yesterday after we raided the town, eh?

SNEAD.—That's right, Pete! An' we ain't let him git out from under our gunsights since then. We ain't takin' no chance with this gent.

RANGER.—What do you want of me?

PETE.—*Why're you so interested in my business?*

RANGER.—Because I want to find a way to *smash* you and your gang!

PETE.—*Wal!* (*Chuckles*) A right outspoken gent, ain't yuh?

RANGER.—Yo're running things with a pretty high hand, Pete, but you won't go on much longer.

PETE.—No? An' maybe you're figgerin' tuh stop me! I heard it *said* that that was what was on yer mind.

RANGER.—Yes, it is.

PETE.—(*Chuckles*) Purty big plans. If yuh cain't git the best of *two* of my men, an' not two of the best ones either, jest *how* d'yew figger on gittin' the best of the hull pack of us?

RANGER.—That can be done, Brogan.

SNEAD.—Brogan, he's got a pal o' some sort that he figgers on trailin' us!

PETE.—*What?*

SNEAD.—Yeah, we figgered yuh'd want tuh git the pal as well, so that uz why we kept quiet when we seen what he was doin'!

PETE.—*What uz he doin'?*

SNEAD.—Wal, it uz yesterday when we got him, yuh know. We rid all night gittin' this far.

PETE.—Yeah?

SNEAD.—He figgered we didn't see him, but I did. He blazed a trail.

PETE.—*He what?*

SNEAD.—That's right. (*Chuckles*) Thought you was puttin' one over on me, didn't yuh, stranger? (*Pause*) All right then, don't answer! But yuh see now that Pete Brogan don't have no *fools* workin' fer him!

PETE.—Take him on tuh the headquarters, gents. Me an' Loomis an' Driscoll will go on an' ride the back trail, watchin' out fer the friend o' his.

SNEAD.—Right. You c'n follow it easy enough. You'll see the marks he put on the trees we rid past.

PETE.—Good enough. Come on, boys. G'lang thar!

VOICE.—*Git up.*

LOOMIS.—*Git.*

SOUND.—*Hoofs start . . . fade out.*

RANGER.—Snead, you're pretty observing, aren't you?

SNEAD.—(*Laughs*) That's the time yuh got fooled.

RANGER.—So you thought I was blazing a trail, eh?

SNEAD.—If yuh wasn't, what *was* yuh doin'?

VOICE.—Nemmine the talk. Let's git back tuh the hide-out.

SNEAD.—Now git ridin', stranger!

RANGER.—And leave Brogan to capture my friend?

SNEAD.—Reckon you an' yore pal will die about the same time. Now git!

RANGER.—Not yet! Hi, Silver!

SOUND.—*Hoofs clatter.*

SNEAD.—Hey . . .

VOICE.—Look out!

RANGER.—At them, boy!

SOUND.—*Shrill whinny . . . clattering of hoofs.*

RANGER.—Down!

VOICE.—(*Scream*) Hi thar . . .

SOUND.—*Shots.*

RANGER.—Get 'em, boy!

ANNOUNCER.—The mighty stallion leaped suddenly at the Lone Ranger's signal and lunged against the nearest of the outlaws. This man, knocked off balance, was helpless as the big white horse reared and lashed down with those sharp forefeet at Snead. Snead, dodging, spilled from the saddle. The Lone Ranger leaped headlong at him, bringing his fist against the heavy jaw of the crook.

SOUND.—*Blow.*

SNEAD.—(*Moans*)

ANNOUNCER.—The other man was firing wildly, blindly, as he fought to maintain his saddle. The Lone Ranger sprang to his feet, as Silver kept charging the outlaw to keep him off balance. Snatching a gun from the unconscious Snead, he fired quickly . . .

SOUND.—*Shot.*

VOICE.—(*Yells*) My hand . . . my hand . . .

ANNOUNCER.—Blasting the gun from the killer's hand. Then he grabbed at the man, jerking him from his horse . . .

RANGER.—*I want you, too!*

VOICE.—*My hand, yuh ain't fair! Yuh* . . .

RANGER.—*Come off that saddle!*

VOICE.—(*Grunts*) *Blast yuh* . . .

RANGER.—(*Struggling*) I'm roping you first!

VOICE.—*My hand is* . . .

RANGER.—Your hand's not hurt! That bullet only struck your gun! *There!* That'll keep your arms down!

VOICE.—Blast yuh, my pals will git yuh fir this! They'll git yuh if it's the last thing they ever do! Yuh cain't git away with this!

RANGER.—(*Tossing rope*) We'll see about that!

ANNOUNCER.—Coil after coil of rope was tossed about the outlaw until he could move neither arms nor legs! Then the Lone Ranger treated the unconscious man in the same way! The two were tied to the trunk of a convenient tree. The Lone Ranger reclaimed his gun belt from the one who had taken it; then when the brace of familiar weapons were strapped in place, he took a mask from beneath his shirt and adjusted it over his eyes. Now he was the masked mystery rider once again. He leaped astride the great horse Silver and shouted . . .

RANGER.—*Hi yo, Silver! Away-y-y-y*

SOUND.—*Hoofs.*

MUSIC.—*Theme song sustain in background.*

ANNOUNCER.—Riding hard along the trail he'd blazed, the Lone Ranger thought only of the safety of his faithful Indian companion Tonto.

RANGER.—*If Brogan gets to Tonto first, he'll make him think we're prisoners! Come on, Silver old boy, stretch out those great legs of yours! We've got to let Tonto understand that we're not captured! Hi yo, Silver, away!*

MUSIC.—*Crescendo to finish.*

ANNOUNCER.—The curtain falls on the first act of our Lone Ranger drama. Before the next exciting scenes, please permit us to pause for just a moment.

(Commercial and Presentation)

ANNOUNCER.—Tonto followed the trail blazed by the Lone Ranger when the masked mystery rider was a captive of Pete Brogan's men. The Indian rode fast, his keen eye catching the small marks on the trees he passed. Then three men loomed on the trail ahead . . .

SOUND.—*Hoofs clattering to halt.*

TONTO.—*Whoa, scout!* Whoa, feller!

PETE.—(*Approaching*) Rein up, boys. *Whoa* thar!

SOUND.—*Hoofs approach and halt . . . ad libbed whoas.*

PETE.—Git ver hands high, redskin. We hanker tuh ask you aplenty of questions!

TONTO.—Who you?

PETE.—I said we'd *ask* questions, not answer 'em.

TONTO.—Ugh.

PETE.—You lookin' fer a white friend that's been captured?

TONTO.—You see-um him?

PETE.—Mebbe we have. Are yuh or *ain't* yuh huntin' him?

TONTO.—Me want um him!

PETE.—That's what we wanted tuh know! Grab him, boys!

VOICE 2.—Right!

TONTO.—What this?

PETE.—Git a rope around him!

LOOMIS.—This'll hold him!

PETE.—Make a move, an' we'll drill yuh here an' now! Now let's git ridin'! Lead the redskin's hoss fer him!

SOUND.—*Ad libbed git ups . . . hoofs start . . . sustain.*

ANNOUNCER.—Tonto, tightly lashed, was compelled to go with Pete Brogan through the woods toward the badlands and the outlaw stronghold. But as the group progressed, the Indian suddenly noted a new sign on some of the trees he passed. It was a cryptic pattern that could not have been cut there in a hurry. His face showed a trace of a grin . . . Suddenly, Tonto ducked low in the saddle, bending far over the neck of his horse Scout. At the same instant the three outlaws were dragged from the saddle and spilled to the ground.

SOUND.—*Hoofs breaking.*

PETE.—(*Gasp*) *What* the . . .

LOOMIS.—Hi . . .

VOICE 2.—G-g-got . . . got me! What's happened?

PETE.—Where . . . shoot . . . shoot it out . . . who roped us . . .

RANGER.—Keep your hands away from guns!

PETE.—Wha . . . what the . . .

RANGER.—You're covered!

LOOMIS.—You!

VOICE 2.—That voice. That's the crittur Snead had . . .

RANGER.—Your pals are already roped and waiting for jail!

TONTO.—Steady, scout!

RANGER.—I'll have you cut loose in just a minute, Kemo Sabay.

PETE.—You stretched a rope between them trees!

RANGER.—Of course, I did! That was the easiest way to catch you without giving you the chance to fire on Tonto! There you are, Tonto.

TONTO.—Now, Tonto, rope um, feller!

RANGER.—This will make five of the Brogan gang to take to the sheriff in town!

PETE.—The jail ain't made that'll hold me!

RANGER.—We'll see about that!

TONTO.—Put um hand behind back.

LOOMIS.—I won't do it! I (*howl*) ouchhh . . .

TONTO.—That better.

RANGER.—Make those ropes good and tight, Tonto! I guess we wont need to use the plan I had in mind to capture the Brogan outlaws.

PETE.—They ain't no plan that man ever made that'll hold me! I'm bigger'n the law! The law don't dare hold me! My men will wipe out every town around here, if I ain't let go!

MUSIC.—*Tension interlude.*

ANNOUNCER.—When the Lone Ranger left the five outlaws, well tied, in the hands of the sheriff, he rode away, not realizing the terror that Brogan's gang had brought to the entire region. Brogan, as a captive, had a lot to say, and the townspeople heard it . . .

PETE.—Keep me in this jail an' yuh wont have a house left standin'! You know what happened yesterday! Wal, that ain't nothin' tuh what our outfit'll do when they hear I'm prisoner here! (*Murmurs of crowd*) You folks better talk it over an' make the sheriff see things right fer yer own good!

CALEB.—(*Back*) Dad-rat it, sheriff. We cain't risk bein' wiped out.

SHERIFF.—Them prisoners ain't gittin' loose!

VOICE.—I dunno but what the sheriff is wrong, this time.

SOUND.—*Ad libbed murmurs increasing.*

MA.—Now don't go agin the sheriff. Hain't none of yuh no spunk?

CALEB.—I got a family tuh think of.

VOICE.—I cain't afford havin' my place burned down.

AD-LIB.—Brogan's men'll do jest what he says . . . They got a reg'lar army out there in the badlands . . . I figger we should turn 'em loose, if they make promises to us . . . I dunno. It calls fer deep thinkin' . . . It's ag'in all principles . . . First principle is self-preservation . . .

SOUND.—*Sustain ad lib.*

ANNOUNCER.—The crowd that gathered outside the jail was deeply impressed by the harsh threats of the men behind the barred windows. They realized that the scant number of able-bodied men in town would be almost helpless against the well-armed Brogan outlaw band. They talked among themselves while Brogan shouted at them from time to time . . .

PETE.—Yuh better let us go right soon, or it'll be too late!

CALEB.—(*Turn*) I'm fer lettin' 'em go free!

VOICE.—Me, too!

SOUND.—*Ad libbed shouts of agreement.*

SHERIFF.—Yuh cain't do it, folks! We got five of the gang jailed, an' we'll git the rest!

CALEB.—Stand aside, sheriff!

AD LIB.—Stand tuh one side! We're turnin' 'em loose! Someone git their hosses. We'll protect our town. Let other folks do the same!

SHERIFF.—(*Ad libbing pleading*) Folks, use yer heads! This ain't right! Yuh can't turn the killers loose. (*Sustain ad libs*)

ANNOUNCER.—The sheriff's pleas were useless. The townspeople stormed the small jail, broke the lock; and in a moment the five gloating outlaws were free to mount their horses and ride away.

CALEB.—Now, remember. Yuh promised tuh leave our town alone!

PETE.—I got aplenty of scores tuh settle! One of them is with you, sheriff . . . fer wantin' tuh keep me jailed!

SHERIFF.—Why, you . . .

PETE.—You'll hear more of us! Come on, boys! Git up.

SOUND.—*Ad libbed git ups . . . Hoofs start and fade.*

MA.—Yuh pack of white-livered jellyfish! What right've you got tuh call yerselves men! I'm leavin' this town! This is a town that ain't fit tuh be on the face of the map!

RANGER.—(*Back*) Come on, Silver!

CALEB.—Who's that ridin' down here?

MA.—Thar's a man! Thar's the masked man that captured five o' them! An' all you lizards put tuhgether ain't the nerve tuh hold 'em when they're captured!

RANGER.—(*Approaching*) Whoa, there . . . whoa, Silver . . .

SHERIFF.—The masked man!

RANGER.—*Sheriff* . . . Have you let the killers go?

SHERIFF.—I had tuh do it, stranger . . .

RANGER.—Why?

SHERIFF.—I wanted tuh hold 'em, but they talked fear intuh the rest o' the folks here!

RANGER.—And they've been released to return to their stronghold?

SHERIFF.—That's right, an' I'm quittin' Smith's Corner's right now.

RANGER.—Quitting! That's not your job! Your job is to make this town a fit one to live in!

CALEB.—All right, what's tuh be done? Maybe you'll ride up tuh Brogan's fort—intuh the *teeth* of *rifles* an' *cannon*—an' clean them killers out!

RANGER.—Is there anyone here will ride with me?

VOICE.—Not me!

MA.—I will, by ginger. As old as I am, I'll ride with yuh.

SHERIFF.—I'll go, stranger . . .

CALEB.—Well, I won't.

AD LIB.—Not me. It's certain death! They aint a *chance* of beatin' 'em!

RANGER.—Two people! One of them an old lady! Your town isn't fit to be saved! But there are other towns to consider! Come on, boy!

SOUND.—*Hoofs clatter.*

SHERIFF.—Where yuh goin'?

RANGER.—Hi yo, Silver . . .

SHERIFF.—Hey . . .

RANGER.—*Away-y-y-y.*

SOUND.—*Hoofs start . . . sustain.*

MUSIC.—*Theme of gallop, faint.*

ANNOUNCER.—Wheeling the white stallion, the Lone Ranger raced away from town and headed back for his camp where Tonto waited to learn if the rumor was right . . . The masked mystery rider came to a rearing halt . . .

SOUND.—*Hoofs clattering to halt.*

RANGER.—Back to the original plan, Tonto! Those folks are helpless! They'll be taught a lesson! To the saddle!

TONTO.—Me ready!

RANGER.—Come on, Silver!

SOUND.—*Hoofs start . . . fade out.*

MUSIC

SLADE.—(*Fading in*) It ain't that the work in this camp is tough, boys; the warden sure ain't rough on us; it's jest bein' a prisoner fer so many years that bothers me . . . we ain't nothin' but a pack of forgotten men!

MUSIC.—*Soft evening theme.*

ANNOUNCER.—One of the prisoners at the camp was speaking to his companions as the warden came up, overhearing him . . .

WARDEN.—I'm afraid that's what you'll be, Slade, fer a good many years tuh come—forgotten men.

SLADE.—Oh, I didn't see yuh come up, warden.

WARDEN.—I'll admit that most of you deserve a better life. There ain't a man in this camp that's vicious or a man that's done anything more serious than tuh protest against the war . . .

SLADE.—We figgered tuh end the war a year before it did end . . . by refusin' tuh carry on the fight. That's all, warden.

WARDEN.—I know your records. Now, boys, I come to tell you somethin'!

SLADE.—Um.

WARDEN.—If I was in any one of your shoes, I'd almost as soon do anything, as live like this!

SLADE.—Me, too.

WARDEN.—Suppose . . . there was a chance fer you to fight!

SLADE.—Is the war started again?

WARDEN.—They's a different sort of war now. A war against crooks that've infested the West.

SLADE.—They's sheriffs tuh take care of that.

WARDEN.—But the lawmen can't! Boys, maybe some of you noticed the man on the white hoss that was around here.

SLADE.—Yeah, what'd he want?

WARDEN.—He brought me a special order. Now I don't know if you'll be needed or not. He's goin' to let us know. But the thing is, you're goin' to be offered the chance to win a free pardon.

SOUND.—*Excited chatter.*

SLADE.—How! Tell us how!

WARDEN.—Wait, boys! Quiet down a minute.

SLADE.—Tell us!

WARDEN.—Pete Brogan's gang is fortified in the badlands. He's too well protected for any posse the sheriff can get together to wipe out.

SLADE.—Is that the same Brogan that sold out the army?

WARDEN.—The same!

SLADE.—Why, that . . .

WARDEN.—Listen to me! There's horses here to equip you. The same ones you've used for work. There ain't one chance in a hundred for a man to live through an attack on Brogan's stronghold; but if you do, you'll earn your pardons!

SOUND.—*Excited chatter.*

WARDEN.—Hold on, boys! I ain't said yet that you was needed.

SLADE.—Of course we're needed! We heard about Pete Brogan! We know his kind!

WARDEN.—He's skilled in army work. He knows fightin'!

SLADE.—So do we! This is a different kind of fightin' than when we was shootin' men the same as us! In some cases our own relations! Give us a fightin' chance tuh be free men! That's all we ask!

SOUND.—*Ad libbing agreement.*

AD LIB.—Let us go! You gotta give us the chance!

WARDEN.—Boys, it's 'most the same as suicide!

AD LIB.—*Sustaining.*

SLADE.—Warden! We're going! We're goin'! You cain't stop us!

SOUND.—*Ad libbing builds.*

MUSIC.—*Fade in chaotic . . . burst . . . then down fast.*

SOUND.—*Clattering of hoofs.*

SLADE.—We're startin' out, boys! Git tuh yer saddles!

VOICE 3.—You take command, Slade!

SLADE.—Whar's that bugler! This is an attack, boys! It's fer freedom or kingdom come! Are yuh mounted? (*Shouting agreement . . . blast of bugle*) Thar's the bugle! Follow me, boys! We're headin' fer Brogan's fort! Git up!

SOUND.—*Blast of bugle . . . shouts and hoofs . . . fade out.*

MUSIC.—*Crescendo.*

ANNOUNCER.—The long pent-up energies of the strange army of convicts found an outlet, as they raced to what was almost certain death in the slim hope that some would live to become free men.

The Lone Ranger came into the convict camp some time later to learn that the men had already gone!

RANGER.—Hi yo! Silver . . .

SOUND.—*Hoofs clattering.*

RANGER.—But they were to wait until I came!

SOUND.—*Hoofs.*

MUSIC.—*Burst.*

ANNOUNCER.—The Lone Ranger realized that the odds would greatly favor the outlaws. Yet he dashed on to be with them when they made their attack. Miles from the convict camp the light of the moon showed Brogan and his men the hard-riding soldiers, and the outlaws behind their rocky fortress opened fire. (*Burst of gunfire . . . hoofs . . . shouts*) The first volley dropped many of the former soldiers. The rest spread out but kept riding up the hill, saving their few precious shots.

AD LIB.—We can't do it, boys. We may's well give up.

RANGER.—*Who said that?*

ANNOUNCER.—The men turned toward the new voice that spoke. The man was masked, and his white stallion showed hard riding.

RANGER.—You keep falling back! That's playing right into Brogan's hands! Keep going! Keep going, and some of you will make the fort! They can't stop all of you!

VOICE 2.—I had enough!

VOICE 3.—Me, too!

RANGER.—All right . . . deserters! Quit! Those of you who are men . . . can follow me!

VOICE 3.—Yuh ridin' up there alone, stranger?

RANGER.—No! I'm not riding alone! There are a lot of men right here who will follow me!

ANNOUNCER.—The Lone Ranger reached beneath his shirt as he spoke. He drew out a brilliantly colored piece of bunting. He unfolded it, and the moonlight showed red . . . white . . . and stars in a field of blue!

RANGER.—I'm flying this flag from inside that stronghold! . . . Come on, boys . . . Who'll follow Old Glory?

SOUND.—*Hoofs.*

VOICE 3.—The flag!

AD LIB.—*Cheers.*

VOICE 2.—Boys . . . I'm ridin' with him!

VOICE 3.—Come on! Git up thar!

RANGER.—Hi yo, Silver! Away . . .

SOUND.—*Ad libbed git ups . . . hoofs very strong.*

ANNOUNCER.—Inspired by the flag the former soldiers thrilled to the task before them. They raced madly up the hill.

SOUND.—*Gunfire.*

MUSIC.—*Chaotic sustaining.*

ANNOUNCER.—This time there was no turning back. The Lone Ranger raced into the very teeth of the outlaw fire. The men with him could not be stopped. Many of them took bullets and still kept going. They gained the fort, then stormed inside.

SOUND.—*Hoofs clattering to halt . . . hand-to-hand fighting.*

ANNOUNCER.—Some leaped from their horses, using their rifles as clubs. Others had bayonets. The Lone Ranger, still astride the mighty Silver, was everywhere. The outlaws, cowards at heart, were disorganized. The attackers had accomplished the impossible! The fortress had offered no defense against the unfaltering spirit, and the sharp hand-to-hand struggle was brief!

MUSIC.—*Burst . . . finish.*

RANGER.—(*Cue*) Now, Brogan, you're going to go back to the prison!

PETE.—D-don't . . . don't take me there . . . they . . . they'll *hang* me now.

RANGER.—And is there anything that's more deserved? *You men* . . . you've showed the people of Smith's Corners what *men* can do! You're going to be granted pardons. Take this flag, and keep it flying out here in the country you conquered.

VOICE 3.—We . . . there . . . there ain't many of us left . . .

RANGER.—It's up to those of you who are left to make this the sort of country your friends would be willing to give their lives for! That is the foundation of America.

VOICE 3.—I . . . I ast the bugler . . . figgerin' on raisin' this flag here . . . if he remembered his calls. He's fixin' tuh sound off.

RANGER.—What call?

VOICE 3.—To the colors.

MUSIC.—(*Bugle*) "*To the Colors*" *fade-out.*

RANGER.—(*Slightly back . . . On cue*) Hi yo, Silver! Away . . .

MUSIC.—*Theme.*

BEST DAYTIME SERIAL

Pepper Young's Family

by Elaine Sterne Carrington

In coming to the first, and perhaps the last, example of a daytime serial that I will reprint, several things need to be mentioned before the actual mechanics of this form of radio writing can be properly comprehended and appreciated by the layman. It is commonly supposed that, because the daytime serial is so often trashy, its writer is likewise a trashy writer. This is true in only a very few cases. Most of the serials of the sort that we are discussing are not only the literary products of definitely professional writers but are the products of writers who were very definitely professional long before they were doing anything of this sort.

It is important to know people and to know how to record what they do and say, if the desired effect of such record is to bring the reader into a close and sympathetic participation with the people whose lives are unfolded before him. This cannot be done by amateurs. It can be accomplished only by the man or woman who has done a great deal of watching and listening and a great deal of recording, too, and who has printed it and watched for the effect on his own readers of what he has printed.

Let us take the case of our present author as an illustration. She is Elaine Sterne Carrington, one of the most prolific and highly paid writers in radio today. Almost all her income during the past few years has been derived from radio. Almost none of it was derived from radio when she was making her living as a fiction writer in the magazine world. Her stories have appeared in *Harper's*, *Collier's*, *Good Housekeeping*, *Saturday Evening Post*, *Woman's Home Companion*, *Pictorial Review*, and *Red Book*. She has published collections of her own short stories and has written a play or two for Broadway.

Since her first radio program (1932) she has done very little magazine work. The mere physical fact that she has ten scripts a week to write makes additional creative effort too hard. In 1932 she wrote a show called Red Adams. It ran for three months as a sustainer and then was bought by the Beechnut Company. This firm changed the name to Red Davis. Under this title it moved to evening time, ran for two years solid, and gained top rating as the most popular serial on the air. It was then purchased by Procter and Gamble, and Red Davis suddenly became "Forever Young." This, in turn, eventually changed once more to Pepper Young's Family, a sample of which I am including this year. With the great-grandmother of all daytime serials, Ma Perkins, the Pepper Young stories have shared top honors for many years. I think, at the present moment, Pepper is shy of Ma by three-tenths of a point.

Miss Carrington's own ideas about the radio phase of her career are illuminating, and I wish to quote her briefly:

I am intensely curious about every form of writing and have always thought I could do anything if I tried. I never seem to be discouraged by finding out I can't. I was intensely curious about radio. It seemed to me it was unlimited opportunity for writing, and for a new form of writing quite different from what I was doing for magazines and the stage. With that in mind, I stopped in one day at the National Broadcasting Company with a one-act play of mine, which Henry Hull always used as a vehicle when he wanted to do a turn in vaudeville. It was called "Five Minutes from the Station." They read it at NBC, and liked the dialogue, and sent for me and asked me if I would care to tackle a serial. The idea appalled me. I didn't feel I could keep any idea going for any length of time, as my true medium was the short story. However, they prevailed upon me to prepare two audition scripts, which I did, and these were the scripts that became "Red Adams." I should have said, when they asked me to do a serial that I had no idea what to write about. I should have said, frankly, that all I knew about was an American family, such as I was trying to raise myself, and that, if this idea appealed to them, I'd take a fling at it. Thus "Pepper Young" was born. It was then, and still is, the story of an average American family doing their darndest to give every advantage to a son and daughter, to understand them, and encourage them and correct their faults. It seemed to me that in this time of flux, the only thing stable was American family life itself. And that is what I built the story around—the very best family life I could possibly offer my public.

Miss Carrington works lying down and dictates all of her stuff, stretched out on a big couch near the waters of Long Island Sound. She starts working each week on Monday morning at ten and sometimes works right through till midnight. She keeps up this pace until all ten shows are written (her other five-time a week serial being "When a Girl Marries") and then takes a day off to revise what she has dictated, to point the dialogue, to cut overwritten pages, to improve transitions, etc. She is usually through by Thursday night. She spends Friday, Saturday, and Sunday recovering from the ordeal of the previous four days and enjoys life quietly with her family over the week end. She puts completely out of her mind all idea of her work, her characters, and her plots when she is enjoying these weekly periods of relaxation. She writes twenty thousand words a week.

Here is episode 1031 of Pepper Young's Family, heard on Christmas Day, 1939, entitled "Back in the Old House."

Pepper Young's Family

ANNOUNCER.—This is a day of special rejoicing for the Youngs. For today Mr. Young is going to take Mrs. Young back to the old house on Union Street and give her the grandest surprise of her life; for he has arranged to rent the house so that the Youngs can move back in their old home again. It's the one thing in the world Mrs. Young wants. Pepper and Peggy are already at the old house fixing it up for the surprise. And Mr. Young is going to try to get his wife to go over to Union Street with him without letting her know the secret. As we join them now, Mr. and Mrs. Young are in the living room of their little house on Harvey Street. Mr. Young says:

FATHER.—What time are you figuring on having dinner?

MOTHER.—Well, I was going to have it fairly early. But, Sam, we can't, not with all the children out of the house and goodness knows where.

FATHER.—Isn't anybody home?

MOTHER.—No. They all shot out of here right after breakfast. Do you know, I never knew that to happen before on Christmas morning.

FATHER.—Oh, I s'pose they've got presents to deliver to their friends and errands to do and . . .

MOTHER.—They've always stayed home on Christmas Day before.

FATHER.—Have they?

MOTHER.—Why, Sam, you know perfectly well they have. And I don't *like* their trotting off this way without a word as to when they'll be home or anything else. I don't like it a bit.

FATHER.—Well, honey, they're growing up, whether you like it or not.

MOTHER.—Now what do you mean by that?

FATHER.—I mean Christmas probably doesn't rate as high with them as it once did.

MOTHER.—Well, it still rates high with me.

FATHER.—And with me, too. But you can't expect Pepper to hang around here all day. He wants to get over to Linda's house and give her whatever he has for her. And Peggy and Edie and Biff are someplace else. Yes, you've got to face it, Mary, they aren't kids any more. Dancing around the Christmas tree and clapping their hands and gurgling are things of the past.

MOTHER.—It's such a nice tree, too. I picked it out myself.

FATHER.—Sure it's a nice tree. But it's for you and me, Mary, not for them any more.

MOTHER.—Sam, stop talking like that. You're spoiling the whole day for me.

FATHER.—All right, I'll stop, then. What time did you say we'd have dinner?

MOTHER.—Oh, I don't know. How can I tell with nobody here?

FATHER.—Can you name an hour?

MOTHER.—Why do you keep on asking me to name an hour? Do *you* want to go someplace else, too?

FATHER.—Well . . .

MOTHER.—Where?

FATHER.—As long as we've got the whole morning ahead of us, I think I'll just take a run over to Elmwood proper.

MOTHER.—And leave me here all alone in Elmwood *im*proper? Not much!

FATHER.—I thought you had dinner to get.

MOTHER.—Well, I don't have to get it this minute. And if you think, Sam Young, that I'm going to stay here alone and twiddle my thumbs on Christmas Day and . . . and think about the past while you're in Elmwood "proper," as you call it, you're very much mistaken. I'm going with you.

FATHER.—All right, dear, all right. Get your togs on.

MOTHER.—Not that I want to go to "Elmwood proper" at *all.*

FATHER.—I've got to go. It's a matter of business.

MOTHER.—Business? On Christmas Day?

FATHER.—Yes, I can catch Phillips in today. Ready? Come on.

MOTHER.—Phillips! You mean you're going to see Mr. Phillips who . . . who lives in our old house?

FATHER.—Yes, sure. Why not?

MOTHER.—Oh, Sam, I couldn't go there on . . . on Christmas Day. I just couldn't, that's all.

FATHER.—All right, Mary, but I'm not quite sure when I'll be back.

MOTHER.—I won't stay here alone. All right, I'll go. But you can leave me parked outside the house while you go in. And I don't see how you can even think of going there on this day of all days.

SOUND.—*Door closes.*

FATHER.—Oh, I don't mind. That house isn't our house any more; it's theirs.

MOTHER.—It'll never be theirs to me, never!

SOUND.—*Door slams . . . car starts.*

FATHER.—I want to talk to him about a tract of land he's interested in over in Winsford. Nice piece of property. He wants to put up a taxpayer on it and . . .

MOTHER.—I don't want to hear about it.

FATHER.—You don't! I thought you'd be crazy to hear about it.

MOTHER.—Well, I'm not. Oh, Sam, do you s'pose all our Christmases from now on are going to be so . . . so bleak?

FATHER.—Bleak? What's the matter with this one? I'm out with my best girl, am I not?

MOTHER.—Sam, I want them to be little again.

FATHER.—*Who?*

MOTHER.—Oh, you know who, you goose, the children, Pepper and Peggy. I want them tiptoeing into our room at daybreak Christmas morning to get their stockings and jumping on the bed and waking us up and yelling, "Merry Christmas."

FATHER.—I prefer to sleep late on Christmas morning, the way we did today, for instance, if you don't mind.

MOTHER.—And I love cleaning up the mess of tissue paper and oranges and sugar candy left in the wake of the stockings. And I love having the living-room doors closed tight and lighting the candles on the Christmas tree and keeping them quiet till you dressed up like Santa Claus.

FATHER.—Till I was suffocated under those confounded masks and stuffy costumes, you mean.

MOTHER.—Oh, you loved those days as much as I did. You know you did.

FATHER.—I was always glad when the candles were out and no major conflagration had taken place. I guess we're about the only people left who use candles. Everybody else uses electric lights.

MOTHER.—And, oh, Sam, I loved it when I'd open the living-room doors wide and call, "Come in, now, children." And instead of coming in they'd just stand there in the doorway with their cheeks so pink from excitement and their eyes popping out of their heads. Sam, I want that kind of Christmas again.

FATHER.—Honey, time doesn't stand still. We might as well face it. Life goes forward. Things change. Little pink-cheeked, wide-eyed children grow up.

MOTHER.—(*Break in voice*) Well, I hate it. I . . . Oh, Sam, why do we have to be back here in this part of Elmwood today?

FATHER.—I'm darned glad to be back here. Looks familiar, doesn't it? Say, there's a pretty tree right in that front yard. Bet it looks nice tonight when they light it up.

MOTHER.—Are you going to be long at the . . . the Phillips?

FATHER.—No, I don't think so. But it's an important deal, Mary. Mighty important. If Phillips wants that land and can get his company in Chicago to back him, it may turn out the most profitable deal I've closed yet and . . .

MOTHER.—Sam, I think you'd better let me stay around the corner from Union Street. I don't want to see the old house today. Not today, please, not today.

FATHER.—Now, Mary, that's just silly and sentimental of you. Of course you're going to see it. That's all part of life, too, having something one day, losing it the next.

MOTHER.—All right, then, I'm silly and sentimental. But I don't want to go near it today just the same.

FATHER.—I'm not going to humor you any more. I'm going to stop in front of the old house, and you're going to get over that feeling the way you do about it. It's just a . . . a phobia with you, Mary. You've got to look at these things reasonably. It *was* our house once. It's somebody else's house now. Just be hard-boiled about it.

MOTHER.—I . . . I can't, Sam. Oh, please don't stop here, please don't.

FATHER.—I'm going to do it, because I want to get you over this mental hazard. Stop covering up your eyes. Look at it.

SOUND.—*Car stops . . . door slams.*

MOTHER.—I . . . I . . . (*voice quivers*) Sam, they've got a tree in the window just the same place we always had our tree.

FATHER.—Um. Yes. So they have. Well, isn't that a coincidence?

MOTHER.—It's almost as if we . . . as if the children . . . as if all of us . . .

FATHER.—Look, honey, I'm going to ask you, for my sake, to do something that's going to be awfully tough for you to do.

MOTHER.—Do what?

FATHER.—For the sake of this deal, Mary, if you just go to the door with me and speak to Phillips and his wife . . .

MOTHER.—Oh, no, Sam, not that! You wouldn't ask me to do that.

FATHER.—You needn't go inside. Just go up the steps and say, "Merry Christmas." It'll put the whole thing on a different basis. What I mean is, the Phillips feel sort of lonesome and out of joint here in Elmwood. And if you'd just be friendly enough to step up and wish them a Merry Christmas . . .

MOTHER.—No, Sam.

FATHER.—If they saw you sitting out there in the car, well, it might make Phillips think you thought he was beneath you or something. Come on, dear. I wouldn't ask you to do it except that it may help put across a deal. And, better than that, it may be a kindly act to a couple of lonely strangers here on Christmas Day.

MOTHER.—I . . . all right, Sam, I'll try. But I'm not sure I can.

SOUND.—*Door slams.*

FATHER.—Good for you, Mary. I know just what a tough thing I'm asking you to do.

MOTHER.—And I'm not doing it because of your old deal either.

FATHER.—I know that.

MOTHER.—This is the hardest thing you've ever asked me to do.

FATHER.—I know it.

MOTHER.—Walking up this path, up these steps, ringing this doorbell . . . (*voice breaks*) Oh, Sam, I can't bear it. It's my house, not theirs. It's my house.

SOUND.—*Door opens.*

CROWD.—Merry Christmas, Mrs. Young, Merry Christmas!

FATHER.—You bet it's your house, yours forever more, I hope.

MOTHER.—What? Who? Where?

PEGGY.—Mama, darling, it's our Christmas surprise for you.

PEPPER.—Yeah, and we thought you'd never get here. Boy, are you late!

LINDA.—It's your house again, Mrs. Young.

MOTHER.—My house? Sam, I don't understand. Sam, I . . . I think I'd better sit down.

PEPPER.—That's right. We've got it back again. And that's what we've been doin' every night, gettin' it ready.

PEGGY.—And Mama, look! Almost all the old furniture back . . .

LINDA.—That's Nick's and Hattie's and Lew's and my Christmas present to you.

HATTIE.—Yes, Mrs. Young, we bought it all and kept it at the time of the auction.

MOTHER.—Hattie! Hattie! Tell me I'm not dreaming all this.

NICK.—You're wide awake, Mrs. Young, which is more than most of us are, after the night we put in getting things to rights.

MOTHER.—But, Sam, how? I don't understand. I don't understand anything. Won't somebody tell me about this? Won't somebody please explain?

FATHER.—The Phillips moved out.

PEGGY.—And we moved in.

PEPPER.—That's all there is to it.

MOTHER.—Moved in? You mean . . . you mean we can stay here, here in this house again? Here? Oh, Sam!

PEGGY.—I told you Mama'd cry.

HATTIE.—I guess we're all cryin'.

BIFF.—Gee, Mrs. Young, if you only knew how we've been waitin' for this minute when you'd see it again for the first time.

EDIE.—It was really I who thought of Mr. Young's renting it.

FATHER.—Yes, Edie, all the credit for that goes straight to you.

MOTHER.—You mean you've rented it, Sam?

FATHER.—Yes. I couldn't afford to buy it, but I may be able to someday.

MOTHER.—I—I can't say anything yet. I can't even think. I can only feel.

LINDA.—Hattie's cooked Christmas dinner over here. We took everything from your kitchen, so it's lucky you didn't start looking for it.

HATTIE.—And I want you to see Butch, Mrs. Young. Only you'll never know him.

NICK.—He's grown 3 miles. Hey, Butch, where are you?

BUTCH.—Here I am. I'm a big boy now.

HATTIE.—You remember Mrs. Young, Butch?

BUTCH.—Merry Christmas, Mrs. Young.

MOTHER.—Oh, Butch! Oh, Hattie! Oh, Nick. Oh, Linda. Oh, Biff. Oh, Edie! Oh, all my dear ones! What can I ever say to you? What can I ever do to show you how deeply grateful I am, how greatly touched. To think that on this day—on Christmas Day itself—all of us should be back here again, here in this blessed house. To think that my dream has come true! I want to say a prayer, Sam, just one little prayer. (*Voice trembles*) Dear God who looks down from heaven above, we, Thy humble servants, thank Thee for the great joy Thou hast brought us on this day of our Saviour's birth. May we be worthy of this great joy and spend our lives to the glory of His blessed name, Amen.

President's Talk to Science Congress

by Franklin D. Roosevelt

"Ladies and gentlemen, the President of the United States."

These few words bring to the microphone the most effective speaker radio has ever presented. The graciousness of breeding, the prescience of stored and inquiring thought, the control of emotion, the clarity of utterance, the overtone of appeal and the undertone of confidence, the intimacy of delivery, the choice of exact words for exact meaning, the great personal sincerity of appraisal, the rhythm of sentence, the flow of figure, the spacing of phrases, all these are present in subdued yet compelling measure. No man equals him in the reach of personal contact or in that subtle and invisible power to disarm or arouse by the simple means of extending his personality, his whole personality, through his voice. Others believe him because he so patently believes himself; and what he says, he says superbly.

One of the finest tributes ever paid to an American statesman for the transporting skill of his public speaking was offered up inadvertently to the President by the late Senator Borah of Idaho, himself one of the greatest orators of this century. "I never listen to the President," the Senator said. "He can persuade me to believe anything he pleases. I read his speeches in the newspapers the next day and then make up my own mind."

Following is the text of the President's address before the American Scientific Congress in Washington, D.C., on the evening of May 10, 1940.

President's Talk to Science Congress

FRANKLIN D. ROOSEVELT.—My fellow servants of the Americas: All of the men and the women of this Pan-American Scientific Congress have come here tonight, I think, with heavy hearts. During the past few years you and I have seen event follow event, each and every one of them a shock, a shock to our hopes for the peaceful development of modern civilization as we know it. And this very day, the tenth of May, 1940, this very day three more independent nations have been cruelly invaded by force of arms.

In some kind of human affairs the mind of man becomes accustomed to unusual actions if those actions are often repeated. But that is not so in the world happenings of today—and I am proud that it is not so. I am glad that we Americans of the free Americas are shocked, that we are angered by the tragic news that has come to us from Belgium and the Netherlands and Luxembourg.

The overwhelmingly greater part of the population of the world abhors conquest and war and bloodshed. It prays that the hand of neighbor shall not be lifted against neighbor. The whole world has seen attack follow threat on very many occasions and in very many places during these latter years.

We have come, therefore, to the reluctant conclusion that a continuance of these prophecies of arms presents a definite challenge to the continuance of the type of civilization to which all of us have been accustomed for so many generations.

I use this American Pan-American Scientific Congress as an illustration, and I could use many similar illustrations. It is no accident that this meeting takes place in the New World. In fact this hemisphere is now almost the only part of the earth in which a gathering can take place. Elsewhere war or politics has compelled teachers and scholars to leave their great calling and to become the agents of destruction.

We, and most of the people in the world, believe still in a civilization of construction and not of destruction. We, and most of the people in the world, still believe that men and women have an inherent right to hew out the patterns of their own individual lives, just so long as they as individuals do not harm their fellow beings.

We call this—this thought, this ideal—by many terms which are synonymous. We call it individual liberty; we call it civil liberty; and I think best of all, we call it democracy.

Until now, up to these days, we permit ourselves by common consent to search for truth, to teach the truth as we see it, and by learning a little here and a little there, and by teaching a little here and a little there to allow the normal processes of truth to keep growing—to keep growing for the well-being of our fellow men.

In our search and in our teaching we are a part of a great adventure—an exciting adventure, an adventure that gives to us a larger satisfaction, I think an even larger satisfaction than our forefathers had when they were in the midst of the adventure of settling the Americas from the Old World.

We feel that we are building human progress by conquering disease and poverty, discomfort, and by improving science and culture, removing one by one the many cruelties and crudities and barbarities of less civilized eras.

In contrast to that rather simple, rather fine, picture of our ideals; in contrast, in other parts of the world, teachers and scholars are not permitted to search for truth lest the truth when made known might not suit the designs of their masters.

Too often they are not allowed to teach the truth as they see it, because truth might make men free. Yes, they become objects of suspicion if they speak openly, if they show an interest in new truth; for their very tongues and minds are supposed to be mobilized for other ends.

This has not happened in the New World. God willing, it shall not happen in the New World.

At the Pan-American Conference at Buenos Aires and again at Lima we discussed a dim and unpleasant possibility. We feared that other continents might become so involved in war, wars brought on by the school of destruction, not construction, that the Americas might have to become the guardian of Western culture, the protector of Christian civilization.

And in those days, not so long ago, it was merely a fear. Today the fear has become a fact.

The inheritance which we had hoped to share with every nation in the world is, for the moment, left largely in our keeping; and it is our compelling duty to guard and enrich that legacy, to preserve it for a world which must be born, reborn, from the ashes of the present disaster.

Today we know—we admit—that until recent weeks too many citizens of the American republics believed themselves wholly safe—physically and economically and socially safe—safe from the impact of the attacks on civilization which are in progress elsewhere.

And perhaps this mistaken idea was based on a false teaching of geography—the thought that a distance of several thousand miles from a war-torn Europe to a peaceful America, that that distance in itself gave us some form of mystic immunity that could never be violated.

And yet, speaking in terms of—what shall I say?—timetables; in terms of the moving of men and guns and planes and bombs, every single acre—every hectare—of all the Americas from the Arctic to the Antarctic, every one of them is closer to the homes of modern conquerors, closer to the scenes of attacks in Europe than ever was the case in those episodes of history that we read about, the efforts to dominate the world in centuries gone by.

It is a shorter distance from the center of Europe to Santiago de Chile than it was for the chariots of Alexander the Great to roll from Macedonia to Persia.

In modern terms it is a shorter distance from Europe to San Francisco, California, than it was for the ships and legions of Julius Caesar to move from Rome to Spain or Rome to Britain. And today it is 4 or 5 hours of travel from the continent of Africa to the continent of South America, where it was 4 or 5 weeks for the armies of Napoleon to march from Paris to Rome or Paris to Poland.

You who are scientists may have been told that you are, in part, responsible for the debacle of today because of the processes of invention for the annihilation of time and space; but I assure you that it is not the scientists of the world who are responsible, because the objectives which you have looked to, all of those objectives, have been headed toward closer and more peaceful relations between all nations through the spirit of cooperation and the interchange of knowledge.

What has come about has been caused solely by those who would use, and are using, your inventions, the progress that you have been making along the lines of peace, but are using them in a wholly different cause—those who seek to dominate hundreds of millions of people in vast continental areas—those who, if successful in that aim will, we know down in our hearts, enlarge their wild dream to encompass every human being and every mile of the earth's surface.

The great achievements of science, yes and of art, can be used to destroy as well as to create; they are only instruments by which men try to do the things that they most want to do. If death is desired, science can do that. If a full, rich, a useful life is sought, science can do that also.

Happily for us, that question has been solved—for in the New World we live for each other and in the service of a Christian faith.

Is this solution—our solution—is it permanent or safe if it is solved just for us alone? That seems to me to be the most immediate issue that the Americas face. Can we continue our peaceful construction if all the other continents in all the world embrace by preference or by compulsion a wholly different principle of life?

No, I think not. Surely it is time for our republics to spread that problem before us in the cold light of day, to analyze it, to ask questions, to call for answers, to use every knowledge, every science that we possess, to apply common sense, and above all to act with unanimity and singleness of purpose.

I am a pacifist. You, my fellow-citizens of 21 American republics, you are pacifists, too.

But I believe that by overwhelming majorities in all the Americas you and I, in the long run and if it be necessary, you and I will act together to protect, to defend by every means, to protect and defend our science, our culture, our American freedom and our civilization.

The Chamber Music Society of Lower Basin Street

by WELBOURN KELLY

IN SOME of its lighter moments, radio has a good time "ribbing" the awesome dignity of its heavier side. Every Sunday afternoon at 4:30, over NBC's Blue Network, a group of superlative instrumentalists gets together to play jazz, swing, boogie-woogie, and sweltering improvisations that float through their heads and hands at the time. The performances of the Chamber Music Society of Lower Basin Street are immensely popular, completely unruly, and full of fun. The announcer, in a composed and analytical manner, discusses the vulgarisms of the music we hear and does so with a straight face. His self-conscious determination to ennoble the swing phase of music by stealing the nomenclature of symphonic programs is one of the best burlesques on the air. The continuities are written by Welbourn Kelly, a member of Lewis Titterton's script staff.

Here is the show for May 26, 1940.

The Chamber Music Society of Lower Basin Street

SOUND.—*Tuning of instruments in background . . . down under.*

ANNOUNCER.—(*Dead pan*) Good afternoon, music lovers—you rascals, you! It is our privilege now, no doubt, to eavesdrop lightly on a concert of the very justly celebrated Chamber Music Society of Lower Basin Street. This means, of course, that once again a small group of musicologists has gathered here in Radio City for the purpose of perpetuating the time-hallowed classics of the three B's—boogie-woogie, barrelhouse, and the blues. We are speaking to you now from the critics' circle, here in the short right-field bleachers, and we note that once again the conductors of the occasion are Maestro Paul Laval, with his turpentine-treated yellow-pine wood winds, and Dr. Henry Levine, with his Dixieland Little Symphony of eight men and no girl. But the guests of this solemn occasion are about to be introduced . . . so—if we know which side our announcer's job is buttered on—no doubt we'd better leave that up to Dr. Gino Hamilton, the society's chairman, whose voice you will hear next . . .

SOUND.—*Three raps of gavel as music background goes out.*

HAMILTON.—As you all know, fellow members of the Chamber Music Society of Lower Basin Street . . . (*pause*) and furthermore we agree with you. As we said, we agree that the classics of our land should not only be revived but preserved intact. And, of course, that's what we're here for. So in pursuance of which, we present as the society's special guests—the distinguished piano virtuoso Professor Michael Joseph Aloysius Xavier Dockerty Sullivan, to whom a grand piano once bowed low, then said in awesome tones, "Quote: Wow! Unquote"; Dr. George Simon, editor of the musicians' magazine *Metronome;* and our own special favorite, Mademoiselle Dinah Shore, the deep South diva from Tennessee, who is said to be a good reason why boys leave home to go into radio . . . Be that as it may, Dr. Henry Levine has now mounted the podium to give his own Dixieland reading of the South Rampart Street Divertimento, "The Jazzme Blues" . . . if, during the reading, you must throw money on the floor, please don't hit the musicians. The "Jazzme Blues."

MUSIC.—(*Levine and octet*). "*Jazzme Blues.*"

HAMILTON.—When the musicians of our society heard that Mademoiselle Dinah Shore was returning to our group, they waxed loud and eloquent, as only a musician can. For instance, Professor Henry Wade, the saxophonist, said—"Yes"! Professor Rudolf Amadeus Adler nodded his head in agreement. Professors Alfred Lewis Evans and Jacque Davide Epstein missed a couple of bars while they were shaking hands. And Professor Harry Grumpy Patent climbed up to the neck of his double bass and said, "I feel it"! So we now present the renowned Tennessee diva Mademoiselle Dinah Shore in the first presentation—as far as we know—of the *lyrics* of . . . "Tuxedo Junction"!

MUSIC.—(*Shore, Laval, and orchestra*). "*Tuxedo Junction.*"

HAMILTON.—Maestro Paul Laval trots out a special arrangement of "Everybody Step," in which all the musicians do. For those who are interested in the score, we might point out that the work opens with an introductory motif in stomp bounce and that special mention should be given to Maestro Laval himself on the bass clarone, Professor Rudolf Amadeus Adler on the English horn, and Professor Angel Barnes Rattina on the subtone trumpet. Here is "Everybody Step."

MUSIC.—(*Laval and orchestra*). "*Everybody Step.*"

HAMILTON.—Just 2 weeks ago, we asked all you members of the Chamber Music Society of Lower Basin Street how you felt about an all-Handy concert, with Dr. William Christopher Handy himself playing the trumpet and singing the blues and perhaps acting as guest commentator. The response shows that you all feel it. In fact, the letters are still coming in to such an extent that we ourselves have begun to feel that perhaps the time has come when we should get Dr. Handy on the telephone and ask him whether or not *he* feels it. So, if Dr. Handy is listening, he can expect a call very soon.

Meanwhile, Dr. Levine gives us an idea of what a W. C. Handy cycle would be like . . . by playing for us the master's . . . "Beale Street Blues."

MUSIC.—(*Levine and octet*). "*Beale Street.*"

HAMILTON.—We have now reached the intermission in today's concert by the Chamber Music Society of Lower Basin Street. Before introducing our guest commentator, we will ask Mademoiselle Dinah Shore to step forward.

SHORE.—Yes, Dr. Hamilton—I have stepped forward.

HAMILTON.—You know of course, Mademoiselle Shore, that we're very glad to have you back. But just to make it more official, we've brought in the editor of the magazine which gave you your first push forward.

SHORE.—Of course, Dr. Hamilton. And if by any chance you should mean Dr. George Simon, editor of *Metronome*, why, here he is. Welcome to Basin Street, Dr. Simon . . .

SIMON.—And whatta street, Dr. Hamilton! It's certainly swell standing here on its sidewalk with you and welcoming back little Miss Shore.

SHORE.—Thank you, Dr. Gentlemen.

HAMILTON.—Well, now that Dinah is here—and we've got our lines straightened out—tell us what it was that first drew your attention to her singing, will you, Mr. Simon?

SIMON.—Two things, Mr. Hamilton: originality and sincerity. I think you'll notice that those qualities are the two most important for an artist's success in the popular field. I'm happy to say that *Metronome* was first to point out these traits in Mademoiselle Shore, and she's gone up ever since.

HAMILTON.—Do those two qualities of originality and sincerity mean success for band leaders, too?

SIMON.—As a matter of fact, for band leaders especially. If you look through the list of successes during the past years, you'll find mostly men who have presented something new and who have believed in what they have been presenting. Take Glenn Miller, as an example. Most of us don't know that for quite a while he was just another trombone-playing band leader who was in danger of being labeled as an imitator of Tommy Dorsey. He didn't like that idea, either. Then Glenn evolved that five-man sax section idea that typified his music, and look at him now!

HAMILTON.—And you imply by that that Tommy Dorsey was successful because he was the first to feature a trombone?

SIMON.—Exactly. None of the many trombone-playing leaders today are as successful. It's not primarily because their bands may not be as good, but rather because the public has accepted Tommy as *the* man in that field. The same goes for Benny Goodman on clarinet and as swing leader, in general, for that matter, and for Eddy Duchin on piano. And, I might add, the same probably will be true of the Chamber Music Society of Lower Basin Street. It brings us music such as we can get nowhere else on network radio today.

HAMILTON.—Thank you, Dr. George Simon, editor of the musicians' magazine *Metronome*. And if you'll just hang your hat on Dr. Levine's embrochure and wait for a moment, we can promise you something special. It's the musical story of the three boys who walked into a fiery furnace some years back . . . three boys by the name of Shadrach, Meshach, and Abednego. The selection was composed by Dr. Bob McGimsey, and you have heard it many times. But just wait till you hear what Maestro Paul Laval does to it now. Here is "Shadrach."

MUSIC.—(*Laval and orchestra*). "*Shadrach.*"

HAMILTON.—As you all know, fellow members of the Chamber Music Society of Lower Basin Street, we take no stock in rumors. Thus we have politely pooh-poohed those who say that Professor Joe Sullivan could not possibly play as much piano as Professor Joe Sullivan plays. For instance, one group maintains that the professor is really triplets. Another group says, no . . . but that he is helped out greatly by the fact that he has fingers on his feet. We recently saw Professor Sullivan playing with his band at the Café Society, here in New York, and, frankly, we couldn't tell which is correct. So we merely present him now, playing his own great work, "The Ginmill Blues."

MUSIC.—(*Joe Sullivan at piano*). "*Ginmill Blues.*"

HAMILTON.—Of course a recital by Professor Joe Sullivan would not be complete without at least a small portion of the work by which he is best known as a composer—the "Little Rock Getaway."

MUSIC.—(*Joe Sullivan at piano*). "*Little Rock.*"

HAMILTON.—Thank you, Professor Joe Sullivan. (*Aside*) Hm-m-m. Do you suppose he *has* got fingers on his feet? (*Prop cough and on-mike again*) At the risk of being redundant, we would like to repeat that we are very glad that Mademoiselle Dinah Shore is back with us again. One very good and sufficient reason is Mademoiselle Shore's Piney Woods treatment of "I'm Coming, Virginia"—a treatment which she is at this moment just before treating. Mademoiselle Shore and . . . "I'm Coming, Virginia."

MUSIC.—(*Shore, Laval, and orchestra*). "*I'm Coming, Virginia.*"

HAMILTON.—A statement which will come as a surprise to a lot of us is the fact that Dr. Henry Levine was a member of the Original Dixieland Jazz Band—having taken Nick La Rocca's place when that master of the trumpet went back to New Orleans. In those days Dr. Levine was known as the "long-lipped short-pants wonder," and he usually played about two bars ahead of the truant officer, at the old Cinderella Ballroom here in New York. To signalize this historic event, Dr. Levine and the Dixieland group will now play the Nick La Rocca-Larry Shields classic "Ostrich Walk." But—and this will come as a surprise to Dr. Levine—he is now being asked to play an ad-lib, unarranged growl chorus, just as he played back in the good old days.

MUSIC.—(*Levine and octet.*) "*Ostrich Walk.*"

HAMILTON.—As is usually the case with all those things which start out with a beginning, we have now reached the ending of our concert. This fact is announced by the familiar strains of "The Basin Street Blues," played in the Haydn "Farewell Symphony" version—with the musicians leaving the stand, one by one, until only the bass player is left, dolefully drubbing on the doghouse.

MUSIC.—(*Levine and octet.*) "*Basin Street Blues.*"

ANNOUNCER.—And so, music lovers, you rascals, you, we have come to the end of another concert by the Chamber Music Society of Lower Basin Street, no doubt. But, knowing which side my announcer's job is buttered on, I think I'd better tell you that next week is another week. Period. And that means, of course, that Mademoiselle Dinah Shore and all our regulars will be back, at which time we will present the sensational new guitarist, Professor Floyd Smith, who plays with Harlem in both hands. Right now, as Dr. Hamilton would say, it behooves me to impart to you the indubitable fact that . . . this is the National Broadcasting Company, RCA Building, Radio City, New York.

The John Kirby Show

by PAUL PHILLIPS

MANY readers will think it strange to find this piece of writing included in this book. To those in radio it will not be strange. The writing is individual and peculiar, and it belongs to a moment that will soon be over. It describes something that is and has been immensely popular, the vulgar music of the late 1930's. The orchestra for which the following pages were written is the versatile Negro sextet put together by John Kirby. It is one of the most successful bands in America today. It will pass; but it is having its day, and it is making its impression. Music changes and decorates speech, and the reader will see some of this influence at work in this continuity. Some of the phrases are as irresponsibly arboreal as the music they seek to explain. Paul Phillips wrote them. His is one of the great talents of radio, one not yet put to its fullest use. Comedians need him and will presently use him, for comedy is his particular gift. But he is a thoroughly sound radio writer in all departments, with a special penchant for describing the special penchants of others. He knows Negroes and Negro talk. He is radio's most inquisitive musical explorer. He understands "ear music." When the special overtone in the phrase "he could play it and say it" first reached his ears in a New Orleans honky-tonk, its full meaning was apparent to Phillips. It moved into his vocabulary, together with many hundreds of other words and phrases, and they have been sprinkled through his writings ever since. He has translated something for the average conscious mind that had belonged theretofore to its instinct alone and never to its expression.

Here is the continuity for the John Kirby show of May 5, 1940. The words are read by Canada Lee, a young Negro actor and prize fighter, the prototype of all the strong and silent men.

The John Kirby Show

ORCHESTRA.—*Figure.*

VOICE.—Flow gently, sweet rhythm, swing low. Let it flow gently, John Kirby said.

People were talkin' about John Kirby's band, askin' questions, askin' how come. Well, you just can't say John Kirby told them, "You just play it good." We made the band our way, and we played the way we felt. We played that way when we started . . . and later on, too. At the Onyx, at the Ambassador, at Perino's Sky Room on the coast. We didn't care about that blast stuff or drivin'. We played like we knew, like we wanted; we made our music up.

MUSIC.—"*Pastel Blue*" . . . *hold* . . . *fade for announcer.*

ANNOUNCER.—And with the theme of "Pastel Blue," ladies and gentlemen, we bring you Flow Gently, Sweet Rhythm, the Sunday program in which Columbia presents the sensational musical organization of John Kirby and his orchestra, called by many "the biggest little band in America." With just six men he's playing a compelling, quiet swing, a new swing with a torrent of rhythm and enchanting color. The Golden Gate Boys appear with him, and again this week our singing voice is the first lady of swing, Ella Fitzgerald.

And now, listen, as John Kirby lets that rhythm flow.

MUSIC.—(*Orchestra*). "*Then I'll Be Happy.*"

VOICE.—Sometimes we picked a tune up like "War Chant," a moody piece, suited to the band. It had ear quality and a dicty way-out harmony that made people laugh. It went pretty good when we fixed it up some.

MUSIC.—(*Orchestra*). "*Hawaiian War Chant.*"

VOICE.—We picked an old piece up in Berkeley. That "Royal Garden" piece, been goin' round for years. We put some hop in it, put some old move in it till it took technique to play.

MUSIC.—(*Orchestra*). "*Royal Garden Blues.*"

VOICE.—It was in Chick Webb's band where we met Ella. We used to go uptown after hours, singin' in the "Braddock" with the lights down low. Billy Kyle at the piano and Ella standing up singin' those knockout songs. All the musicians would come around to hear Ella Fitzgerald.

FITZGERALD.—"*Sugar Blues.*"

VOICE.—We opened ensemble playin' sextette from "Lucia." Nice, easy rhythm, movin' good. The "singin' sextette" we called it. "I don't know who this Lucia is," Buster said, "but she sure had good music."

MUSIC.—(*Orchestra*). *Sextette from* "*Lucia.*"

(*Guitar and Quartet*).
"*Kentucky Babe*" . . . *very soft effect.*

VOICE.—If you ever hear one note reachin' for another, you're hearin' those Golden Gate Boys. They got scripture music. They got a beat like hittin' a bass.

MUSIC.—(*Golden Gate Boys*). "*Job.*"

VOICE.—They sing like they got the call. They got another song they do this time. It's about rockin' and rollin' on the "Rock Island Line."

MUSIC.—(*Golden Gate Boys*). "*Rock Island Line.*"

VOICE.—We got some bite into this one. Got some drum licks in it in O'Neill's style. "It's just a little jump number," John Kirby said, "just a little rhythm number itself." We liked it, so we named it "It Feels So Good."

MUSIC.—(*Orchestra*). "*It Feels so Good.*"

VOICE.—Ella made a star. Had her name in bright lights. Got her own band. We surely liked to see her get attention, like when Mr. Winchell gave her one of them orchids for singin' "Starlit Hour." It's just what we always said—that Ella's a natural. That gal can do it.

FITZGERALD.—"*Starlit Hour.*"

VOICE.—We played the "St. Louis Blues" lightly, played it softly and gladly blue. You had to hear Buster Bailey's clarinet to believe it. He got stuck on a note and held it right on through.

MUSIC.—(*Orchestra*). *"St. Louis Blues" . . . segue to "Nocturne" . . . hold under.*

VOICE.—"Well, that's music," John Kirby said. You take a band and you work hard. You play and you think and you talk your music and pretty soon it gets right, the rhythm flowing, the reeds deep, the bass beating behind to let the horns ride over. We felt good, we felt right, and our music kept comin'. Russ Procope we had on sax, and John himself on bass, and we played 'em down the way we made them, the way John Kirby said.

MUSIC.—(*Orchestra*). *Theme up and down for*

ANNOUNCER.—Ladies and gentlemen, you've been listening to Flow Gently Sweet Rhythm, a new Columbia series featuring John Kirby and his orchestra. With the six men who make that marvelous music, you heard the Golden Gate Boys and the first lady of swing Ella Fitzgerald. John Kirby's numbers today included: "Then I'll Be Happy," "Hawaiian War Chant," the sextette from "Lucia," "It Feels so Good," and "St. Louis Blues." While Ella Fitzgerald sang "Sugar Blues" and "The Starlit Hour." "Job," from the "Old Songs Hymnal," and "Rock Island Line" were by the Golden Gate Boys. Join us again next Sunday. This is the Columbia Broadcasting System.

BEST NEWS REPORTING

VERY few radio listeners really understand or appreciate how splendid the radio coverage of news is in this country or how difficult it is to keep the service going, especially under the conditions prevailing in Europe at the present time.

As an illustration of the trouble to which radio goes to get all the news it brings you, here is the way it was done by CBS during the Russian invasion of Finland; and this is a standard example, not an exceptional one, of the setups necessary whenever the situation, as regards terrain, distance, climate, existing facilities, national laws, etc., is as vexed and worried as was the one in Finland. Radio handles every day, and many times a day, remote jobs of equal difficulty and many that are considerably worse.

News of the Russo-Finnish War came to American listeners in this way: If the actual point of origination was somewhere behind the Mannerheim Line, the announcer's voice (very frequently William L. White's) was carried from the spot by telephone line to Helsinki. From Helsinki, it was carried under the Gulf of Finland and under the Baltic Sea by submarine cable to Stockholm on the east coast of Sweden. From Stockholm, Mr. White's voice next went by land lines (overhead telephone lines) 420 miles to the foot of the Swedish peninsula, then under water again for 60 miles (across the stretch of the Baltic estuary that runs east of Denmark's island of Zealand). This brought his voice to the northern coast of Germany, and it would have been perfectly simple to carry it from that point overland to Berlin and from there to short-wave it to America. It would have been simple because Berlin has the finest short-wave facilities in Europe today, but CBS could not use them. Germany will permit her Berlin facilities to carry only those programs that originate within the borders of her own country. She will not allow them to be used for broadcasts coming from some other country. However, in these instances, she does permit the use of her telephone lines to carry programs across her territory, provided the point at which the broadcast finally reaches the air is not on German soil. In the case of the news shows from Finland, therefore, it was necessary to transmit the program across Germany, from her most northern to her most southwestern border, then to order Swiss lines to carry the show an additional 140 miles past the shoulder of the Alps to Geneva. Here it reached the air for the first time. Geneva shortwaved it to the receiving towers at Riverhead, Long Island. At Riverhead it was once more put back on telephone lines and brought to master control in the studios of WABC, the New York station for CBS. Master control put it on another line running to a little town in New Jersey about 19 miles from Manhattan Island, the town of Wayne, and at Wayne it finally reached the air as a broadcast. That is how the bad news was brought from Viborg or Abo or whatever Finnish town it might have been and how it finally got on the air in America and into your living room. I believe any reader can see what an effort this was.

The human problem is often as bad as or worse than the problem of physical facilities. Edmond Taylor, CBS correspondent in Bordeaux following the French government's evacuation of Paris, recently returned to the United States with an illuminating story about the type of problem he had to cope with over there. He writes:

In Bordeaux and Tours, facilities were primitive, to say the least. In Tours we could not even get a time check, and when Eric Sevareid (chief of the CBS Paris bureau) and I protested to an unsympathetic French engineer, he pointed to a kitchen clock on the wall of the improvised studio and said, "What's the matter with that?"

In Bordeaux, we used a reasonably well-appointed French studio, but in the general confusion we were left to shift for ourselves. The night that the Reynaud government fell, Sevareid and I, after a wild dash without headlights through a mile of winding, inky black streets, arrived panting in the studio and announced we had a flash for America.

The studio engineer said it was all right with him, but there was a lady playing the mandolin to South America and she was to be on for another fifteen minutes. We burst into the studio, and, after an acrimonious argument, which was probably heard all around the world, persuaded the indignant musician to yield us the microphone.

On the other hand, the radio censors somehow evaporated in the general confusion; the authorities simply forgot all about us; and for three days we were able to go on the air whenever we liked and say anything we pleased.

The elaborate system for bringing to CBS listeners the news of the world is controlled from a central office in the Columbia Broadcasting System's building in New York. The office is presided over by Paul W. White, a former United Press executive, and one of the most resourceful and indefatigable newsmen in this country. About fifty people work under him directly, and the number who are responsible to him in other parts of the world varies according to the news volume and news distribution of the moment. As many as thirty can be "on call" for any assignment, and a minimum of ten are kept on the permanent staff in Europe alone.

Columbia's news staff is basically like that of any large metropolitan newspaper, with editors, reporters, rewrite men, and columnists or news analysts. The staff is composed of experienced newspaper men of wide journalistic background. The very nature of the work, embracing as it does affairs of international importance, demands judgment and a fine capacity for instant and accurate decision that comes only with extensive training in this field. Under Paul White are his chief assistant, Bob Wood, and his assistant daytime editor, Bill Dunn. The newsrooms are equipped with tickers, and the wire services available for this are the United Press and International News Service. A shortwave listening post is located on the same floor, and here a vast number of unusual items being broadcast from foreign countries and in foreign languages are intercepted and translated by a twenty-four-hour-a-day staff, all of whom are themselves newspapermen or women, and all of whom are expert linguists.

In New York the news-announcing and news-analyzing staff includes such outstanding experts as Major George Fielding Eliot, Elmer Davis, Linton Wells, and Bob Trout;

the regular announcing staff includes Jack Knell, Tony Marvin, Jackson Wheeler, and John Reed King.

In Europe the staff is headed by Edward R. Murrow. Under him are men in every key city on the continent: Vincent Sheehan and Erland Echlin in London; David Anderson in Stockholm; Russell Hill in Budapest; Eric Sevareid, Larry Laseuer, and Thomas Grandin in France; Cecil Brown in Rome; Farnsworth Fowle in Ankhara; William L. Shirer in Berlin; and Spencer Williams in Bucharest. These men all move about a great deal, the staff in France already having been obliged to leave that country and either go on to other spots or return to America. Increasing interest in the affairs of Central and South America has sent CBS radio correspondents to Mexico City and Buenos Aires. They are Clarence Sorenson and Herbert Clark.

The six men whose broadcasts I have decided to print this year are Major Eliot, Elmer Davis, Edward R. Murrow, William L. Shirer, Wythe Williams, and Raymond Gram Swing. They are all well known not only as radio voices and personalities but as newsmen of very high rank. The conditions under which radio news reporters and news analysts must frequently do their work, especially these men broadcasting from abroad, can be envisioned by what I have already quoted from Mr. Taylor.

George Fielding Eliot.—He was born in Brooklyn in 1894. His family moved to Australia when he was an eight-year-old, and he was graduated from the University of Melbourne in 1914. He served during the entire World War with the Australian Imperial Force, seeing action in Egypt, at Gallipoli, and on the Western Front. He was elevated to the rank of major and served in the Military Intelligence Reserve, United States Army, for the eight years between 1922 and 1930. His comprehensive study of American national defense, "The Ramparts We Watch," was published in 1938. "Bombs Bursting in Air" (the influence of air power on international relations) appeared a year later. He is co-author (with Major R. E. Dupuy) of "If War Comes." He has contributed articles on military and naval affairs to *Harper's*, *The Saturday Evening Post*, *American*

Mercury, Foreign Affairs, Infantry Journal, U.S. Naval Institute Proceedings, Life, Fortune, New Republic, and many others. He is the military and naval correspondent of the *New York Herald-Tribune*. He has been the military analyst for the Columbia Broadcasting System since the outbreak of the present war.

Wythe Williams.—Mr. Williams is one of the most thoroughly trained reporters in American journalism. He has been a foreign correspondent for American newspapers for twenty-six years, serving at one time or another the *New York World* (from London), the *New York Times* (from Paris). For the war years he was chief war correspondent for the *Times*. He was general European director for the *Philadelphia Public Ledger* and the *New York Evening Post* and special correspondent for the *Saturday Evening Post*. He has written quantities of good fiction and two non-fiction books: "Passed by the Censor" and "Dusk of Empire." His broadcasts are heard over the Mutual Broadcasting System.

Elmer Davis.—Mr. Davis was engaged by CBS on August 23, 1939, to analyze the domestic side of the news picture while H. V. Kaltenborn journeyed to London to be on the scene as the crisis developed. Mr. Davis's analytical reports were so shrewd and so vivid that he was immediately engaged as a permanent member of the staff. His own background is unusually full. From 1914 to 1924 he worked as a reporter and editorial writer for the *New York Times*. He left his post there for world travel, research, and free-lance writing. He became a very popular and prolific short story writer, published two or three novels, and contributed innumerable articles on national and international affairs to the best magazines in the country. He writes clearly, and he writes well. He can be caustic and ironic, but he is never splenetic. He can cover more ground in shorter time than any other man on the air, and although he makes most of his broadcasts from prepared copy, he is one of the best ad libbers in radio.

Raymond Gram Swing.—I wrote rather fully of Mr. Swing's talents in last year's anthology. His peculiarly individual skills are known to all those who catch his nightly ten o'clock programs over MBS, and most people are acquainted with his intensive newspaper experience in Europe.

Edward R. Murrow.—Mr. Murrow is chief of Columbia's European staff. He is thirty-four years old. Prior to his appointment to the London office he was for two years the CBS Talks Director. Before his radio career began, he was for several years the assistant director of the Institute of International Education, working with the internationally famous Stephen Duggan. His responsibilities in this interesting connection took him all over Europe and acquainted him with most of the important men and important movements of both England and the Continent.

William L. Shirer.—Mr. Shirer is considered by Mr. Murrow and by *Time* magazine to be the most effective news reporter in the entire foreign field. He came to radio after twelve years on the Continental "beat" for the *Chicago Tribune* and Universal Service. He was their European correspondent from 1925 to 1937. His broadcast, which I am reprinting, someday will become a historical document.

Major George Fielding Eliot

June 14, 1940

ANNOUNCER.—And now Columbia's military analyst, Major George Fielding Eliot, gives you the military picture of the war—Major Eliot.

MAJOR ELIOT.—Both from political and military indications the possibility that French resistance may be nearing its end has to be taken into account. The Germans appear to have broken through the French center. They report that their troops are advancing from Chalons-sur-Marne towards Romilly. On the French left the German advance across the Seine continues, with the effect of British intervention in this sector still in doubt. Despite British reports that every possible man and piece of equipment is being sent to France, it is necessary to consider from the point of view of the British High Command the possibility that every man and every gun dispatched to France may be completely lost and that Great Britain will unquestionably be the next point of attack.

Under these circumstances, what is the duty of the British High Command? To endeavor to make a possibly hopeless resistance in France, or to hold back as much as possible for the defense of Great Britain herself?

It is not a decision with which I should like to be charged, and that it is the cause of great heartburning in high British circles there can be no possible doubt. On the one hand, if France goes down, when she might have been saved, Britain will be in deadly peril which might perhaps have been avoided. On the other hand, if the French case is already hopeless, then every man sent to France now is so much loss to the defense of Britain.

As a tragic dilemma this has few parallels in history. Meanwhile, French resistance still continues. Always provided the Germans do not reach the point of exhaustion and have to stop to consolidate and bring up fresh troops and supplies, there seems little hope tonight for the worn-out French armies. Already threatened with division in the center and without flanking on the left there is no possibility of any worth-while aid from the United States, and British aid is questionable as to quantity and efficiency.

A great part of the French industrial regions have been already lost. Paris, the chief railway and communication center of France, is gone. The tactical mobility of the Germans seems to preclude the chance of a successful retirement behind the Loire. A shadow of defeat hangs darkly over France.

If France is compelled to make peace, the exact terms on which that peace is made will be of great importance to the British and to the world. What will be the status of the French colonies? What will be the status of the French fleet? This last may be of great interest to Americans as well as to others. France has three modern battleships in the west and three others, as well as two aircraft carriers and a number of smaller ships under construction. Will these fall into the hands of the Germans? What will become in particular of the French positions in the new world? Of Martinique, Guadeloupe, French Guiana, of St. Pierre, Miquelon, south of Newfoundland? It is clear from this very brief summary that the possibility of French defeat contains serious questions for all the world, questions which may soon be answered, which must meanwhile receive the thoughtful consideration of us all.

Elmer Davis

June 21, 1940

Davis.—The German armistice terms, handed to the French delegates at Compiègne today, have been received by the French government, which is still in Bordeaux, and are being studied; action on them may not be taken till tomorrow. We still have no information as to what they are, except that the preamble, read to the French delegates by General von Keitel, Hitler's chief of staff, said that their purpose was to prevent resumption of fighting, to give Germany full security for continuance of the war against England, and to create prerequisites for the construction of a new peace. This sounds as if the terms were only preliminaries, like the armistice of 1918; but from Bordeaux it is reported that they are a lengthy document including the Italian claims, which a French source describes as even more pretentious and embracing than those of the Germans.

The terms were handed to the French delegates in the same railroad car where Marshal Foch handed the armistice terms to the Germans in 1918. The car had been moved from the museum in which it was housed to the exact spot, a short distance away, which it occupied 22 years ago, and a studied effort seems to have been made to reproduce the conditions of that meeting in reverse, in order, as the preamble stated, to eradicate a memory which was felt by the German people to be the deepest shame of all time. In style and content this document is pretty plainly the work of Hitler himself, and he left the car as soon as it had been read. Hitler's touch is also apparent in the stage setting and in the fact that the railroad car and the monument on the scene are going to be taken to Berlin as trophies.

Fighting still goes on in France, chiefly in the east, where French troops in a vast square are holding out in the Vosges mountains, and also at Clermont-Ferrand in south-central France. The Germans report the capture of much war material, but the story that they have seized France's two newest battleships under construction in the shipyard at Brest comes only from Dr. Goebbels's newspaper, the *Angriff;* and, as one of the ships is known to be in service, the story is open to suspicion.

A revolution in Estonia raised the Red flag, under protection of the Russian army of occupation, and formed a government more satisfactory to Russia. King Carol of Rumania remodeled, or at least renamed, his single totalitarian party apparently to make it more satisfactory to the Nazis. And the Swedish Riksdag met in secret session to receive a special message from the king.

German air raiders again attacked England tonight, but we have no details of the action, which apparently is still going on. Today British planes bombed gun emplacements at Calais, from which it was reported German long-range guns were preparing to bombard England, and also attacked German air fields at Rouen in France, Amsterdam in Holland, and Paderborn in Germany.

The Italian editor Virginio Gayda again warned the United States against participating in a war which, he said, is solely a European affair and does not concern us. The Monroe doctrine, he said, excludes American intervention in European affairs as well as European intervention in American affairs, so that American intervention now would mean destruction of the Monroe Doctrine. Our Rome correspondent Cecil Brown reported that no one could recall that this argument was advanced in 1917, when America intervened on the same side as Italy.

In Washington the objection of isolationists to the resale of American military equipment to England and France and of Republicans to the appointment of Henry L. Stimson as Secretary of War and Frank Knox as Secretary of the Navy flared out in sharp criticism of the President. Senate committees will examine Stimson and perhaps Knox, too, before they can be confirmed in office, and this will probably not take place before the Republican convention. Representative Carlson of Kansas demanded investigation of published reports that Secretary of War Woodring had resigned because of his opposition to the resale policy. Senator Walsh of Massachusetts said that men of property were agitating for warlike policies in this country against men of no property and said he could understand the feelings of the German people, who had lost territory in the last war. Senator Nye went farther and demanded that the President resign on the ground that he had lost the confidence of Europe and said he would not be surprised if Mr. Woodring had resigned because he refused to give up the army's secret bomb sight. Mr. Nye adduced no proof of this, and Senator Barkley said the chief of the air corps had told him the bomb sight is, and will be kept a secret.

Edward R. Murrow

June 17, 1940

ANNOUNCER.—The eyes of the world are focused on London, the nerve center of the British Empire, and in order to give you the latest developments direct I'm going to call on Ed Murrow, chief of the CBS staff in the British capital. Go ahead, London.

MURROW.—This is London! It would be quite easy on a day like this to exhaust one's vocabulary and breath in describing British reaction to the French decision to give up the fight. It would be easy but inaccurate, because the British impulse when something happens is to do nothing, say nothing, until all the facts are known. The only official statement was made by the Foreign Office spokesman when he said that Britain would continue the fight. Another statement, reaffirming that position, is expected later today. London is awaiting the answer to a number of questions before it can assess the full measure of the disaster. There is no news of the British Expeditionary Force in France and no indication of the terms that will be imposed by Germany aside from the Berlin announcement that Hitler and Mussolini will confer before terms are settled.

The one comment that one hears in Parliamentary circles this afternoon is that, of course, Britain will continue the fight, and the hope is expressed that America will not conclude that it's now too late for any help to be effective. I went into my club a few minutes ago with the intention of asking some of the members what they thought about continued British resistance. I listened to the conversation for 15 minutes and left without asking my question. The whole trend of the conversation was: send away as many children as possible, evacuate the coastal areas, and prepare to fight. No one has even considered the possibility of making peace. If you were to say to most Britishers, "The battlefield is gone, there is no place to fight," they would reply, "We'll fight here in these islands and before long."

Sir Nevile Henderson, former British Ambassador in Berlin, prophesied this afternoon that Hitler will invade these islands this month or next. Hitler could only win this war, he said, by starving us out, by bombing us into submission, or by coming and invading this country, and in Sir Nevile's opinion Hitler is going to try all of the three methods.

London this afternoon wears a serious face, but it's perfectly calm. Walking up Regent Street a few minutes ago, I saw a nice, comfortable armchair in a shop window with the sign on it saying: "Make your air-raid shelter comfortable." I heard a well-dressed lady say to her companion: "How irritating! About the French, I mean." There is, so far, no tendency in official circles to criticize or malign the French. Most Britishers are quite willing to admit that the French have fought this war so far almost alone, except at sea, while to the British it's been something of a luxury war. All that is ended, but I can find no one here willing to advocate that Britain should die without battle. I think above everything else the British people are waiting now to hear from Winston Churchill tomorrow. When he assumed office he offered the people of this country "blood, sweat, and tears." No one expects him to retract that offer tomorrow.

I return you now to Columbia in New York.

William L. Shirer

June 21, 1940

ANNOUNCER.—At this time, as the French government considers Germany's terms for an armistice, Columbia takes you to Berlin for a special broadcast by William Shirer in Germany. We take you now to Berlin. Go ahead, Berlin.

SHIRER.—Hello, America! Hello, CBS! William L. Shirer calling CBS in New York.

William L. Shirer calling CBS in New York, calling CBS from Compiègne, France. This is William L. Shirer of CBS.

We've got a microphone at the edge of a little clearing in the forest of Compiègne, 4 miles to the north of the town of Compiègne and about 45 miles north of Paris. Here, a few feet from where we're standing in the very same old railroad coach where the armistice was signed on that chilly morning of November 11, 1918, negotiations for another armistice—the one to end the present war between France and Germany—began at 3:30 P.M. German summer time this afternoon. What a turning back of the clock, what a reversing of history we've been watching here in this beautiful Compiègne Forest this afternoon. What a contrast to that day 22 years ago. Yes, even the weather, for we have one of those lovely warm June days which you get in this part of France close to Paris about this time of year.

As we stood here, watching Adolf Hitler and Field Marshal Goering and the other German leaders laying down the terms of the armistice to the French plenipotentiaries here this afternoon, it was difficult to comprehend that in this rustic little clearing in the midst of the forest of Compiègne, from where we're talking to you now, that an armistice was signed here on the cold, cold morning at 5:00 A.M. on November 11, 1918. The railroad coach—it was Marshal Foch's private car—stands a few feet away from us here in exactly the same spot where it stood on that gray morning 22 years ago, only —and what an "only" it is, too—Adolf Hitler sat in the seat occupied that day by Marshal Foch. Hitler at that time was only an unknown corporal in the German Army, and in that quaint old wartime car another armistice is being drawn up as I speak to you now, an armistice designed like the other that was signed on this spot to bring armed hostilities to halt between those ancient enemies—Germany and France. Only everything that we've been seeing here this afternoon in Compiègne Forest has been so reversed. The last time the representatives of France sat in that car dictating the terms of the armistice. This afternoon we peered through the windows of the car and saw Adolf Hitler laying down the terms. That's how history reversed itself, but seldom has it done so as today on the very same spot. The German leader in the preamble of the conditions which were read to the French delegates by Colonel General von Keitel, Chief of the German Supreme Command, told the French that he had not chosen this spot at Compiègne out of revenge but merely to right a wrong.

The armistice negotiations here on the same spot where the last armistice was signed in 1918, here in Compiègne Forest, began at 3:15 P.M., our time, a warm June sun beat down on the great elm and pine trees and cast purple shadows on the hooded avenues as Herr Hitler with the German plenipotentiaries at his side appeared. He alighted from his car in front of the French monument to Alsace-Lorraine which stands at the end of an avenue about 200 yards from the clearing here in front of us where the armistice car stands. That famous Alsace-Lorraine statue was covered with German war flags, so that you cannot see its sculptured works or read its inscriptions. I had seen it many times in the postwar years, and doubtless many of you have seen it—the large sword representing the sword of the Allies, with its point sticking into a large, limp eagle, representing the old empire of the Kaiser, and the inscription underneath in front saying, "To the heroic soldiers of France, defenders of the country and of right, glorious liberators of Alsace-Lorraine."

Through our glasses, we saw the Führer stop, glance at the statue, observe the Reich war flags with their big swastikas in the center. Then he strolled slowly toward us, toward the little clearing where the famous armistice car stood. I thought he looked very solemn; his face was grave. But there was a certain spring in his step, as he walked for the first time toward the spot where Germany's fate was sealed on that

November day of 1918, a fate which, by reason of his own being, is now being radically changed here on this spot.

And now, if I may sort of go over my notes—I made from moment to moment this afternoon—now Hitler reaches a little opening in the Compiègne woods where the armistice was signed and where another is about to be drawn up. He pauses and slowly looks around. The opening here is in the form of a circle about 200 yards in diameter and laid out like a park. Cypress trees line it all around, and behind them the great elms and oaks of the forest. This has been one of France's national shrines for 22 years. Hitler pauses and gazes slowly around. In the group just behind him are the other German plenipotentiaries—Field Marshal Goering, grasping his Field Marshal baton in one hand. He wears the blue uniform of the air force. All the Germans are in uniform. Hitler in a double-breasted gray uniform with the Iron Cross hanging from his left breast pocket. Next to Goering are the two German army chiefs, Colonel-General von Keitel, Chief of the Supreme Command, and Colonel-General von Brauchitsch, Commander in Chief of the German Army. Both are just approaching sixty, but look younger, especially General von Keitel, who has a dapper appearance, with his cap slightly cocked on one side. Then we see there Dr. Raeder, Grand Admiral of the German Fleet. He has on a blue naval uniform and the invariable upturned stiff collar which German naval officers usually wear. We see two non-military men in Hitler's suite—his Foreign Minister, Joachim von Ribbentrop, in the field gray uniform of the Foreign Office, and Rudolf Hess, Hitler's deputy, in a gray party uniform.

The time's now, I see by my notes, 3:18 P.M. in the Forest of Compiègne. Hitler's personal standard is run up on a small post in the center of the circular opening in the woods. Also, in the center, is a great granite block which stands some 3 feet above the ground. Hitler, followed by the others, walks slowly over to it, steps up, and reads the inscription engraved in great high letters on that block. Many of you will remember the words of that inscription. The Führer slowly reads them, and the inscription says "Here on the eleventh of November, 1918, succumbed the criminal pride of the German Empire vanquished by the free peoples which it tried to enslave." Hitler reads it, and Goering reads it. They all read it, standing there in the June sun and the silence.

We look for the expression on Hitler's face, but it does not change. Finally he leads his party over to another granite stone, a small one some 50 yards to one side. Here it was that the railroad car in which the German plenipotentiary stayed during the 1918 armistice negotiations stood from November 8 to 11. Hitler looks down and reads the inscription which merely says: "The German plenipotentiary." The stone itself, I notice, is set between a pair of rusty old railroad tracks, the very ones that were there 22 years ago.

It is now 3:23 P.M., and the German leaders stride over to the armistice car. This car, of course, was not standing on this spot yesterday. It was standing 75 yards down the rusty track in the shelter of a tiny museum built to house it by an American citizen, Mr. Arthur Henry Fleming of Pasadena, California. Yesterday the car was removed from the museum by German army engineers and rolled back those 75 yards to the spot where it stood on the morning of November 11, 1918. The Germans stand outside the car, chatting in the sunlight. This goes on for 2 minutes. Then Hitler steps up into the car, followed by Goering and the others. We watch them entering the drawing room of Marshal Foch's car. We can see nicely now through the car windows.

Hitler enters first and takes the place occupied by Marshal Foch the morning the first armistice was signed. At his sides are Goering and General Keitel. To his right and left at the ends of the table we see General von Brauchitsch and Herr Hess at the one end, at the other end Grand Admiral Raeder and Herr von Ribbentrop. The opposite side of the table is still empty, and we see there four vacant chairs. The French have not yet appeared, but we do not wait long. Exactly at 3:30 P.M. the French alight from a car. They have flown up from Bordeaux to a near-by landing field and then have driven here in auto.

They glance at the Alsace-Lorraine memorial, now draped with swastikas, but it's a swift glance. Then they walk down the avenue flanked by three German army officers. We see them now as they come into the sunlight of the clearing—General Huntziger, wearing a brief khaki uniform; General Bergeret and vice-admiral Le Luc, both in their respective dark-blue uniforms; and then, almost buried in the uniforms, the one single civilian of the day, Mr. Noel, French Ambassador to Poland when the present war broke out there.

The French plenipotentiaries passed the guard of honor drawn up at the entrance of the clearing. The guard snapped to attention for the French but did not present arms. The Frenchmen keep their eyes straight ahead. It's a grave hour in the life of France and their faces today show what a burden they feel on their shoulders. Their faces are solemn, drawn, but bear the expression of tragic dignity. They walked quickly to the car and were met by two German officers, Lieutenant Colonel Tippelskirch, Quartermaster General, and Colonel Thomas, Chief of the Paris Headquarters. The Germans salute; the French salute; the atmosphere is what Europeans call "correct"; but you'll get the picture when I say that we see no handshakes—not on occasions like this. The historic moment is now approaching. It is 3:32 by my watch. The Frenchmen enter Marshal Foch's Pullman car, standing there a few feet from us in Compiègne Forest. Now we get our picture through the dusty windows of the historic old *wagon-lit* car. Hitler and the other German leaders rise from their seats as the French enter the drawing room. Hitler, we see, gives the Nazi salute, the arm raised. The German officers give a military salute; the French do the same. I cannot see Mr. Noel to see whether he salutes or how. Hitler, so far as we can see through the windows just in front of here, does not say anything. He nods to General Keitel at his side. We can see General Keitel adjusting his papers, and then he starts to read. He is reading the preamble of the German armistice terms. The French sit there with marblelike faces and listen intently. Hitler and Goering glance at the green table top. This part of the historic act lasts but a few moments. I note in my notebook here this—3:42 P.M.—that is, 12 minutes after the French arrived—3:42—we see Hitler stand up, salute the three with hand upraised. Then he strides out of the room, followed by Goering, General von Brauchitsch, Grand Admiral Raeder is there, Herr Hess, and, at the end, von Ribbentrop. The French remain at the green-topped table in the old Pullman car, and we see General Keitel remains with them. He is going to read them the detailed conditions of the armistice. Hitler goes, and the others do not wait for this. They walk down the avenue back towards the Alsace-Lorraine monument. As they pass the guard of honor, a German band strikes up the two national anthems "Deutschland über Alles" and the Horst Wessel song.

The whole thing has taken but a quarter of an hour—this great reversal of a historical armistice of only a few years ago.

CBS ANNOUNCER.—You have just heard a special broadcast from the Compiègne Forest in France where on the historic morning of November 11, 1918 representatives of the German army received from the Allies the terms of the armistice which ended the first World War, and where today, June 21, 1940, representatives of the French government received from Führer Adolf Hitler the terms under which a cessation of hostilities between Germany and France may be reached. As you know, the actual terms presented to the French plenipotentiaries have not yet been made public.

MUSIC.—*Organ.*

ANNOUNCER.—This is the Columbia Broadcasting System.

Wythe Williams

June 13, 1940

WILLIAMS.—Observers here still marvel at the positively uncanny ability of the German High Command to pick the weakest links in the French defense system and to break through them with clocklike regularity. This correct advance knowledge by the Germans has been attributed to the excellent Nazi intelligence service and to the Fifth Column activity behind the French lines. Both these assumptions are incorrect. The facts that I now am about to report have reached me from a source close to the German general staff—an authority which may be considered unimpeachable. The general staff has for some months been in possession of maps containing the minutest details of the entire French defense system. While a Fifth Column was the medium through which the Nazis obtained these maps, the Fifth Column in question is not anywhere near the French army, but is safely ensconced behind the high walls of the Kremlin at Moscow.

You will recall that as late as last August France had a military alliance with the Soviet Union . . . This alliance was strongest when the Front Populaire, made up principally of communists and socialists, conducted the affairs of the French Republic. An interchange of military missions between France and Russia took place, with Red generals invading Paris in considerable numbers. These officers were received with open arms by the communists then strongly entrenched in the French Chamber of Deputies. They were taken wherever they wished to go and shown whatever they desired to see. So great was the political power of the deputies in those days that it overruled all and any objections raised by the helpless military authorities.

The Generalissimo during this hectic period was Maxime Weygand, and his objections then against political interference with the army resulted in his retirement in favor of General Gamelin. The Red officers, under the protective guidance of their French comrades, did a thorough job. They mapped every bit of French fortifications that was worth mapping. They secured a comprehensive picture of the entire organization of the French army. They carried this information to Moscow, and they dumped it on the desk of Stalin. When Stalin found himself in dire distress at one moment of the Finnish campaign, he had but one place where he could turn for help—and that place was Berlin. He needed German military advisers and technical experts to help him make a breach in the Finnish Mannerheim line. Hitler sent this help, and it proved highly effective. But Hitler had his price—the complete information gathered by the Red army mission in France. And Stalin, without batting an eyelash, turned the secret maps and other details of the French defense organization over to Adolf Hitler.

Today the allied governments still seem incapable of drawing conclusions from past mistakes. Again they are trying to play marbles with Stalin. Again they are courting the man who gave Hitler the initial dagger with which to stab France. The mass production of German airplanes is something else that one of these days may be the subject of international consternation.

How do these supposedly almost bankrupt Nazis manage to turn out thousands of planes every month against the few hundreds manufactured by the Allies? Well, they didn't think up *all* of the plans *all* by themselves. Their success in this line again results from the successful penetration of secrets—secrets of great foreign manufacturers, some of them engaged in turning out automobiles by the hundreds of thousands, and who also are able to turn their industries overnight into the building of airplanes . . . And it may become publicly known before very long that among the most successful German spies is a young man of great rank in Germany, formerly distrusted but now highly approved by Hitler, who traveled extensively abroad—including the United States.

Yesterday and today I have received hundreds of letters, urging the necessity of full speed ahead on a real program for our national defense. Mothers, fathers, and sons unite in approving a great American army of soldier mechanics, selectively drafted, and who at the end of their service would be sufficiently expert to run the machines of expanding industries. Under this scheme these men would eventually take the places of their elders in all key industries and provide stamina and inspiration for those who follow them. In short, these men would lay the foundations for lasting prosperity throughout the Western Hemisphere. Just before this broadcast, I received word that the French government, meeting tonight in special emergency session, has given permission to General Weygand to abandon the Maginot line, if in his opinion the military situation makes this step necessary for the preservation of the army of France. That's about all, except that Hitler *again* has changed his address. Tuesday he was at St. Quentin. Today he is at Laon.

Good night.

Raymond Gram Swing

May 10, 1940

SWING.—This is a day to think, first of all, of the simple people who didn't merit the doom that befell them this morning, who hadn't made a botch of their personal lives nor of their collective lives and brought this doom upon themselves as a retribution. I refer to the honest, plain people of Holland and Belgium and Luxemburg, the sons at their posts, the families in their threatened homes. Every one of them is in danger of death; all of them already are gripped by the terror that strikes from the skies. If there are feelings left that can sympathize, these people command sympathy.

In the last 31 days, five peaceful, neutral, unoffending nations have been invaded: Denmark, Norway, Holland, Belgium, and Luxemburg. No 31 days in all history can duplicate that record. To conquer and rule has been the theme of ambitious men and oligarchies throughout history. But never before has it operated on so many small and innocent nations so quickly. Of the 21 small nations of Europe, only 8 survive with their sovereignty intact. They are Switzerland, Greece, Rumania, Sweden, Jugoslavia, Hungary, Bulgaria, and Portugal. And all of them but Portugal may be invaded before another month or another week are past. For this war is not like any preceding war; it had a remarkable prelude before it really began. That was the prelude of conquest. Most wars are waged for conquest. In this one the conquests were made, some of them, before formal war even began, as of Austria, Czechoslovakia, and Albania, the others before the real war started today. There was a detached episode in which the Soviet Union reduced the sovereignty of four of its neighbors with and without bloodshed. There may be a further Italian episode like it quite soon. Now the real war begins, which will decide whether those countries are to be retained. That is the meaning of the final violation of the innocent states, which were invaded this morning. The war now is being carried to Britain, over their dead bodies, since they have chosen to risk death to defend their independence.

It also is being carried to France; for in attacking Belgium and Luxemburg the Germans have released France from its inactivity, and the French army was advancing as rapidly as conditions allow into Luxemburg to reinforce the Belgians. Germany cannot hold any of its conquests and cannot extend conquest beyond Europe unless Britain is crushed and unless France shares and accepts defeat of its ally.

The war as it began this morning was at once christened a blitzkreig. Probably the name doesn't apply. What has begun today will be much longer than lightning and much deadlier. The blitzkreig did work against Poland which was beyond the reach of assistance. But both Holland and Belgium are within reach of it. They are getting it. The British sent fighter planes, also bombers to bomb Dutch airfields held by the Germans. The French had motorized troops moving into Belgium within 30 minutes after the receipt of the Belgian government's appeal for help. But the extent and strength of the aid is still impossible to judge. A spokesman of the French general staff today said that if Hitler was aiming to get the channel ports, this is the beginning of the greatest battle in history. Chancellor Hitler in his order to the German troops in the west used these words: "The hour of the deciding fight for the future of the German nation has come." And at the close of the order are these words: "The fight beginning today decides the fate of the German nation for the next thousand years." But the French spokesman said that the Germans might be carrying out another plan, and from the military operations so far it isn't clear whether the objective is the channel ports or whether it is to crush and shut off only Holland. That wouldn't alter the full force of what Hitler meant by this being the decisive fight. For from Holland the war would be carried by air and submarine, possibly by landing operations from sea and air to the British Isles. It simply isn't clear as yet which objective the Germans have. If they try to drive through to the channel ports, they are pitting their army against the French and are challenging what the experts consider the finest army in the world. If they are striving only to get Holland, they will have an easier time; for the Dutch are not a military nation, their army is not trained intensively for modern war, and it is underequipped. It is too early to judge how effective the Dutch resistance can be. The defensive floodings have started; some of them take a few hours to be effective; others need 2 to 3 days.

One must distinguish in the news today between three kinds of operations in Holland: bombings, landings of parachute troops, and straight invasion. Most of the news has been made by the bombings and the parachute troops. The first report that The Hague had been taken was only a brief episode with parachute troops. Other captures claimed in the interior of Holland and Belgium are all in this category. No doubt parachute troops have done some damage, and they have somewhat disrupted the Dutch defense. But despite them the real defeat of Holland would have to be accomplished by infantry on the ground. And the Dutch front proper is fairly intact at all points tonight, to judge by official Dutch reports. The fighting in Belgium may have as its purpose a shielding operation for the expected advance into Holland. Or it may turn out to be a major drive. The Belgian defense minister today told his parliament the Germans had failed of their first objectives and said that Belgium had scored a point. But in both Belgium and Holland, German bombing was severe and destructive, with heavy casualties. This has been war aviation's greatest day, to judge, not from actual accounts of the air battles, but from the Dutch and Belgian's claim that a hundred German planes have been brought down and the German claim that a hundred Allied planes were put out of action. And this must be regarded with great foreboding, for the bombings in Holland and Belgium were not the whole story. At least 15 towns or cities in France were bombed today, and incendiary bombs were dropped near a village in Kent, England. The Allied governments at once announced that they would consider themselves free to inflict reprisals if these bombings were not stopped. Then the Germans announced that the open town of Freiburg had been bombed, resulting in 24 civilian casualties, and they promised that they were going to bomb five British and French towns in reprisal. This means the opening of unrestricted warfare in the air. And the dismal wanton cruelty that lies ahead for British and French civilians, particularly the British, is dreadful to contemplate. Only the Finns and, to a lesser extent, the Poles and the Norwegians have had a taste of it. Tonight Winston Churchill is Prime Minister of Great Britain. He has been an ambitious man, but not in any flight of fancy could he have wished what has been committed to him today. For 5 years Winston Churchill lifted his eloquent warnings in and out of parliament against the German menace and the crime of

British unpreparedness. A minority in the House of Commons believed him. The rest refused to be disturbed. Then came Munich, a sell-out whose only excuse was British and French air inferiority. Thereafter the British prepared. But they did it without great speed or efficiency, and they were too late. They are far from catching up. Today has begun the decisive campaign of modern times. The Allies are handicapped, perhaps "handicap" is too kind a word, in the air and on land. It isn't Churchill's fault. And he takes charge in modern Britain's darkest hour. He has to guide the country through the reverses that are foredestined, which he would have averted, and he must hold it together while the slow work of forging strength proceeds. It will be no day of elation for him, no day for congratulations, a day for those sturdier words "duty" and "devotion." The new Churchill cabinet is still to be named. It will have Labor and Liberal ministers. Chamberlain, who finally submitted to his defeat, will be Chancellor of the Exchequer and member of the war cabinet. That is the one appointment that is sure tonight. France's cabinet crisis was quickly over today, too, as Premier Reynaud took into his government two members of the extreme right and so finished his cabinet of national unity.

In this country there has been much thought today about the status of the Dutch Indies, east and west. It is well to have clear the documentary status of the Dutch possessions as far as the Germans are concerned. They handed a memorandum to the Dutch minister in Berlin, explaining why his country had to be taken under protection to forestall invasion by the Allies. In this they said: "Germany does not intend by these measures to attack the integrity of the kingdom of Belgium and the kingdom of Holland or their possessions or property in Europe or in the colonies now or in the future." You see there are no "ifs" and "ands" about it. It is a promise. But to the Dutch foreign minister at The Hague the following threat was delivered by the German Minister. "We announce that an enormous German force has been put into action. Any resistance is senseless. Germany guarantees that if no resistance is offered, Holland will retain her possessions in Europe and overseas. If resistance is offered, there is danger of the complete destruction of the country and the state's organization." The Dutch have offered resistance; so the promise made in Berlin already is gone.

Let me close by summing up such news of today which is better than dismal. The flaming proclamation of the Queen of The Netherlands with its indomitable spirit is one. I want to quote most of it, for, as President Roosevelt said, it is worth reading. "To my people: Despite the fact that our country all these months has maintained strict neutrality with utmost conscientiousness, German troops last night made without any warning a sudden attack upon our territory. I am making herewith a flaming protest against this unexampled violation of good faith and what is considered decent between civilized nations. I and my government will do our duty now, too. Do yours, everywhere and under all circumstances, everyone in the place to which he is assigned, with utmost watchfulness, with inner calm and devotion to which a pure conscience entitles us."

Britain today has attained national unity under a great leader. France also has ended its political crisis and has been galvanized into solidarity. The Allies today have the cooperation of about a million troops who yesterday were neutral, and of these the Belgian army of six hundred thousand is well trained, though like the Dutch it is not sufficiently well equipped. The Allies today, too, are enriched by the accession of resources in the United States, for the Dutch and Belgians between them have a billion three hundred million dollars worth of assets in this country. This sum will be available for the purchase of supplies. And the French army is in action, which is by no means the least of these items. The news isn't all hopeless. But, for all the hope, it is predominantly and inexpressibly tragic.

BEST SPOT NEWS REPORTING

The Graf Spee

by James Bowen

James Bowen, who made this remarkable report, is, I believe, the manager of the American Club in Montevideo, Uruguay. The naval battle, which took place a few miles east of the mouth of the La Plata River a few days before the *Graf Spee* scuttled herself, could be seen clearly, in many of its phases and maneuvers, by spectators on the Uruguayan shore. After being badly mauled by the *Exeter*, the *Achilles*, and the *Ajax*, the German pocket battleship *Graf Spee* retired and sought refuge in the near-by neutral waters of Montevideo Harbor. Not all the King's men in the whole of British diplomacy could determine her exact status in a neutral port. Would she repair her damages and come out for another round? Would Uruguay intern her until the war ended? Would Germany send help? The Englishmen cruised up and down, waiting. Uruguayan authorities hospitalized the German wounded and buried the dead. One afternoon at sundown, after five days of anchorage, the *Graf Spee* steamed out of the harbor without warning, slowed down offshore about four miles, and there, within sight of half a million people, blew out her insides and sank in shallow water. There were no casualties connected with this theatrical finale, the *Graf Spee's* powder magazines having been detonated by her bridge officers from the comparative safety of a remote control in their lifeboats. But that night Hans Langsdorff, her commander, committed suicide in his hotel room in a gesture that seemed more oriental than necessary.

The first explosion was neither caught nor carried by radio; but James Bowen, who was standing by ready to short-wave the story to NBC, shouted for the air and began the following vivid ungrammatical account of what he saw only thirty seconds after it started to happen. It is, without doubt, the most exciting "on the scene" piece of radio reporting of the war so far. It took place between 6:01 and 6:13, Sunday afternoon, December 17, 1939. Here is what he said.

The Graf Spee

Bowen.—There's been quite a little of excitement all day. It's been going back and forth—being pushed around. I had to cut off of one broadcast, due to almost falling in the water with the amplifier and microphone and all the equipment—it's being pushed by the crowd. There's been a crowd of 70 to 100,000 people or more pushing around the dock in and around the Maldonado all day long.

It looks now that the War of Nerves is absolutely over. We just gave you the Flash News Report since the *Graf Spee* had scuttled the ship—as we call it—had blown itself up. What method was used we can't tell you at the moment. The ship is 5 miles out, and all we can see at the present moment at the shore here is a lot of smoke and flame. The launches leaving the ship—we tried to get it with the glasses. The smoke seemed to overcast the action. She's still afloat; pieces of her have gone up; the hull is still afloat, and the *Tacoma* which left, as we wired you a short time ago, left shortly after the craft, is trying to stand by her. It's without doubt that the *Tacoma*, also being loaded with fuel oil, will very possibly take fire and also go up.

The launches trying to get away. Evidently, the report that we gave you of scuttling the ship was the truth, and the crew being transferred suddenly seemed to be in a terrible position being aboard the *Tacoma*.

The quest of burning to death instead of being blown to death. It's been quite a time down here. A question of nerves—postponements of sailing hours, incoming ships, outgoing ships, everything being used as a method of postponing the inevitable.

The *Graf* left here a short time ago this afternoon before it began to get dusk and dropped anchor 5 miles off the coast. At that time there were two Argentine ships very close to the entrance of the La Plata River. The crew was standing off. The cruisers were known to be very close to the English banks just to the South.

The ship is moving—rolling from side to side. There goes another explosion! The bow is brought up. Evidently, the powder magazine has caught fire. She's going down! She's going down by the stern! The stern is completely under water! Flames are still shooting up in the air! Smoke! Evidently, this wasn't what we call exactly scuttling the ship, because nautical term scuttling a ship is opening the sea valves and letting in the water. These boys evidently are making a good job of it and leaving nothing but the pieces. They aren't going to leave anything anyone can reclaim whatsoever.

Without a doubt there'll be no reclamation for any of the sailors. This afternoon in our broadcast we told you of the transfer of some of the sailors to the hospital, a transfer of 31 sailors to the hospital. It may be possible that those are the only sailors who'll remain of the pocket cruiser *Graf Spee*.

She's going down by the fore part. The bow is under! She seems to raise a little bit at the stern. That is possibly due to seeing it from here. Naturally, that would throw her bow a little bit in the air. Now she seems to be settling—going down a little bit. She's just about where we can see the aftstern gone completely. Part of the superstructure is gone. The stack is still there. She's down in the water due to the low depth of water. Her superstructure is out of the water. She is absolutely on the bottom. Only thing showing now is her superstructure, her stack, and part of her battle tower above water.

We have just received information here which is not official and will probably need a long time to be confirmed. The confirmation or rumor is, or the advice which we'll have to accept as the rumor at the moment, the advice is that the explosion of the *Graf Spee* was done at the dictation of Mr. Hitler—absolutely. That of course will have to be proven in time like a number of things in the last war that we waited 20 years to find the truth. However, the first naval battle in this war fought in South American waters has probably come to its conclusion. And the heroism of all the sailors who took part in that battle is very well-known, especially the boys who are now in hospitals. They will have some memory, and the other boys will have none. We may possibly have another battle, if maritime reports are correct that the *Admiral Scheer* and the *Deutschland* are en route to South American waters with a convoy of submarines and will be met by at least one-third of the British Fleet.

The flame—the *Graf Spee* is still a-flame so it's very hard to say whether or not anything will be saved due to the water action—possibly the action of the water will save something. It's a very strange sight having, as I have, seen the *Graf Spee* about 4 hours after her arrival in Montevideo, having made at least 10 trips around the *Graf Spee* in the last 3 days—noticing the changes and the checking up of the shell holes, repainting—and as we described last night, the work, the welding of plates. It brings about the logical suggestion that the decision to blow up the *Graf Spee* must have been made as a last-minute resort.

We are unable at the moment to determine what is happening to the crew even with glasses, due to the movement of launches and the movement of two or three tugs which left the harbor here after the *Graf Spee* had gone out. All the launches seem to be getting to the *Tacoma*. Whether the *Tacoma* is unloading the sailors that were transferred to her to the launches, it's impossible to define at the moment even with glasses. There's a lot of action, and the crowd around here are just about crowding us into the water. We are in a very bad way. However, we'll do the best we can. It's awfully hard to describe this. We know more or less what is going on, but we don't want to tell you what we think is going on. We want to tell you what we can see, and we can't see a great deal, due to the excessive action and movement.

At least 300,000 people are here on the "rambler" as we call it—a wide highway such as the wider even than the boardwalk at Atlantic City—and it's absolutely blocked—it's impossible to move.

You can't walk in one direction or another—you just have to follow the swing of the crowd. It's completely full of automobiles and people—accidents are happening. Now here come the tugboats from Montevideo. All the tugboats that have fought are borrowed to go to the assistance of the sailors. It's very hard for the tug to go on after the search. They're doing what they can. I think they're going to get very little myself, because I don't think they'll pick up much except pieces. It'll be sometime before there's anything done about the hull unless she's a menace to navigation. If she is, at that time they'll just give her a little more dynamite, and that will be all.

The *Graf* seems to be settling a little bit at the moment. It may be possible that the rest of her may go.

It looks bad. However, we'll come back later.

ANNOUNCER.—This is NBC in New York. You've been listening, ladies and gentlemen, to another in the series of the NBC On the Spot broadcasts. James Bowen, NBC's representative in Montevideo, Uruaguay, has told us of the sinking of the *Graf Spee* and of the condition of the German supply ship *Tacoma*. The voice of Mr. Bowen was heard in the United States via RCA Communications.

Keep tuned to your favorite NBC station for the latest news.

This is the National Broadcasting System.

The Belmont Stakes

by TED HUSING

THE amazing, almost prodigious, talent of Ted Husing is known to every radio listener in this hemisphere. Very few know the man himself. He is nervous, quick of movement, crepuscular, and physically as tough as raffia. He works about twelve hours a day and has a wonderful time in his special corner of the radio industry. He has played semiprofessional baseball, basketball, and football. He has the keen eyes of a hunter, great ebullience of spirit, and fine self-control. Nothing scares him; nothing passes before his vision without being completely observed; nothing moves too fast to be made articulate to the listener. He is radio's master of ad libbing.

His book "Ten Years before the Mike" (Farrar and Rinehart) reveals many of the secrets of his craft and is full of the color of radio's early foliage.

Here is his broadcast (with Bill Corum) of the Belmont Stakes, June 8, 1940.

The Belmont Stakes

HUSING.—Good afternoon, everyone, everywhere. The spring meeting of the Westchester Racing Association, a span of two dozen days, comes to a successful close this afternoon with the seventy-second running of the Belmont Stakes, third of the classics comprising the triple crown for three-year-olds.

Columbia, which began the racing season with the exclusive description of a Kentucky Derby and which since has presented the New York state racing season classics at Jamaica and Belmont, turns its microphones today to the mile and a half racing strip at beautiful Belmont to recount the running of the Belmont Stakes. Six of the nation's three-year-olds are going to go to the post. Two of them, Colonel Bradley's Bimelech, winner of the Preakness, and Mrs. Ethel Mars' Gallahadion, winner of the Kentucky Derby, will match each other in a rubber contest. Pitted against them will be the surprising winner of the Withers, Corydon, which beat Bimelech in that stake; Andy K, which romped to victory in the Peter Pan Handicap; Your Chance, also a galloping winner of the Delhi purse here the other day; and Century Note, stable mate of Corydon and favored over Corydon at this long distance.

The Belmont, which closes down the spring get-together of the Westchester Association, is decidedly the richest and the most important of the races run here the past 3 weeks. It is also the classic which will decide the establishment of the three-year-old champion, or at least the leadership of the three-year-old division, a title now considerably in dispute. This race includes no geldings; and while fillies are permitted to run, none have been entered, leaving the filly title in the present good hands of Damaged Goods.

Now here is the field which will go to the post: Greentree Stable has two horses running in the race. They are Corydon and Century Note. That is to say, if you bet on one or the other and they should win, you will be paid off. Corydon will be ridden by Eddie Arcaro, and all of the colts will carry 126 pounds. Century Note will be piloted by Johnny Longdon. That is the Greentree entry: Corydon and Century Note.

Then we have Colonel Bradley's Bimelech with Freddy Smith aboard; Milky Way Farm's Gallahadion, with Georgie Woolf aboard (Carol Bierman was injured and could not ride); Millsdale Stable's Andy K, with Basil James aboard; and Mrs. George D. Widener's Your Chance, with Harry Richards aboard.

And now I want to present Bill Corum, the renowned sports columnist of the *New York Journal-American*, to you in a discussion of this race, for the horses are coming on the track.

Bill is my good luck omen. When he nears my microphone, I know that things will hum correctly; so each big event always finds Bill at my side by special request. And here he is, ladies and gentlemen, Bill Corum.

CORUM.—Thank you, Ted, and I'm always glad to be here, you know, and especially on such a lovely day as we have here at Belmont this afternoon. The field for the seventy-second running of the great Belmont Stakes is on the track. Up the track there now I see Bimelech galloping away in front of them, bouncing around a little, with little Freddy Smith, whom the other jockeys call the "Feather Merchant," and in the back I see the horse that I'm going to pick for Ted on his good luck omen; but I don't pick many winners for him, and I'm sorry we didn't hear from Mark Hellinger, because maybe some of you who are listening will remember that Hellinger sent Ted a telegram at the Kentucky Derby which Ted turned over to me to read, and ever since then I've been taking bows on Gallahadion, which I didn't even know was in the race and thought Hellinger probably got out of a seed catalogue. And I'm sorry we didn't get a wire from him today because if Snow Ridge hadn't been scratched, he'd have picked him, I'm sure, and with his luck he might have won. But the horse I really like in this race is Mrs. George Widener's Your Chance. He's a dark chestnut, a kind of a muddy chestnut or chocolate-colored; and Alfred Vanderbilt was saying to me the other day that he didn't like the horse's color, he didn't think he could be a great horse because of his color. And I said to him, "Well, Alfred, I haven't seen that stopping the heavyweight champion of the world yet." He's a little brown, too, the Brown Bomber is, but he gets along pretty good; and I don't think color has much to do with what's going to happen in races. Now, the Greentree pair look awfully good. That's Corydon and Century Note. Century Note is the full brother of that great horse Twenty Grand. Perhaps it's an indication in the change of times that when Twenty Grand was a Derby winner, people talked twenty grands and now they talk century note; but Mrs. Whitney names her horses beautifully, and I just saw her here a minute ago, the First Lady of the turf. And it's a great day for racing when she comes out. And this is her first visit this year, and just a moment ago I saw her walk in on her son's arm, Jock Whitney of the Jockey Club and of the Racing Commission.

I also saw Colonel Bradley a minute ago getting up to walk back. He sits down here under where we're broadcasting, where Ted's booth is, and he was getting up and stretching his legs and walking back, a gentleman now eighty years old, to try to get a peek through the trees at this little horse he loves, this grand little Bimelech; not so little, a medium size horse—was little last year, and they called him "Little Bimey," but he grew over the winter. Only beaten twice and has run great races both times. Now he's six to five over on that odds board. The horse I like, Your Chance, is five to two; the Greentree pair, Corydon, Century Note, four to one; Gallahadion, the winner of the Kentucky Derby, is six to one. If Mrs. Mars is here, every owner of the horses in this race is at this track this afternoon. I'm not certain about her, but Mrs. Ethel V. Mars does own the Milky Way Farm and Gallahadion the Derby winner and is probably here. Andy K, the sidewise horse, the crab, he's a 10-to-1 chance on the board and a long shot of the field.

Now, before I came up here, I did a little televise broadcast before the National Saddle Stakes, and I picked a horse called Attention, and Attention won; and maybe that's what I've been needing all this time, Ted, is television. But anyhow, I'm going to tell you that I think this race will wind up between Your Chance and the Greentree horse, one or the other of them, probably Corydon; and I don't quite believe, until he proves it to me, that Bimelech is going to like to go a mile and a half with this great race.

It's a pleasure to be here; it's a gorgeous day. Down in front of us is the beautiful Belmont Bowl being contested for, for the seventy-second time; and it's a great thing to live in a country like this and be at a spot like this, and just think how grateful we all should be for it, and I am, and I'm happy to be here, and I thank Ted for giving me this opportunity to talk to you, and don't forget Your Chance might be your chance. Good-by.

HUSING.—Thank you very much, Bill Corum. Ladies and gentlemen, in bringing this field together winners of events which saw favorites beaten and tumble to startling defeats we feel that the Belmont Stakes will prove a contest of unusual interest for the throne of the three-year-olds of scrambled and very muddled style. The six principal horses have given one indication or another that they possess enough to come through here today in an open race. They have already paraded and are probably approximately three-sixteenths of a mile away from the starting gate.

This is a mile and half oval. This is the seventy-second running of this great race. That means they'll go once around the track from the starting wire back to the finish wire. Bimelech won the Preakness, the Blue Grass, and the Derby trial, as you recollect, and he is the son of Black Tony. Gallahadion was winner of the Kentucky Derby and the San Vincentes handicap at Santa Anita. Corydon was the surprise winner of the Withers, Andy K the winner of the Peter Pan but third in the Delhi, which was run Monday; Century Note, which is green at the gate yet and breaks in a tangle, needs a half a mile for his best stride and is the horse figured to be the color bearer for the Greentree stable, with Johnny Longdon up who blew in from California, was second in the Delhi on Monday and won two straight overnight events before that race. Your Chance, a long striding colt which hit his ankle in the work before the Preakness and wound up fourth, with Harry Richards aboard, won the Survivor Stakes at Pimlico and the Delhi stakes here at a mile and an eighth the other day, galloping, and was fourth in the Preakness.

Now the horses have approached the post. I don't think we have much more time for any discussion regarding the race excepting to see what they do. And as they come up to the post, we'll just take a good look at them. We see right now that Corydon is going to be the first one into the gate—Corydon with Eddie Arcaro aboard, wearing the black cap, the pink and black stripes of the Greentree Stable. Century Note is still behind and ready to move in, and we see Andy K, Gallahadion, and last but not least we find Your Chance, which is still back of the barrier. This is the Clay-Puett electric starting gate with the electric front, you know, which springs open when starter George Cassidy releases the button. The crowd has crowded down to the rail. There are 26,000 people here who have bet almost three quarters of a million dollars today, probably betting a quarter of a million dollars alone on this race to make it another million dollar day; and the horses are moving in.

As they go in there we find that Bimelech is in post position one, Gallahadion in two, Corydon in three, Andy K in four, Century Note in five, and Your Chance on the outside. And Bimelech is acting up a little bit at the gate now. Your Chance comes in. They'll be away very shortly. They're all locked in there.

They're just moving back and forth. Gallahadion is the last one to actually get in as they put the backboards up. The crowd is tense now. You can hear the nervousness and the excitement, and we're ready to go the minute George Cassidy sends them on their way. It's a beautiful sunshiny afternoon. The weather is clear, and the track is fast. Now the crowd is beginning to talk it up a little bit because they see Your Chance backing out. They also see Century Note, the Greentree one, backing out. Bimelech is acting up in post position number one, and the crowd is talking from behind, as down the stretch they can see the horses going into the gate. They are obscured from in front, of course, and they'll be off in a second. They're in there a little bit more quietly than they were a moment ago. Uh-uh, now, Bimelech, don't throw him. The crowd roars as we just said that, because Bimelech begins to back out and Freddie Smith has a time holding him in. Gallahadion is standing quietly. So is Corydon, Andy K. Now Century Note is acting up a little bit. Your Chance is standing very quietly. Your Chance moves forward and moves back again. Bimelech is still nodding his head in there. He just didn't like the gate at all. Bimelech is being the fractious one in there, and Freddie Smith finds him backing out a little bit.

Now they're moving in. They're going to back the backboard across the back of the Clay-Puett gate. Cassidy is standing still. He is just watching it. Now Bimelech has backed out. A mile and a half in this race. This is going to decide the triple crown, that is, the three-year-old crown—I shouldn't say the triple because two-thirds have already been run of the triple crown, and Gallahadion and Bimelech have won one each. Now Your Chance is standing there for a second, as he watches Century Note back out. Century Note has now moved in again. Aboard Century Note is Johnny Longden who flew in from California and requested that he be given this horse. He is the more favored horse of the two of the Greentree entry and should give a long run to this race. We are a little bit late as I see it now.

Now we have Bimelech backing out. And they're off, and breaking right on top are Andy K, Bimelech and Gallahadion. Andy K takes the lead on the outside. Bimelech along the rail is running with him. Gallahadion is running third. Then come the Greentree pair, and last is Your Chance. And they're spread out as they go up that track. Now as they run one-eighth of a mile, it's still that way. Along the fence we find in there that Andy K has moved into the rail, Bimelech is second; and as they round the turn, we are obscured for a moment—in case there's a foul. As they come out, it's Andy K on the outside, Bimelech on the inside, Gallahadion running third; and Andy K takes a straight lead now, as they go a quarter of a mile.

Then behind comes Corydon, Century Note, and Your Chance; and that's the way they run. Now as they go for the three-quarter mile mark on that first turn, the clubhouse turn, going around the center of it it's still in the front Andy K by one length. Bimelech along the rail is being lapped over by Gallahadion, which now takes a clear place at second and taking a shot at the one up on top. Corydon is making a beautiful run to get in there fourth. Century Note is fifth, and Your Chance is last.

Now going into the back stretch. We'll watch them very carefully. Andy K is on the front end by three-quarters of a length. Gallahadion on the outside of him by a length over Bimelech; Bimelech by a length and a half over Corydon; Corydon by five lengths over Century Note; Century Note a half length over Your Chance. Going down the back stretch now, the boy sitting up on Andy K is giving a beautiful ride, riding him very nicely. Bimelech has gone on the outside now of Gallahadion, and Corydon is making a run for it. And it's Bimelech second now with Corydon on the outside, and the three of them are up there.

It's Andy K on the rail, Bimelech and Corydon. And now Bimelech and Andy K are fighting it out on the backstretch, and Bimelech is taking the lead from Andy K by about a nose. A length behind comes Corydon, then Gallahadion, Century Note, and Your Chance. Now they are going into the mile mark, and they'll soon be turning in the stretch. It's Andy K back on the front end again by a half a length; Bimelech, second; Gallahadion running third; Corydon, fourth; Century Note, fifth; and Your Chance is beginning to make his move now. Your Chance has moved up from sixth to fifth.

Now on the front end is Bimelech, having a fight again with Andy K, and the two of them are lapped over three lengths in front of the field, and Your Chance is moving up from fifth to third, and Your Chance is moving around Corydon and Gallahadion. But on the front end with approximately a half a mile to go it's still Bimelech and Andy K, with Bimelech a half a length out in front on the outside—Andy K with Your Chance now moving into third place, Gallahadion running in fifth. Century Note is in there running last.

And now as they come to the head of the stretch, it's Bimelech on the front end with Andy K fighting him along the rail; Your Chance on the outside; Gallahadion, fourth. And now we'll watch this race down the homestretch, as Bimelech takes a clear lead of a half a length on Andy K. Your Chance is running up both of them. And it's Bimelech by a half a length out in front, now a length, with a quarter of a mile to go; and Bimelech is going away with Your Chance coming the fastest. Your Chance is running at Bimelech now and coming hard—the three of them looped together. And as they come down to the wire Your Chance is making a great run for it, but Bimelech is going to win by a half a length over Your Chance, Andy K, Century Note, Gallahadion, and Corydon.

The winner: Bimelech reestablished as the three-year-old champion. A beautiful race with Andy K which ran him all the way, and Your Chance in there at the same time. And the official numbers go up, but it does not mean the race is official, as Bimelech is declared the winner. Then comes Your Chance which ran by Andy K, and then comes Corydon.

Well, that was a race. 2:29⅗, and the crowd of 26,000 had gone absolutely wild as the great and mighty Bimelech, Colonel Bradley's horse, ridden beautifully by Freddie

Smith, was able to stay on the pace of Andy K as ridden by Basil James, who was shaken up very badly in the preceding race when he was thrown off Maeda. Andy K faded in the last pace. Your Chance, which was running last with Century Note, made up plenty of ground, came wide at the outside, and ran down that second one, Andy K, but could not have enough to come up on Bimelech who never had to worry about disposing of anybody excepting Andy K, which he did in time. He got rid of Gallahadion early in the race. The rest of them were never in there for any contention whatsoever. So your winner, Bimelech, and reestablished on the front end now as the three-year-old colt, of the year striding alongside of the three-year-old filly Damaged Goods; and a beautiful race it was, called all the way around as the calls were called almost at every quarter mile.

Again, Bimelech the winner, in 2 minutes, 29⅗ seconds, exceeding good time, approximately 1 full second behind the track record. Your Chance, Mrs. George D. Widener's horse, was second. Third was Andy K, and fourth was Century Note. I called Corydon, but I meant Century Note, the one with the green hat.

And so, ladies and gentlemen, we have come to the conclusion of the spring meeting at beautiful Belmont Park. On Monday afternoon we resume our race broadcasting directly from Aqueduct, the third stop in the parade of five race tracks here in the metropolitan area where the Mutuels have now taken hold and where the crowds get bigger and better and enjoy everything that goes on in racing. It is not an official result, but Bimelech is the winner.

This is the Columbia Broadcasting System. Good-by, all.